A CONSTELLATION OF AUTHORITY

IBERIAN ENCOUNTER AND EXCHANGE
475–1755 | Vol. 8

SERIES EDITORS
Erin Kathleen Rowe
Michael A. Ryan

The Pennsylvania State
University Press

ADVISORY BOARD
Paul H. Freedman
Richard Kagan
Marie Kelleher
Ricardo Padrón
Teofilo F. Ruiz
Marta V. Vicente

The Iberian Peninsula has historically been an area of the world that fostered encounters and exchanges among peoples from different societies. For centuries, Iberia acted as a nexus for the circulation of ideas, people, objects, and technology around the premodern western Mediterranean, Atlantic, and eventually the Pacific. Iberian Encounter and Exchange, 475–1755 combines a broad thematic scope with the territorial limits of the Iberian Peninsula and its global contacts. In doing so, works in this series will juxtapose previously disparate areas of study and challenge scholars to rethink the role of encounter and exchange in the formation of the modern world.

OTHER TITLES IN THIS SERIES
Thomas W. Barton, *Contested Treasure: Jews and Authority in the Crown of Aragon*

Mercedes García-Arenal and Gerard Wiegers, eds., *Polemical Encounters: Christians, Jews, and Muslims in Iberia and Beyond*

Nicholas R. Jones, *Staging Habla de negros: Radical Performances of the African Diaspora in Early Modern Spain*

Freddy Cristóbal Domínguez, *Radicals in Exile: English Catholic Books During the Reign of Philip II*

Lu Ann Homza, *Village Infernos and Witches' Advocates: Witch-Hunting in Navarre, 1608–1614*

Adam Franklin-Lyons, *Shortage and Famine in the Late Medieval Crown of Aragon*

Sarah Ifft Decker, *The Fruit of Her Hands: Jewish and Christian Women's Work in Medieval Catalan Cities*

A CONSTELLATION OF AUTHORITY

CASTILIAN BISHOPS AND THE SECULAR CHURCH
DURING THE REIGN OF ALFONSO VIII

KYLE C. LINCOLN

THE PENNSYLVANIA STATE UNIVERSITY PRESS
UNIVERSITY PARK, PENNSYLVANIA

Library of Congress Cataloging-in-Publication Data

Names: Lincoln, Kyle C., author.
Title: A constellation of authority : Castilian bishops and the secular church during the reign of Alfonso VIII / Kyle C. Lincoln.
Other titles: Iberian encounter and exchange, 475–1755 ; v. 8.
Description: University Park, Pennsylvania : The Pennsylvania State University Press, [2023] | Series: Iberian encounter and exchange, 475–1755 ; vol. 8 | Includes bibliographical references and index.
Summary: "Examines the role of bishops in Castilian politics in the High Middle Ages, focusing on the reign of Alfonso VIII"—Provided by publisher.
Identifiers: LCCN 2022046289 | ISBN 9780271094373 (hardback) | ISBN 9780271094380 (paper)
Subjects: LCSH: Bishops—Spain—Castile—History—To 1500. | Church and state—Spain—Castile—History—To 1500. | Castile (Spain)—Church history. | Castile (Spain)—History—Alfonso VIII, 1158–1214.
Classification: LCC BX1586.C3 L56 2023 | DDC 322/.109463—dc23/eng/20221118
LC record available at https://lccn.loc.gov/2022046289

Copyright © 2023 Kyle C. Lincoln
All rights reserved
Printed in the United States of America
Published by The Pennsylvania State University Press,
University Park, PA 16802–1003

The Pennsylvania State University Press is a member of the Association of University Presses.

It is the policy of The Pennsylvania State University Press to use acid-free paper. Publications on uncoated stock satisfy the minimum requirements of American National Standard for Information Sciences—Permanence of Paper for Printed Library Material, ANSI Z39.48–1992.

Contents

ACKNOWLEDGMENTS   vii

1   "A Constellation of Authority": Using Episcopal Sources to Recover Castilian History in the Time of Alfonso VIII   1

2   The Importance of Being Archbishop: Celebruno, Bishop of Sigüenza and Archbishop of Toledo   17

3   *Homo Ignarus* or *Reparator Regni?* The Curious Case of Ramón II de Minerva of Palencia   35

4   A Milanese Lawyer at the Castilian Court: Alderico di Palacio of Sigüenza and Palencia   51

5   A Reformer and a Gentleman: Martín Bazán of Osma   69

6   "His Name Was Martín Magnus": Martín López de Pisuerga and an Archiepiscopate for the Thirteenth Century   85

7   A Mozarab? A Reformer? A Saintly Professor? Julián ben Tauro of Cuenca   101

8   How to Get Away with Murder: Rodrigo de Finojosa, Bishop of Sigüenza   113

9 *Palea, Comparanda,* and Conclusions   129

APPENDIX: SUMMARY PROFILES OF THE CASTILIAN
EPISCOPATE, 1158–1214   143

NOTES   153

BIBLIOGRAPHY   193

INDEX   213

Acknowledgments

This volume could not have been completed without the substantial assistance of too many colleagues to thank appropriately without producing a second volume to describe my many debts to them. There is not enough space to enumerate all those that deserve my thanks.

John Wickstrom and Damian Smith, as my undergraduate and graduate history mentors, respectively, were instrumental in setting me down this path of scholarship and teaching me to avoid my many self-imposed pitfalls along the way. Elizabeth Manwell's guidance in the learning of Latin and Greek has paid more dividends than I can count on this long road. Steven Schoenig, S.J., and Atria Larson helped nurture my interest in legal history at a time when I needed more to substantiate the support of my investigation of prelates, and shiny objects like legal history were more than enough to grow my interest. My classmates at Saint Louis University were constant companions in the early process of discovery, and Amy Boland, Samantha Cloud, John Giebfried, Edward Holt, Matt Parker, and Kathleen Walkowiak deserve special mention. Although not at SLU properly, Miguel Gómez has been a constant collaborator, and he deserves mention among my classmates and fellow travelers *pro causa honoris*.

Beyond Saint Louis University, I benefitted from many colleagues that helped refine my focus and sharpen the quality of my work. Janna Bianchini's work and friendship made this volume's argument stronger and better connected to the wider world of scholarship; she deserves a second vote of thanks for providing the splendid phrase that became this book's title. Miriam Shadis and Lucy Pick helped refine some of my technique in reading sources for information that lay beneath their surfaces. Simon Doubleday has provided enormous support for the ongoing process of this work; he knows well how meaningful his guidance has been. Jerrilynn Dodds offered thoughtful questions while she was working on projects of her own, took time to explain their context, and enriched my understanding of clergy in the meanwhile. Jessalynn Bird gave thoughtful answers on liturgical questions that I had during the process, and she was always a friend when my bishops seemed more quotidian than hers. Evan Gatti played a role of similar enthusiasm, as did our colleagues in Episcopus. Peter Linehan was kind and thoughtful in his comments about the work that I was doing in the summer of 2015 and gave me some especially useful advice about surviving the work of archival research in Castile. Simon Barton read many of the chapters of this volume before his untimely death, and I have been fortunate enough to count his students among my friends as a lasting tribute to his legacy.

In Spain, I was lucky to find a great many colleagues that renewed the intensity of my investigation. Carlos Ayala and Martín Alvira were constant patrons of my work, and they deserve to be listed in a place of honor. Francisco Garcia-Serrano gave me some important suggestions as this project made major transitions in its interest and focus, for which I am still very grateful. Flocel Sabate was gracious enough to host many AARHMS sessions at his International Medieval Meeting in Lleida, and several chapters in this book were worked out as conference papers. The team of archivists at Toledo were always patient with my inquiries, as was Angel de la Torre Rodriguez in Palencia, Matías Vicario Santamaría at Burgos, and most especially Felipe Gil Peces-Rata at Sigüenza. The staff of the Biblioteca Nacional in Madrid were capable of finding volumes from the seventeenth century that were not digitized but whose words pepper some of the pages and epigraphs of this book.

The librarians of Saint Louis University, Kalamazoo College, Western Michigan University, the University of Wisconsin–La Crosse, Norwich University, and Oakland University deserve the highest praise. Too often, I asked for obscure dissertations from the 1930s or rare offprints from defunct journals, expecting a delay of some months but finding them waiting for me after a long weekend. The administrator that cuts the budgets of librarians is a fool and a charlatan. George Milne, a kind and generous colleague at Oakland University, drew the map for this book with quickness and grace, despite my peculiar requests for its elaboration. This project received funding from several institutions, even while they were under their own financial strain. Saint Louis University's History Department offered 1818 and Matthews Fund grants to support the project in its infancy, and Kalamazoo College's Faculty Development Fund sent me to a number of international conferences where the conclusions were refined. Most importantly, the kingdom of Spain's Hispanex program provided key funding for this project and a subsequent one.

Last, but perhaps most importantly, this book is a testament to the support of my family, and most especially to my mother and my maternal grandmother, who taught me to read. I still read things, even if they require a different kind of help, and this book is proof that their struggles meant a great deal to someone, even if he was none too appreciative at the time.

I

"A CONSTELLATION OF AUTHORITY"
Using Episcopal Sources to Recover Castilian
History in the Time of Alfonso VIII

These bishops are almost inarticulate. They do not tell us what ideals they held, nor how they tried to put them into practice. We have no collections of their letters . . . no treatises on the office of a bishop, no penitentials, no codes of ecclesiastical custom. . . . What we can perceive about episcopal thoughts and aspirations must be apprehended by the flickering light.
—Richard Fletcher, *The Episcopate in the Kingdom of León in the Twelfth Century* (1978)

Despite being called "the key institutional element" by Bernard Reilly, bishops rarely play a central role in Castilian historiography.[1] Others have noted that supporting cast members—such as Gonzalo Gutiérrez Girón of Segovia, a son of a lesser nobleman and brother of the royal *majordomo*—constituted a kind of "constellation of authority."[2] In part, this tension highlights what is actually under examination here: in what institution did bishops play a key role? Conceptualizing a monarch as a singular figure may work etymologically, but medieval monarchies were inherently plural agencies. Janna Bianchini notes that "the definition of who might share in this plural monarchy was flexible and often expansive . . . it was never static. . . . The 'reigning monarch' was considered the only constant, the central figure in a constellation of authority."[3] Figures like Gonzalo, then, may be the key to unlocking a much broader understanding of history, especially in kingdoms like Castile, where the records might be less than desirable. There were forty or so other bishops who were "lunch-pail" workaday prelates, who showed up and did their work, and yet (thanks to the poor preservation of records) scholars cannot flesh out that work with the kind of rich historical treatment that some of the bishops' more famous contemporaries receive. Thus their histories are mostly still unwritten. This study reframes how we conceive of the extant material on bishops like Gonzalo to provide microhistories of important individuals, even those too often overlooked, during the reign of one of Iberia's longest-serving kings, restoring lost details of the period.

For most of those better-recorded bishops, the data are rich enough to track the most important balancing act that shaped medieval prelates: the tripolar relationship of their diocesan work, their political sovereign, and the bishop of Rome. The relationships bishops cultivated with the Castilian royal family always existed in tension with their relationships with the reigning popes. This book argues that that complex negotiation of relationships was a kind of zigzag—first toward Rome, then toward Castile—that gradually drew king and pope closer together. As a result, this monograph will provide both a revised narrative foundation and an important corrective for historiography that still overlooks the importance of Castilian historical evidence. Historians of the episcopacy have demonstrated that ecclesiastical history could fill important gaps in the records of secular institutions, and as Melissa Julian-Jones has recently written, "Bishops as figures of authority were, throughout previous decades of the twentieth century, often overlooked as embodiments of authority and intolerance, but gradually the tide of scholarship has shifted into making explorations of the bishop as a personality and a persona far more nuanced."[4]

In addition to their religious function and identity—a factor that was, for most medieval people, more important than it is in the twenty-first century[5]—the bishops of Latin Christendom played many other roles. Cathedrals owned huge tracts of land, had their own fortifications (manned by secular and religious figures alike), collected rents, taught lessons in Latin, copied books, and sang masses. Being a cleric in the medieval Latin West was no less complicated than being a count. (In fact, one might argue that canon law made things even more complicated than the various local legal systems.) The activities of bishops are no less historically important than those of aristocratic knights or urban patricians.

It is hard to speak of formal organs of government in most medieval kingdoms before the thirteenth century, and the origins of modern states and their precursors in the medieval world remain hotly debated. For example, some scholars might label the kingdom of England the first "constitutional monarchy" because of the baronial party's presumptions at Runnymede in 1215.[6] For others, the March Pact of 1204 represents just such a precedent for the Latin empire of Constantinople.[7] Still others would have the Cortes of Valladolid's limits on the power of Alfonso IX of León in 1188 serve as the starting point for the story of constitutional monarchies in the Latin West.[8] In all of these cases, we know that prelates were present and that bishops brought their own ideas into the conversations about the way that monarchies were supposed to function, and that these decisions had an impact on churches, dioceses, and clerics. Even where bishops were present, their role in this dynamic is unfortunately understudied, leaving a major gap where records could support more extensive research.

In twelfth-century Castile, Toledo was a metropolitan archbishopric that controlled a province of six suffragan dioceses and their bishops.[9] These were the dioceses of Palencia, Osma, Segovia, Sigüenza, Cuenca (after 1179), and—outside Castile but still under Toledan jurisdiction—Albarracín-Segorbe.[10] In the north of the kingdom was the diocese of Burgos, whose privileged status as an exempt diocese meant that while it might be swayed politically and economically by factors internal to Castile, it was responsible to the Roman pontiff alone.[11] Also within Castile but subject to a foreign metropolitan archbishop were the dioceses of Ávila and (after 1189) Plasencia, which were suffragans of Santiago de Compostela after that archdiocese had assumed the rights of Mérida in the early twelfth century.[12] Adding to the dioceses and their cathedrals, of course, were the many powerful monasteries and collegiate churches that competed for the patronage of lay lords and the pious bequests made by Christians seeking to ameliorate the conditions of their immortal souls. All of these diocesan administrations produced records, but what makes them an especially fruitful field of study is the fact that records of ecclesiastical purchases, sales, quarrels, and bequests survive more plentifully than those of other entities in medieval Castilian archives.

So who were these prelates of Castile? What world did they occupy, and how did their relationships with superiors and colleagues shape their work? What does recovering their history from the extant sources contribute to larger conversations about medieval history and its pertinent themes? To answer these important questions, the bishops under study here need to be first placed in their historical context before they can be better appreciated as historical actors in their own right. As stars in a "constellation of authority," each prelate had his own gravity and body of orbiting figures, all of whom revolved around the great pull of the centralizing figure of the Castilian monarch.

Scena Frons: The Reign of Alfonso VIII of Castile

The long trajectory of Alfonso's reign (r. 1158–1214) saw a major shift in the fortunes of Castile—from a component in a growing Leonese empire toward becoming one of the major powers of the Iberian Peninsula. Examining the "constellation of authority" of the reigns of Alfonso VIII and Leonor provides a more complex portrait of a kingdom that normally gets short shrift.[13] Bishops were a key part of the Alfonsine constellation, and the tripolar relationship between the local diocesan see, the Roman pontiffs, and the Castilian monarchy serves as a lens through which scholarship can better examine the work of the Castilian prelates. While other thematic elements, such as frontier construction or crusading culture, were closely connected to this tripolar nexus, the core relationships among the kings, pontiffs, and prelates remain a powerful focal point for scholarship. The history of the bishops of medieval Castile is used much too rarely, and without careful scrutiny, for the long reign of Alfonso VIII.[14] That history deserves to play a part in the larger conversations of medieval historians going forward and is this book's primary task.

At Alfonso VII's death in 1157, there were many contenders for the title of "Emperor of the Spains" in the Christian kingdoms of the Iberian Peninsula: a powerful king reigning in a growing Portugal, two ambitious brothers on the thrones of Castile and León, a wily upstart ruling in Navarra, and a messy solution to a succession crisis that created a precarious possibility in the nascent Crown of Aragon.[15] The second *taifa* period in al-Andalus was likewise a scene of competition and struggle, but Murcia swallowed up many of the smaller *taifa* kingdoms in his efforts to stave off the surging Almohads.[16] Sancho III was king of Castile for only a year and ten days, and his son was left in the hands of the two most powerful families in the kingdom. What should have been a long minority was commandeered by the king of León, likely because of both legitimate security concerns for his southern and southwestern borders and his own personal ambition to be acclaimed as "king of the Spains."[17] Given these factors, the survival and expansion of Castile during the fifty-six years of Alfonso's reign appears quite remarkable in hindsight.[18]

Scholars of lordship and queenship have elsewhere shown that medieval kings had help from a wide array of family members, extended social networks, and hereditary and appointed potentates within their midst.[19] The orphaned toddler-king was alone in his personal body, but not in the body of his kingship.[20] This volume will argue that prelates were integral collaborators who guided Alfonso's reign from their cathedral sees, and their careful work to bring the papacy and the kingdom closer together was the foundational effort that supported the Castilian church's lasting success.

From the earliest days of his rule, Alfonso VIII was watched over by two bishops, both of whom figure prominently in this study: his great-uncle Ramón de Minerva of Palencia and his godfather Celebruno, first bishop of Sigüenza and later archbishop of Toledo.[21] Scholarly consensus marks the decade of Alfonso VIII's minority (1158–69) as a time of considerable internal conflict, especially between the two families charged by Sancho III with protecting the orphaned king.[22] With two noble families grappling for control and two clerics trying to keep the peace, outside intervention would seem inevitable, and the interjection of Fernando II of León, both as an uncle and as the presumptive heir of Alfonso VIII's crown, created real problems. By 1166, the fortunes of the Castilian elites—especially with respect to Toledo, where a Leonese-appointed governor held the city—had deteriorated enough that the clergy of Castile were forced to take decisive action in concert with the count of Lara and probably several other unnamed aristocrats.

At Segovia in 1166, the archbishop of Toledo convoked a synod in which the bishops included several items of prime political importance. The first item affirmed was the allegiance and homage (*hominium*) owed to Alfonso by "anyone who might hold an honor within the kingdom of Alfonso and who was his vassal."[23] Because the young king was threatened, this was a critical guarantee of his nascent political legitimacy. The second item made anyone who invaded Alfonso's kingdom a military target and granted a full crusade indulgence to those who repulsed invading forces.[24] This may be the first instance of a crusade indulgence issued against other Christians, given the fact that León and Navarra had recently swallowed up parts of Castile.[25] Even if it was not the first instance of crusade indulgences leveraged to repel fellow Christians, it was still a profound statement of ecclesiastical backing for Alfonso's kingship. The third item in the synodal canons declared that bishops should excommunicate anyone in the kingdom who dared to wage war without the royal nod.[26] Effectively, these canons ensured that when action was taken against a threat, it secured a directly royal interest. The occupation of much of western Castile by Leonese forces being the backdrop for such a gathering, it is safe to say that the bishops meant the king of León and his vassals most of all when they said "anyone." Although the chronicle evidence is murky in the period, it seems unlikely that the contemporary witnesses were not better informed than much later chronicles.[27] The agenda of the synod—pro-papal, pro-Castilian, and anti-Leonese—makes clear that Castilian bishops were aligned with the king. Because they were not at

Toledo (then under Leonese control) but at Segovia, the importance of those common bonds was heightened. The bishops used their own gravity as prelates to pull Alfonso closer to themselves and to Rome.

Alfonso VIII's minority ended with a celebration of a gathering of the *cortes* in 1169 at Burgos, often called the "head of Castile."[28] While the king had knighted himself, taking his arms from the altar of San Zoilo of Carrión, he shored up major political support by announcing his betrothal to the daughter of the most powerful secular leaders in Europe: Leonor Plantagenet, daughter of Eleanor of Aquitaine and Henry II Plantagenet.[29] In the same flurry of activity, Alfonso gave the monastery of San Zoilo a charter to provide for the foundation of the first Castilian fair (*feria*) at San Zoilo de Carrión in 1169.[30] Every scholar working on the meetings of the Castilian *cortes* (*curia regis*) has made clear the importance of this gathering for Alfonso and new bride, with some calling it a political master stroke.[31] Some forty-six years later, Alfonso and Leonor would die within weeks of each other, surviving their numerous tragedies and expanding the fortunes of Castile many times over; the Cortes of Burgos in 1169 was an auspicious, but not unchallenged, beginning.

The early 1170s were a major turnaround for Castile. Two wars, against León and Navarra, reclaimed major territory in the kingdom of Castile's border regions that had been poached during Alfonso VIII's minority. Military campaigns against the two rival kingdoms were endorsed by and even employed bishops, and this signals how close these prelates were to the royal court because it shows them collaborating on an explicitly royal project couched in ecclesiastical idioms.[32] Francisco García Fitz has shown that Castile's wars against its neighbors were one of the sources of a major recovery of its political fortunes in the period.[33] It is also clear that Castile secured these advancements, in part, with a clever arbitration between the kings of Navarra and Castile at the court of Henry II Plantagenet.[34] Beyond these less well known campaigns, the celebrated conquest of Cuenca in 1177 was so powerful a political motivator that Powers has suggested it was a crowning achievement, and several historians have patiently untangled the degree to which its capture was commemorated in charters for a long time thereafter.[35] Even the visit of Cardinal Hyacinth Bobone brought Iberia, Castile included, into closer cooperation with the papacy, a feat mirrored in the foundation bull of Cuenca and subsequent papal approval for the new diocese.[36] These were major political achievements and swelled the fortunes of Castilian dioceses, and some have even suggested that the archbishops of Toledo had helped finance the conquest of Cuenca in order to add another suffragan diocese to their province.[37] The impact of these campaigns on Castile was enormous, as both the expansion of territory and the recovery of prestige laid the groundwork for the 1180s and brought the papacy, bishops, and crown closer together in pursuit of mutually beneficial goals.

If the decade after Alfonso and Leonor's marriage was successful, then the decade after that was a mixed bag. Foundations of both the important royal monastery of Las Huelgas—perhaps the most important women's monastery in Castilian history—and a new diocese at Plasencia saw the increase of clerical fortunes.[38] Despite unusually high infant mortality in early pregnancies, several children—including Alfonso's eventual heir, Queen Berenguela of León and Castile, and her sisters Urraca and Blanca, who would become the queens of Portugal and France, respectively—would ensure the biological future of the dynasty.[39] The new diocese centered on Plasencia, carved out in part from territory from the diocese of Ávila; it continued Alfonso VIII's gradual process of checking Leonese expansion into Extremadura and provided a launching pad for further wars against the southwest.[40] The often-discussed Cortes of Carrión in 1188 saw Berenguela of Castile's betrothal to a German prince and the knighting of the new king of León by the king of Castile (who humiliated the Leonese monarch, forcing him to kiss the hand of his elder Castilian cousin).[41] Having stepped onto the wider stage of European affairs, the end of the 1180s was also the start of a decade of monumental highs and lows, punctuated by the September 1189 birth of the first healthy son—Prince Fernando—and a truce with the Almohads.[42] The connection between the papacy's geopolitical objectives, the growth of the episcopal ranks and the number of dioceses, and the royal expansionist agenda would find a great new backer from an old familiar face.

The election of Cardinal Hyacinth Bobone (whom Alfonso VIII and his court had known during his legations to the Iberian Peninsula) as Pope Celestine III brought the holy wars against the Almohads into renewed focus for the papacy.[43] Celestine III dispatched his nephew, Cardinal Gregory of Sant'Angelo, as a legate to the peninsula with a clear mandate to secure peace between the Iberian Christian powers and further the wars against the Almohads.[44] The high-water mark of this process was the Treaty of Tordehumos in 1194, which secured a peace between León and Castile for ten years.[45] Martín López de Pisuerga, a young archbishop of Toledo, led a major raid into al-Andalus, breaking the truce and launching a new holy war against the Almohad caliph Yaqub al-Mansur.[46] The Crusade of Alarcos in 1195 was an enormous undertaking: the bishop of Sigüenza lent the count of Molina money to pay his soldiers; the pope sent a number of letters (one of which was suppressed) to clerics in Castile; and, after the Castilians were defeated, two bishops were even found dead on the battlefield.[47]

After the defeat at Alarcos, the great reversal in fortunes brought a Leonese invasion (prompting a crusade against Alfonso IX in 1196) and a pair of raids from the Almohads, both of which would only be reversed with major assistance from the Crown of Aragon.[48] Even the military orders, legally independent but politically invested, were "pressured to take up arms against Alfonso [IX] and wanted to avoid doing so."[49] Retaliating against those who had wronged him in the aftermath of the defeat at Alarcos meant taking revenge on both León and Navarra. Major conquests of territory in Navarra closed out the military achievements of the decade, and a number of reforms of cathedral chapters helped reshape the spiritual practice of the kingdom just as its borders were expanding.[50] The closeness of the connections between Alfonso VIII and the church in his kingdom had taken many forms, but at the close of the twelfth century they were perhaps the closest they had been since the conquest of Cuenca nearly twenty-five years earlier, even as the papacy had a lower-than-usual opinion of the king of Navarra, in part owing to his alliance with the Almohads.[51]

At the start of the thirteenth century, the Castilian monarchs were enjoying a phase of considerable strength. New children brought increasing survival chances to the dynasty and a great increase in the number of available diplomatic markers to play on the international scene.[52] While Alfonso's brother-in-law, John of England, was struggling against his own internal dissension and against a reinvigorated Capetian monarchy in France, the Castilians sought to seize Queen Leonor's dower lands of Gascony.[53] Although Alfonso and Leonor's hold over the southwestern parts of modern-day France was short-lived, the mere fact of passing over the Pyrenees to exert dominance in what was traditionally an Aragonese and Angevin zone of influence was a powerful political statement of ambition by Leonor and Alfonso.[54] The charters from this period make clear that the bishops of Castile were at Alfonso's side, and for a short time, prelates from Gascony even appear as witnesses to charters from Castile.[55] The end of the first decade of the thirteenth century saw a huge shift in the population of the bishops of Castile: of the forty total prelates serving under Alfonso and Leonor, nine of them were appointed during this decade.[56] Replacing a quarter of the bishops—and thus a key segment of the administrative operations of Castile—should have stunted the Castilian's progress, but not even the king's fever, causing him to draft his will in 1204, would slow the pace of Castilian expansionism in the early thirteenth century.[57]

Iberian Peninsula circa 1200 CE

The last half decade of Alfonso's life and reign was also the most successful. In 1210, Alfonso's eldest son, the Infante Fernando, joined with Aragonese forces to raid Murcia and soften up the Almohads, strengthening the Aragonese-Castilian alliance in the process.[58] By 1211, the *infante* (likely with an archiepiscopal ghostwriter) was corresponding with the pope and helping plan a major international crusade against the Almohads, prompted by the Almohads' capture of the Castilian fortress of Salvatierra.[59] When the prince died of a fever in late 1211, a heartbroken Alfonso and his allies from Navarra, Aragon, the Toulousain, and Portugal led a massive campaign against the Almohads.[60] Even the death of a bishop, Juan Mathé of Burgos, on the field could not stunt the wars.[61] The Crusade of Las Navas in 1212 was a pivotal moment, and while scholars have rightly questioned how "inevitable" the collapse of Andalusi independence was in the century that followed, contemporary chroniclers made it the crowning achievement of a monarch nearing the end of his life.[62] The impact of the crusade was enormous, but Alfonso and Leonor lived only a few years after this crowning glory.[63] Although the monarchs faded into memory, the prelates of their kingdom would all live long enough that Leonor and Alfonso's grandson, Fernando III, would take the throne under the watchful eye of their daughter, Berenguela; most would stay well into the second decade of his reign as King Fernando III.[64]

The Challenge of the Sources

Naturally, the question must be why no other volume has presented episcopal history if it is so relevant for filling in the historiography of the High Middle Ages. The general answer is that many medieval studies and their *comparanda* are still profoundly centered on Anglo-French historiography and the themes pertinent to its study; the specific answer is that the Castilian sources are fewer in number than for other regions, and most private archives are lost. Indeed, the sources that are preserved are primarily ecclesiastical or royal ones, so the task of writing an ecclesiastically centered history that plays out as a constellation of authority around the monarchy is less difficult than it might seem.

Take, for example, this complaint between two dioceses whose archives are coincidentally the poorest preserved in long-twelfth-century Castile. Sometime between July and December 1188, the archbishop of Compostela responded to a complaint, assigned to him by the pope, from the bishop of Ávila about the conduct of his former archpriest and now subject archdeacon of Plasencia, Pedro de Taiaborch.[65] An internal conflict of this type for a walled city like Ávila on the southern edge of Castile—only a few hundred kilometers from a major Almohad stronghold at Cáceres—could have spelled disaster if such dissension spilled over.[66] Although the letter from the archbishop of Compostela to the archdeacon of Plasencia is a short text of a little more than one hundred words, it does suggest that Rome had heard from Compostela about the problems between Ávila and Plasencia. The first letter was matched by a similar papal letter to Archdeacon Pedro de Taiaborch himself about the controversy.[67] The added wrinkle of the text is that Plasencia was in the early stages of being organized as a new royally sponsored diocese.[68] Although we even have a chronicle of the exploits of the men of Ávila in Extremadura, there are no mentions of even a single chaplain in their raiding parties, nor whether the conflict with Plasencia provoked any infraclerical violence, as had happened elsewhere.[69] The same could not be said for the conflict between Sigüenza and Osma from a few decades earlier, which occasionally broke out into the hostile occupation of border parishes.[70]

What appears, at first glance, to be a squabble between a bishop and one of his archdeacons takes on a much larger role in the history of secular and ecclesiastical politics in the late twelfth century. As Roman pontiffs wrangled to get some renegade bishops to abide by their writs, so too did bishops attempt to secure obedience from their own clergy, a feat mirrored by royal attempts to bring aristocrats to heel.[71] Even the short text from the archbishop of Compostela betrays the ways in which a diocesan bishop and his archdeacon could be pulled between the royal initiative to found a new diocese and the Roman pontiff's desire to see peace maintained in the churches.

Unfortunately for historians wanting to know more about the back-and-forth of Ávila's life on the frontier and the cast of characters that must have populated the busy diocesan landscape, the Ávilan archive contains only forty-seven documents from the whole of the twelfth century.[72] There were, by most historians' reckonings, a dozen bishops of Ávila, which suggests that a great deal of historical data has simply been lost.[73] In the history of the long twelfth century in Castile, the archive of that episcopal city is not alone in having a smallish collection of records. Plasencia's archives do not exist in the twelfth century, and, in fact, nothing whatsoever before 1238 is preserved in the archive—the entire first half century of the diocese archive's existence is missing.[74] The documentation for Osma—which produced no less than the founder of the Order of Preachers, Saint Dominic, from within its bounds—is as poorly preserved as the records of Ávila.[75] Sources cannot be conjured from thin air, but the history of dioceses with records that are scarcer *can* be filled in from a more oblique angle through the reconstruction of the history of their diocesan colleagues.

Although not every diocese had archives that survived as poorly as those of Osma or Ávila, there are oases amid the undeservedly desertified archives; these are flukes of fortune. At Sigüenza—where the archives were damaged by Franco's forces in the Civil War—many of the same documents still sit in their *armaria*, divided into sections of pontifical and particular texts, or in the codices on the large shelves.[76] Better still, the catalogs of the archives at Burgos, Toledo, Palencia, and Segovia contain considerable amounts of their medieval records.[77] My task here is revive the stories that historians too rarely listen to but are in fact waiting high in a cloister tower at Sigüenza, where the archives now sit.[78] Reanimating each of these dioceses fully would take more historical material than has been preserved, but there are some instances where a real contribution might be made. This book takes up that task.

Since Richard Fletcher's 1978 study of the episcopate in the kingdom of León, no English-language scholar has provided a comparable treatment for Castile despite the need to provide careful examination of the similarities between the church in Iberian kingdoms and their trans-Pyrenean contemporaries.[79] This is in spite of the considerable contributions of Carlos de Ayala Martínez, who has shown that the sources from the Castilian church do provide a substantive base on which serious historical investigation might take place.[80] Reconstructing the history of the church of Castile will add substantial and worthwhile nuance to the history of Castile as a whole. Reilly argued that the development of many of the mechanisms of royal power were cultivated by the high clergy and that the episcopate was the "key institutional element" in León and Castile during the early twelfth century.[81] Peter Linehan made clear his opinion that the church of Castile in the thirteenth century had a free hand from Fernando III because the conqueror's success bought him papal leniency.[82] These three factors suggest that the study of the church in the kingdom of Castile would be worthwhile, but because of the poor preservation of the sources in several archives, such a treatment has not yet appeared. This study will remedy that deficit by showing that bishops and their administrations are an underrealized opportunity to unlock the history of medieval Castile.

So bishops and their clergy present avenues to study a multitude of roles, and the sources for their careers are better preserved than other archival documents (most notably private noble archives and municipal archives) in the history of Castile.[83] As a result, the episcopates of Castile's bishops present a doubly fortunate resource: there are many avenues of historical research preserved in their records, and there are many records in which to pursue these inquiries. It is for this reason that the study of the Castilian episcopate seems to be such a viable object to be undertaken here. Why, then, should such a study be limited to the reign of a single king—Alfonso VIII of Castile?

At first, Alfonso VIII and his age appear rather daunting as a subject. In his massive study of Alfonso's reign, the twentieth-century Spanish scholar Julio González provided more than eleven hundred pages of commentary, drawing further on some two thousand pages of edited archival sources, but he devoted only sixty or so to the study of the bishops themselves and even then was only interested in prosopographical work.[84] The fifty-six years during which Alfonso VIII was king provide two advantages, then, that recommend it as a period of study. First, it creates a natural chronological boundary in the reign of one king, which allows for a bit of narrative cohesion. Second, it makes the actions of that king—themselves the subject of two major domestic chronicles and many other narrative sources, as well—into a kind of historical frame onto which a larger canvas can be stretched and a portrait of historical life in the medieval episcopate can be painted. Yet to many historians of the period, Alfonso VIII is still a lesser-known king, and his reign needs still more explication for nonspecialists and lay readers alike.[85] As a key element of the constellation of authority around Alfonso VIII, the bishops deserve special attention and can offer real improvements for our general picture of the period.

I have endeavored to write a history of those prelates about whom substantial data—from archival and narrative sources—might be compiled and have examined the roles that certain major themes play in their respective episcopates. For some prelates, surviving sources recommended the writing of a more legal history, so that was the history against whose historiography my findings might be tested. It seems right, then, to situate the potential of such an approach against the major scholarly contributions that have shaped this study.

The pioneering work on long-twelfth-century Castile and León in English for "church history" was done in the twentieth century by Peter Linehan and Richard Fletcher. Although his later project *History and the Historians of Medieval Spain* is referenced more frequently as a kind of omnibus compendium of medieval Hispanist scholarship, Linehan's *The Spanish Church and the Papacy in the Thirteenth Century* argued for seeing a close cooperation between the monarchy and church at the beginning of the thirteenth century that was transmogrified into royal control by the end of the same century.[86] Fletcher's first contribution, *The Episcopate in the Kingdom of León in the Twelfth Century*, had two main goals.[87] First, his project created a series of topical narratives that demonstrated that regional ecclesiastical history could be written about the medieval Iberian kingdoms without relying, as Linehan had done, quite so heavily on papal sources. The second goal was to provide a rich reference for the key players and themes preserved in the sources. Frequently, these two goals worked together to demonstrate that the project itself was valid, as were many that Fletcher had hoped would follow. The second of Fletcher's two major monographs on the subject was his biography of the great Compostelan archbishop Diego Gelmírez, which was more in the style of the then-in-vogue microhistories creating a kind of test case for many of the major themes of the period.[88] Carolina Carl has much more recently examined the case of a diocese and its bishop that existed on the frontiers of Navarra, Aragon, and Castile and grew in response to a variety of influences from those regions and larger social forces.[89] In many respects, this volume will connect the work done by Fletcher on the kingdom of León and Carl's project on Calahorra in the long twelfth century with the scholarship of Linehan on the wider Iberian Peninsula's ecclesiastical landscape in the thirteenth century and its connections to one of the major sources of its appellate authority.

Although the number of scholars cited in this volume reveals a widespread interest in the religious history of the Iberian Peninsula, *A Constellation of Authority* complements and nuances other scholarly treatments. In a handful of published articles, Ayala Martínez has begun to synthesize the available scholarship and edited sources to correct a large number of erroneous elements in extant historiography and provide a coherent, cohesive narrative on which later scholarship might be based.[90] Adeline Rucquoi, in both articles and a recent book, has explored the cultural and religious revival of the long twelfth century in Castile with special attention to the historical development of Saint Dominic of Osma.[91] In his extensive project, Andreas Holndonner has chronicled the legal and political history of the metropolitan province of Toledo in order to demonstrate that Toledan clerics had to fight to achieve their distinction as "Primas Hispaniarum," as the theoretical administrative suzerain of the Church in the Iberian Peninsula.[92] There is also a considerable body of *comparanda* against which the preliminary conclusions of this study can be contrasted. Whether in David Foote's study of Orvieto, Maureen Miller's work on Verona, Paul Freedman's investigations of Vic, Graham Loud's histories of the church in Sicily, Bernard Hamilton's scholarship on the Crusader States, or Jane Sayers's research into Canterbury, ecclesiastical sources have been used by a wide array of scholars to show that bishops can be key windows onto historical developments, providing special perspectives not in evidence in lay sources.[93] Where the body of sources from the lower classes and middling aristocratic archives does not survive, scholars can use ecclesiastical sources to fill the gap. Even where important scholars have carefully unlocked alternate viewpoints, bishops' histories build meaningful contrasts.[94] This study takes up exactly that project—using bishops to unlock a "history from the middle" and to show the manner in which the church in Castile was drawing closer to Rome in a variety of ways.[95]

Taken as a whole, scholarship has already made clear the ways in which this study might provide a welcome addition to discussions of major social and cultural themes. Ecclesiastical historians, working both within and outside the Iberian Peninsula, have shown that the history of church institutions could fill important gaps in the records of secular institutions. Although chroniclers may often mention only the king or his close confidantes, studies of Castilian history have demonstrated that the figures "in the background" of traditionalist historiography are not only plausible subjects for study but also reveal a great deal about broader and deeper societal and cultural developments. Moreover, the sources for Castilian history can support and satisfy the questions posed by scholars working on the subject. A brief outline of this book's principal questions, and their answerers, sets the stage for the rest of the volume.

The Questions Posed in This Study and Their Answerers

In this project, I have tried to recover the voices of the bishops of Castile and present them in their own context. By necessity, only the long-serving prelates appear in any detail here, simply because the records preserved from their episcopates were extensive enough suggest how they engaged with the great ideas and movements of their day. The sources do not always answer all the questions one would like to ask, of course. Each of this book's chapters focuses on single bishop to flesh out the history of an individual who might provide something of a case study to help build a new, more comprehensive narrative synthesis.

In every way possible, I have described their encounters with broader pan-European trends and themes, but the overarching theme is the complicated balancing that bishops had to achieve between the monarchy and the papacy, managing their relationships with both to suit their needs. It is my intention that this narrative synthesis will open up more conversations about the historical impact of Castile and its clergy. The biographical studies here, offered in chronological order, offer a revised narrative for the period and its players. (To that end, forty individuals appear here, though some are only mentioned as single points of data at this project's conclusion or in the prosopographical appendix.)

The seven bishops studied here interacted with their colleagues, some of whom we have very little information about, and produced a great deal of records about their activities. They show themselves to be quite like their peers in other kingdoms, a fact that will make the conclusions of this volume useful for comparative studies and will surely lay the ground for future work on the Castilian church.

In the chapter that follows, Archbishop Celebruno of Toledo invites us to see the ways in which he served in the complicated roles that his position as Primate of the Spains demanded. In chapter 3, Ramón de Minerva, a bishop of Palencia, reminds us that in an age of changing clerical norms, the old guard still stood its post (even with a handful of reprovals from the papacy), continuing to fulfill its duties as a great political force in a more rough-and-tumble era. In the fourth chapter, an Italian cleric called Alderico di Palacio demonstrates that the churches of kingdoms were not a homogenous lot; nor were the bishops, as his encouragement of the school at Palencia tells us, purely political. Alderico's contemporary Martín de Bazán is the subject of chapter 5. He belonged to the nobility from a neighboring kingdom and changed his diocese considerably, but his greatest achievement was in carrying out the reforms that recruited Domingo de Caleruega—and thus set the Order of Preachers well on their way to shaping Latin Europe. In the sixth chapter, Martín López de Pisuerga, a scion of a noble family, forever alters the ways in which Toledan archbishops took on all comers, on all fronts, at all times. Chapter 7 details how Julián ben Tauro, a Toledan Mozarab, was elected to the new diocese of Cuenca, his body and diocese acting as living, breathing frontiers that demonstrate the inherent challenge of medieval and early modern sources presenting very different historical narratives. In the eighth chapter, the career of Rodrigo de Finojosa, bishop of Sigüenza for more than three decades, illustrates how a cleric blessed with a long tenure can expose many of the different tensions experienced by bishops in medieval Christendom.

These case studies of about one-fifth of Alfonso VIII's bishops represent a sample of those whose careers can be reconstructed. The early death in battle of a young clergyman, only a few weeks after he was elected to be bishop of Segovia, is an evocative reminder of the fragility of life in the Middle Ages, but it hardly makes for the stuff of a whole chapter, for example.[96] Nor, for that matter, do the bishops of Plasencia; one bishop may have been captured by the Almohads in 1195 or 1196, and the diocesan archives appear to have been completely erased of any material predating 1238, when the diocese itself was entering its fifth decade of existence.[97] An appendix to this volume records the names and backgrounds of all those clerics who served during the reign of Alfonso VIII, but a comprehensive study of every bishop and every act they performed would surely be as dry to read as the fields of Extremadura in August—and not even half as pleasant to write.

Focusing on singular figures preserves narrative cohesion but also gives future scholars a foundation for the study of other important themes uncovered in the building of the narrative. As a result, I have attempted to provide the most comprehensive, but not tedious, treatment of each of the prelates' careers to fill out the portraits of the background stars in Bianchini's "constellation of authority."[98] This kind of personal focus can be very illuminating for larger conversations while avoiding the problems posed by "great man histories." The biographical treatments offered in this volume provide a base on which larger, more complex narratives can later rest.

2

THE IMPORTANCE OF BEING ARCHBISHOP
Celebruno, Bishop of Sigüenza and Archbishop of Toledo

The person of Cerebruno, such a subject, he alone could fill up the great emptiness that would result in Spain from the lack of such a great man. He was Cerebruno the Noble, . . . he was French by nation, and because of his virtue, letters, and such great prudence, it was he that deserved to be master of the child, King Don Alonso [VIII].
—Diego de Castejón y Fonseca, *Primacia de la Santa Iglesia de Toledo* (1655)

Royal minorities were dangerous, both for the parties competing for favor during a regency and for the royal youth. The minority of Alfonso VIII, in particular, was plagued by the contest between two aristocratic clans, the Lara and the Castro, and by the predations of Alfonso's uncles, Fernando II of León and Sanç VI of Navarra.[1] During Alfonso's minority, two groups—the *concejos* of the towns of Castile and the bishops of Alfonso's kingdom—supported the Orphan King against those attempting to divert royal resources for their particular goals.[2] The clerics standing around Alfonso in the early days were a group of men with common backgrounds who rose to meet the challenges of the unexpected early death of Sancho III of Castile. Although he was not the leader of the group in those early years, Celebruno, first as bishop of Sigüenza (r. 1156–66) and later as archbishop of Toledo (r. 1166–80), rose to receive substantial praises from his godson, Alfonso VIII, and his superiors, especially Popes Adrian IV and Alexander III. If the clerics around Alfonso were, as scholars have shown, vital for preserving Castile's independence (and perhaps for even saving Alfonso's life), then Celebruno deserves considerable praise for his efforts on behalf of the Orphan King.

This chapter explores the ways in which Celebruno's episcopate and archiepiscopate serve as an entrée into Alfonso's early relationship with the Church and the bishops of the kingdom of Castile. Celebruno's tenure as a bishop illustrates the nuanced, symbiotic relationship that the kings of Castile would build with the clergy in their realm, a relationship that may have saved Alfonso's life as a boy and dramatically improved his fortunes as a man. We know a great many details about Celebruno's career as a cleric, and in this chapter (as well as the one that follows it), it becomes clear that the early clergy in the kingdom of Castile were some of the Orphan King's closest allies and most effective agents. Celebruno serves as one of the very best examples of this phenomenon.

"My Godfather, Celebruno"

In the medieval world, where parental (and particularly maternal) mortality was a distinct possibility, godparents occupied an important post that guaranteed the safety of young children. Should a child be orphaned, godparents were to step in and fill the void left by the too-early passing of natural parents, with a special focus on instruction in the Christian faith and the assurance that the child would progress through the sacraments in proper fashion.[3] The bonds formed between parents and godparents through their common participation in a child's baptism were no small matter. Studies of cases from the later Middle Ages demonstrate that naming practices, social connections, and strategic alliances were solemnized, in part, by the mutually binding actions at the baptism.[4] The *Historia Compostellana* records that, when he was about to become king of León and Castile, Alfonso VII—later to be called "el Emperador"—received his unction and sacraments from his godfather, the archbishop of Compostela, before taking his arms from the altar of Santiago.[5] Even in the lives of kings, godparents played a crucial role.

In the case of Alfonso VIII of Castile, we can be certain about the identity of his godfather, if less so about his godmother. In 1166, Alfonso donated a substantial endowment to the church of Sigüenza and "you my godfather Celebruno bishop of that same church [of Sigüenza]" (vobisque patrino meo Celebruno ejusdem ecclesie episcopo).[6] The relationship between the two men went far deeper than that single gift in the 1160s, but the story of their interconnectedness starts more than a decade earlier, when Alfonso VIII was not yet born and Celebruno was not yet a bishop.

For a mid-twelfth-century archbishop on the external frontiers of Christendom, we know a great deal about Celebruno. He was likely from the region around Poitou and appears in Toledo as a canon in the early twelfth century, in the company of one its more famous archbishops, Archbishop Raimond of Toledo (r. 1126–52).[7] Celebruno was one of the Toledan cathedral canons who had been promoted to the episcopate, and his first post was to Sigüenza, where a number of ultramontane prelates had served as bishops from its refoundation in the early twelfth century.[8] It was during this decade-long term as the bishop of Sigüenza that Celebruno must have been made Alfonso VIII's godfather, but the reasons behind his appointment and the political context of the time need some unpacking.

Celebruno was elected to the episcopate of Sigüenza during the last months of the reign of Alfonso VII "el Emperador," while his sons Sancho and Fernando served as cadet-kings in Nájera and Galicia, respectively.[9] The diocese of Sigüenza was far closer to Sancho's power base on the Castilian side of the Leonese empire of Alfonso VII, and it may very well be that Sancho's influence propelled Celebruno to the head of the diocese. Unpacking the internal dynamics between father and son is difficult, but Reilly has argued that Alfonso VII exercised overwhelming influence over the Church in his era. We may thus suspect that Sancho acted as one of his father's chief deputies in the Castilian territories, including in the backing of certain clerical candidates.[10] We have confirmation from two sources (epigraphy and necrology) that Celebruno's predecessor, Pedro de Leucat, died on 20 May 1156 and that Celebruno himself begins to appear by 15 December.[11] The Toledan canon's relatively quick confirmation and elevation were likely aided by the fact that Archbishop Juan de Segovia (also called "de Castellmorum") knew Celebruno well—and by the fact that the choice seems to have been favored by Sancho III before his election.

Alfonso VIII was born on 11 November 1155, about six months before Celebruno could have been elected to Sigüenza.[12] Unfortunately, we do not know where Alfonso VIII—or most of the twelfth-century Iberian monarchs—was baptized, but we might suppose that Toledo hosted the ceremony. There are two reasons this seems likely. First, Juan de Segovia was a commanding presence in the Castilian and Iberian church, and both Alfonso VII and Sancho III were later buried in the cathedral of Toledo.[13] Second, Celebruno was a canon of Toledo at the time, which make his presence as Alfonso VIII's godfather seem directly connected to Toledo. Why

Sancho III would choose a canon of Toledo as the godfather of his first-born son is not known, but it seems possible that the move had three supporting points. First, the examples of royal chaplains occupying high offices early in their clerical careers are few, but the trend of chaplains being "elected" to a see after years of faithful service is well attested enough that we may suspect that Celebruno was Sancho's chaplain or perhaps his confessor.[14] Second, Celebruno was one of the number of imported clerics favored by Sancho III's father, the Leonese emperor Alfonso VII.[15] The fact that Celebruno was elected in early 1156, late in the reign of Alfonso VII and early in the period where Sancho III was likely gathering influence, suggests that the Poitevin Celebruno was favored by the Leonese emperor and his "Castilian" son. Third, it seems that Celebruno was also the godfather of Pedro Manriquez de Lara, a key member of the Lara family and southern frontier lord (including possessions around Toledo) who was integral to the Lara efforts in the regency of later Alfonso VIII's minority.[16] Although we cannot say for certain that the cathedral of Toledo was the site of Alfonso's baptism, it does fit into the larger focus of the period. The importance of this connection to Toledo from the early period of Alfonso's minority suggests that both Celebruno and his godson maintained a close connection to Toledo.

While he was bishop of Sigüenza, Celebruno was by no means inactive, even if the records preserved from the period allow us to reconstruct less of his activity than would be ideal. Early in his episcopate, Celebruno received a donation from Emperor Alfonso VII of the revenues and rights over the monastery of San Salvador of Atienza, a town later favored as a residence by Alfonso VIII.[17] In 1158, the Infanta Sancha Raimúndez, sister of Alfonso VII, gave to the church of Sigüenza a mill in Toledo as part of her larger program of donations for her soul and for those of her brother and parents.[18] There were few sightings of Celebruno in the royal texts of the late 1150s or early 1160s, but correspondence from Alexander III's curia suggests that he was hard at work fighting with the bishop of Osma over ownership of a handful of border towns. This correspondence included at least nine letters and may well have been heard in a side session of the Council of Tours in 1163, discussed in greater detail below.[19] Yet these conflicts suggest that Celebruno was becoming increasingly familiar with the inner workings of the curia and that conciliar gatherings presented chances to cultivate contacts with the Roman church and ensure that he was aware of any developments. This closeness with Rome was not in conflict with his relationship with the crown; rather, it evinces the complicated ways in which the two relationships were occasionally covalent and the ways that bishops acted as mutual go-betweens for both their kings and the bishops of Rome.

In early February 1155, while Celebruno was still a canon of Toledo, Cardinal Hyacinth Bobone had held a council at Valladolid.[20] What Celebruno thought about the council in 1155 is beyond the reach of the sources, but it seems quite likely that the drama of the gathering made an impression on him. We know that at the council, Alfonso VII expressed his outrage that Cardinal Hyacinth gave the archbishop of Braga any preferential treatment on jurisdictional matters, not least because it tacitly underscored the growing independence of Portugal.[21] We also know that the canons promulgated at the council in 1155 bore a striking resemblance to those issued by Lateran II, which, far from being as authoritative and widely accepted as its eponymous successors in 1179 and 1215, was a deeply political affair within the papacy of Innocent II.[22] If anything, the council of 1155 likely showed that a lot could happen at a great gathering of clerics and that royal and episcopal interests could easily fall by the wayside if not given considerable defense. The back-and-forth of the 1155 gathering was also evidence of the ways in which relationships between pope and king, king and clergy, and clergy and pope could be put in conflict.

Whatever the impact of the 1155 Council of Valladolid, Celebruno seems to have ensured that he was present at the next major papal council. Thanks to Robert Somerville's reconstruction, we can definitively place Celebruno at the Council of Tours in 1163, headed by Alexander III, as one of the three members of the province of Toledo who attended the assembly.[23] In fact, all of the clerics of Alfonso VIII's kingdom attended, save the bishop of Osma and Bishop Ramón de Minerva of Palencia, who was the Orphan King's tutor and likely wished to secure the royal adolescent from nefarious influences.[24] At Alexander's council, Celebruno had a specific topic that required papal intervention: on several occasions over the past decade, laymen and clerics loyal to the bishop of Osma had forcibly invaded and held churches in a series of towns along the border between the dioceses of Osma and Sigüenza.[25] The half-dozen letters that proceeded from Tours and from Alexander's curia there were a substantial rebuke of the bishop of Osma, and it is noteworthy that Juan of Osma was absent from the council's list of attendees, perhaps anticipating such a result.[26] Even if larger issues were on the docket for the rest of Alexander III's summer council, Celebruno's trip to the court was off to a solid start, and cultivating a relationship with the curia was bearing legally significant fruit.

The clerics gathered in Tours were there to discuss the important issues of the day, and judging from the canons promulgated at the council, those issues covered a wide array of topics. Most notably (for a Castilian cleric in that era), among the questions raised at the Council of Tours were those canons that dealt with the preservation of peace among Christians, and especially the peaceful preservation of ecclesiastical goods and properties. Given the political allegiances held by the clergy of Castile—oversimplified as pro-Alfonso VIII and anti-Fernando II—it is no surprise that these same issues would be repeated in the Synod of Segovia, held three years later (and discussed in greater detail below) and under similarly tense political circumstances. These canons should have been received with particular importance by the contemporary Castilian church, given their ability to provide legal and political cover for any cozying up that the clerics of Castile might do to the young Alfonso VIII. Involving themselves in the political fortunes of the kingdom of Castile was risky, but the guarantee of some legal cover in the form of the canons of the Council of Tours shored up any attempts by other clerics to undermine the Castilians' support for their Orphan King.

The culmination of this pattern of involvement in the affairs of both the kingdom and the church of Castile is represented, albeit metonymically, by Alfonso VIII's 1166 donation to the church of Sigüenza (and thus to his godfather). Felipe-Gíl Peces Rata offered a terse, if perfectly apt, summary of the charter: "On the 25th of October, 1166, King Alfonso VIII . . . made a donation to the Church of Sigüenza, to the bishop Don Cerebruno and his successors in the same [church] . . . making grand elegies about his godfather Don Cerebruno and about the Church of Sigüenza which had done great services [for him]."[27] While Peces Rata's summation is accurate, it does not provide all the detail necessary for unpacking the depth of expressed feeling between the Orphan King and his godfather. The charter's opening lines—after the usual Trinitarian invocations—offer a rare glimpse into the personal relationship between Alfonso VIII and his godfather. The king's scribes wrote, "It is befitting to royal power that it reward with gifts those who serve it faithfully and to transfer from their own good possessions into the lordship and use of those serving God, having been inspired by piety and mercy."[28] Alfonso then proceeded, in usual fashion, to donate the village that was the subject of the charter, before concluding the body of the charter with a notation that he did so not just for his own soul and that of his parents but also because of Celebruno's loyalty to the young king: "I give the aforementioned village with the said things that pertain to it, I say, to you my godfather and to your church, on behalf of the many things, even damaging things, which the church of Sigüenza has sustained on my behalf, that you and your successors might freely, peacefully, and quietly hold and possess it in perpetuity."[29] The 1166 charter was given to Celebruno not just because he was Alfonso's godfather but because Celebruno had rendered many services—some of which were "dampnis"—for which Alfonso had to make amends. It seems likely that it was the clergy—particularly Toledo and its suffragans—that held together the kingdom of Castile for Alfonso VIII while it was beset by Leonese and Navarrese ingressions during his minority.[30] The closeness of the relationship between the king and the clergy was not in conflict but rather in concert with papal dicta issued at Tours; the two relationships were not mutually exclusive.

Five months before the privilege in which Alfonso VIII had lauded the efforts of his godfather, the bishop of Sigüenza and the other prelates of the kingdom of Castile gathered in Segovia. The 1166 synod was one of the most telling markers of this internal cohesion within the kingdom of Castile during the Orphan King's minority. In describing his discovery of the synod, Linehan once remarked that it smacked of a gathering of politically Castilian, rather than archiepiscopally Toledan, provenance: "[The clergy at the 1166 Synod of Segovia] described themselves not as suffragans of Toledo—however large the affairs of that church may have loomed in the minds of some of them—but as 'bishops of the kingdom of King Alfonso.' The well-being of all their churches could only be secured in the shadow of a secular settlement."[31] An examination of this synod and its importance for underscoring some of the themes expressed during the last years of Celebruno's tenure at Sigüenza—and thus just before his elevation to Toledo—provides a critical matrix onto which we can map Celebruno's later activities as an archbishop in his own right.

The first two canons of the Synod of Segovia express the direct connection between the young Alfonso VIII and the vassals of his kingdom, but they do so with the explicit backing of ecclesiastical censure. Essentially, as Linehan has argued, these elements give us a portrait of a mixed assembly—partly royal and pseudo-parliamentary, partly ecclesiastical and conciliar—that undertook a blended royal-clerical agenda for the mutual security of both parties.[32] The support of the clergy (often linked to aristocratic families loyal to the Orphan King) was key to maintaining Alfonso's tenuous grip on his patrimony; a royal cause gave the clergy the terms by which they could resist the incursions of Fernando II of León and Sanç VI of Navarra with the support of noble families allied to the young king.[33] It is worth noting that several but not all, of the canons of the Synod of Segovia echoed a number of earlier councils that had been celebrated both within and beyond the Iberian Peninsula.[34] Connections between both the political context of the gathering and its legal precedents from earlier church councils suggests that the response was not some *pro forma* parroting of earlier gatherings and promulgations, but rather an event inspired by contemporary acts. Examining these canons gives us a better glimpse into the hazy world of the royal minority, a formative period in Celebruno's career as a bishop, and one in which the tripolar relationship of the king, pope, and local bishops grew stronger. This appears to have happened in part because of mutual interests to protect ecclesiastical property, which was royally governed territory, and in part because of the vouchsafing of the rights of Christians living in the region, which was the duty of the king and papal appellate jurisdiction.

It is rhetorically tricky ground to divide the canons promulgated at Segovia in March 1166 along the lines of "royal" and "clerical" or "lay" and "ecclesiastical" categories, but we can sense the concerns of multiple parties in the recorded canons. The invocation that precedes the canons themselves offers us an insight into the heterogeneity of those assembled: "A synod was celebrated at Segovia by the lord Juan, Toledan archbishop and Primate of the Spains, and by all the bishops of the kingdom of King Alfonso, and we convened for reaffirming as much for the honor of God and the exaltation of the lord pope as for the peace of the kingdom of our Alfonso."[35] Appealing to a variety of parties underscored the legality and legitimacy that the Castilian clergy sought their synod to convey: P[etrus?], a papal subdeacon, attended the gathering, the young Alfonso VIII and his noble vassals were there, and so was the Castilian clergy. Communal assent to the promulgated canons that followed such an invocation demonstrated their common "buy-in," underscoring their mutual commitment to the legislation that followed and the growing strength of the tripolar relationship. As a result, dividing canons up into royal and clerical categories fails to show anything of great merit, simply because the gathering itself was a mixed gathering from the start. Although it is hard to know exactly what intervened between this council and his election, it seems wholly unlikely that Celebruno was anything less than impressive there, because he was made the archbishop of Toledo before the year was out.

For the five years that passed between the early days of Celebruno's archiepiscopate and the period where his activities became most diverse, there was still much to do in the kingdom of Castile. The wedding of Alfonso VIII to a Plantagenet princess, Leonor, in 1169 was an enormous political affair to which Celebruno would necessarily have devoted much attention.[36]

Moreover, there were still many issues that commanded his attention. A record of significant patronage from Alfonso VIII attests to the archbishop's continued importance at the court, and we know that Celebruno was busy securing confirmation of his rights at the papal court as well as contesting the primacy question that was endemic to his archiepiscopal post.[37] To maintain any claims about the primacy of Toledo, the archbishops both relied on the support of the monarchs and cultivated the favor and legal sympathy of the papacy.

The Salty Work of Archiepiscopal Lordship

Having spent nearly five years in his post as archbishop, Celebruno appears to have been rather comfortable with the burdens and prerogatives of his post. One of the best indicators for his knowledge of his domains and the ways in which his position empowered him to influence the growth and development of his province is in the issuing of *fueros*, municipal law codes issued by a lord but (usually) negotiated with the *concejo* (municipal council). In 1171, Celebruno issued a *fuero* of his own for a town under his jurisdiction, but the town in question, Belinchón, was different from most in Castile.[38] Belinchón was a highly valued territory with significant salt mines that produced large sums for their feudal lords.[39] The *fuero* issued by Celebruno specifically acclaimed him as the "Señor in Belinchón, Archbishop Don Celebruno," and a number of archdeacons and noblemen confirmed the *fuero*, as did Joscelmo—Celebruno's successor at Sigüenza—effectively reinforcing the terms of the code.[40] (It is worth noting that twenty-seven years later, Martín López de Pisuerga would add a handful of terms to the *fuero* of Belinchón.) Although it is likely that the code's contents were negotiated in a process involving the parties concerned, some elements in the *fuero* speak to concerns of an identifiably clerical and explicitly archiepiscopal nature, worth noting given the infrequency with which clergy appear in other (archi)episcopal *fueros* from the second half of the twelfth century.[41] While it was a code for all the inhabitants of the town, it still represents a nexus of the exercise of secular power (as delegated to Celebruno by his royal godson) and his implementation of larger clerical understandings of the proper ordering of society.

By the modern editions of the 1171 *fuero* of Belinchón, there are nearly forty clauses in the code.[42] Within the text of the *fuero*, there are a few key thematic elements that betray the qualities of the lordship sought by Celebruno for the important and wealthy town of Belinchón. Namely, military, juridical, and economic concerns come to the fore, emphasizing the kinds of "feudal" concerns that were typical of lords in the medieval world.[43] Other contemporary bishops exercised similar authority in their own dioceses across the territories of Latin Christendom, although not in exactly the same ways.[44] Effectively, Celebruno wanted stable control of the territory without surrendering too many of the inherent benefits of controlling the salt-rich region of Belinchón.

There were a series of exemptions from taxes and exactions typical of frontier Castilian towns. In only the second clause of the *fuero*, Celebruno mandated that one-third of the urban knights (*caballeros villanos*) but none of the peasants of the town would venture with him when the archbishop went with the royal army, and that those knights who refused to go would pay a fine equivalent of the cost of three rams.[45] Moreover, he exempted the townsfolk from paying any of the "wall-building" *fazendera* taxes typical of frontier towns in the period.[46] James Powers has noted that these scutage taxes were frequently used to supplement the defensive works of the town, and that in practice, they were usually levied only on those men who were capable of participating in the town's defense but did not do so.[47] That military and economic concerns were connected intrinsically in this code shows clearly that Celebruno saw the town as a military and economic power and that those two elements reinforced each other.

As a law code, juridical and jurisdictional concerns were naturally given extensive and detailed treatment in the *fuero* of Belinchón. For example, Celebruno's *fuero* ordered that the lower nobility (*infanzones*) were subject to the same laws as the townsfolk themselves, despite their difference in status.[48] The same, he later noted, applied to any Jews who might inhabit the *terminos* of Belinchón.[49] Maya Soifer Irish has shown that equality under the law is a complex but generally presumed facet of *fueros* in Castile and León.[50] The archbishop also reserved jurisdiction in cases between Christians to his own curia, but he required litigants from the town to venture to one of a select few locations within the archdiocese (e.g., Toledo or Madrid) and noted that cases between Christians and Muslims did not devolve to the archiepiscopal court, because they were expressly cases for the royal court.[51] The code of Belinchón also included notations about the procedure for major cases like homicide and provided certain instances in which cases would not be brought (accidental death by animal, for example).[52] There was, however, a certain degree of autonomy in the town's governance: Belinchón was allowed to elect its own major officials, including its own judges and *alcaldes*, annually.[53] Included in the number of these provisions was the essential function of a self-operating town, where minimal archiepiscopal interference was necessary to allow for a well-ordered municipality with ample resources.[54]

Although it was hardly the only concern of the archbishops of Toledo, there were a number of economically important provisions in the *fuero* of Belinchón. For example, Celebruno's code set out a series of tax obligations—namely, the wall or public works tax (*fazendera*), forest- or pasture-use tax (*montazgo*), portage-customs tax (*portazgo*), and the assumption of the goods of the intestate by the lord (*mañería*)—that members of the town would not pay under certain conditions.[55] Inhabitants who, having worked lands outside the bounds of Belinchón, brought bread or wine into Belinchón to sell there were exempt from any taxes that would normally be levied there.[56] Despite so many exemptions, Belinchón's inhabitants were required to hand over a share of their plunder in war (either one-fifth from *caballeros* or one-seventh from peasants) to the archbishop as well as one-half of the usual taxes that were taken from outsiders.[57] The ways in which Celebruno asserted his authority in these cases suggests that he sought to receive a steady stream of revenue and soldiers from a mostly autonomous town.

The composite picture of the kind of lordship exercised by Celebruno and laid out for the town of Belinchón has a few key features. First, there is a clear emphasis on demonstrating the authority of the archbishop to collect taxes and revenues from certain activities—and by excusing the inhabitants from these taxes, Celebruno was reminding the townsfolk that he *could* collect those duties but was providing them an incentive to remain obedient to him. Second, several clauses deal specifically with military obligations, suggesting that there was an archiepiscopal need for military service to be reliable (one out of every three urban knights), even if it was not exhaustive (two out of every three stayed home). Third, the number of exemptions and privileges afforded to the people of Belinchón suggests that the town's obedience (and thus its regularly delivered resources) was highly sought after by the archbishop and his clergy because Celebruno was not exacting exhaustive taxes from the town. Taken together, we can observe that Celebruno's *fuero* provided for a reliable base of archiepiscopal power in the region and that his lordship was a complex, if not terribly complicated, exercise. These composite legal codes, issued by the archbishop in negotiation with the town, suggest that he was imitating contemporary royal practice while maintaining clerical control of the city, thus connecting royal and archiepiscopal practices more closely.

Reformers in a Dangerous Time?

Although his municipal lordship was surely a major component of the work done by Celebruno and his archiepiscopal *familiares*, we know that there were also a number of important clerical cases that required his attention in the 1170s. A series of cases concerning his suffragan bishops help underscore how many of the controversies that set major power brokers in the kingdom against one another ended up in Celebruno's archiepiscopal court. Two of these stand out as being particularly worthy of comment and emblematic of Celebruno's work as an archiepiscopal appellate judge. First is the often-discussed case of Bernardo of Osma, a bishop accused and later deposed for acquiring his see after having bribed many of the canons in the chapter of Osma—a clerical crime called simony. Second is the reform of the number and conduct of the canons of Toledo in a series of moves designed to keep the archbishop and his clergy on good working terms in their various affairs. (The case of the "clerical discipline" of Ramón de Minerva, bishop of Palencia, is treated in the next chapter; there are, of course, many others whose records were lost.) These two cases demonstrate Celebruno's concerns for both the internal health of his own diocese as well as the health of the church of Castile at large. Taken together, they make clear that Celebruno was not avoiding the larger papal emphases on the reform of the clergy and the elimination of simoniac clerics that dominated the early twelfth-century politics of the church. As part of his larger program of activities, they represent a way of cultivating close ties to Rome while maintaining the favor of the royal godson and his courtiers.

The case of Bernardo, prior of the cathedral chapter of Osma, is well studied for a case of its size and period. We know relatively little about the conduct of the high clergy in Castile in the early 1170s and even less about Osma between the reign of San Pedro de Osma in the early twelfth century and the times of Martín Bazán (studied in chapter 6) at the end of the same century.[58] Despite these unfortunate gaps in our knowledge, scholarship has established many of the key facts in the case, and they appear relatively straightforward.[59] In late 1173, the elderly bishop of Osma, Juan Téllez, died; the prior of his cathedral, Bernardo, bribed a significant (as yet still unknown) number of the other canons in the chapter to elect him on Juan Téllez's death. Some scholars have gone so far as to read a passage of Alfonso VIII's 1208 will—bequeathing a sum of five thousand maravedíes to Osma—as a way of restoring the funds that might have been paid in bribes to comital and royal officials, some of which wound up in Alfonso's fisc, although the evidence for this is suggestive but inconclusive.[60] Reports of Bernardo's simony prompted almost immediate commands from Rome for investigations by Celebruno.[61] The result was evident in later letters, if for no other reason than the conclusion appeared unavoidable and the law on the question was quite clear. Gratian's first recension of the *Decretum* was well on its way to being disseminated in a second, expanded incarnation by this time, but revised definitions of simony were unnecessary for so cut-and-dried a case: "Because they insinuated themselves through simony, they ought not be held amongst the bishops; if they should have been expelled from their sees, which they would seem to hold, they are unable to seek restoration [to their position] before they have been called for the case [of their crime]."[62] Cases of simony were high priority for the twelfth-century church.

No wonder, then, that the case was set upon so quickly. Bernardo remained as the bishop of Osma (as evinced in subscriptions of royal charters) for a little under two years, but not before a full investigation appears to have deposed him so completely and with so few objections that a larger problem came into view.[63] For Bernardo to have purchased the votes of several powerful canons within the chapter—in short, to have committed simony—he would have had to find canons willing to sell their votes. Such a grave mistake, from a papal perspective, betrayed a rotten core in the cathedral chapter of Osma and set in motion a drive to reform the chapter's membership, one that would take nearly thirty years.[64] Eventually, Bishop Martín Bazán of Osma completed the reform of the canons of his cathedral (a process described in full in chapter 5), but Celebruno's role in the early days of this process must have been considerable. As Osma's metropolitan (and with the chapter held under considerable suspicion of corruption), the reform of the chapter would have fallen to the archbishop during the episcopal interregnum.

In 1176, Alexander III dispatched a letter ordering Celebruno to investigate the clerical discipline of the chapter at Osma and make whatever changes were necessary to restore good order.[65] Two years later, Alexander III had to further instruct Celebruno that Bernardo would be allowed to retain his presimoniacal *officium* (i.e., as archdeacon of Soria) even after his conviction and that, if Bernardo had wrongfully been deprived, he should be restored to that position. The letter further noted that it was the second such order, suggesting that either Celebruno or the new bishop of Osma, Miguel (formerly the abbot of San Pedro de Arlanza), had been overzealous in punishing Bernardo for his crimes.[66] The case appears to have provoked no further papal instruction from Alexander III, but it does show that the archbishops of Toledo were engaged in a back-and-forth with their suffragan dioceses and with the papacy over matters of mutual concern. If the case was, as Linehan suggests, instigated by bribes accepted by Alfonso and his counts, then removing Bernardo would have represented a step toward the papacy and potentially a step away from the young king. Celebruno, like his ultramontane peers, participated in the still inchoate process of incorporating the legal and cultural reforms in the church while attempting to maintain a degree of local autonomy and connection to the local monarchy in the process. Negotiating the boundaries between the papacy, monarchy, and archiepiscopate was not simple.

While the case of Bernardo was still in its early stages, Celebruno was handling another, more internal but equally taxing case. The cathedral chapter of Toledo might not have been the wealthiest in the Iberian Peninsula, but there were few that could claim similar prestige or political influence, as Celebruno's own career illustrates.[67] A series of charters, issued by Celebruno but likely prompted by his cathedral chapter, attests to the archbishop's attempts to reform a few key issues that routinely plagued the chapter: penury, inflated numbers, and a widely varying set of clerical norms among the canons. These issues would not be halted by Celebruno's efforts—given the state of the chapter in the thirteenth and fourteenth centuries, they appear endemic—but the archbishop's efforts do speak to a concerted effort to effect meaningful change within his archdiocesan administration.

The first indication that some change had been needed came from the reform of the number of canons in the chapter. At first glance, this would seem a relatively simple change; it was anything but. Canons were required by canon law to have a prebend, which meant that the number of canons was also an indication of the costs with which the cathedral's patrimony was burdened.[68] Moreover, these prebends also came with a number of other funds available to canons—vestimentary payments, for example, to support the buying of clothing and clerical garb befitting their status as cathedral canons.[69] In fact, these funds were so crucial to the complex compensation package represented by a prebend at Toledo (one typical of high-profile posts in cathedral chapters in Christendom generally) that Celebruno was forced to record that only full canons could receive a vestimentary payment.[70] So when Celebruno set the number of canons in the chapter to forty, he was attempting to balance the prestige and human capital of having a large cathedral chapter of capable clerics with the need for resources to support the canons' incomes, as petitions from the canons indicate. Because one of a prelate's key tasks in the period was to cultivate a patronage relationship with local magnates, it is relatively simple to read the donations to Toledo by both nobles and the monarchy of monasteries and villages as an effort by Celebruno to improve the health of the diocesan fisc.[71] The reform of the chapter required Celebruno to cultivate close ties to the papacy (to underline and encourage the reform as a legal enterprise) and to the king and his court (to guarantee that new endowments could support the realignment of resources that reform required). A delicate balance like this ensured that Celebruno's chapter was compliant with his larger goals while serving as a vital resource of human capital to support his work.

Further complicating the issue of *how many* canons were enrolled in the chapter of Toledo was the question of *who* those canons were. In addition to the competition among noble families that was endemic to the inner workings of a cathedral chapter in the twelfth century, Toledo's cultural diversity added another wrinkle to the deeply political question of which young clerics were appointed to the chapter. We know that during the time of Rodrigo Ximénez de Rada, the Mozarabic canons in the chapter appear to have revolted against the young Navarrese archbishop, and we have no reason to suspect that their influence appeared overnight in the early thirteenth century, especially since the Mozarabic population had a deep hold on the city of Toledo after the late eleventh-century reconquest of the Visigothic *urbs regia*. Moreover, there is substantial evidence that the Mozarabic population of Toledo represented a vital macroeconomic element within the city, and we can trace several members of the cathedral chapter whose commerce with the Mozarabic inhabitants of Toledo left numerous records of sales and exchanges. Canons like Nicolás the Priest and Domingo ben Abdallah al-Polichení bought at least nine properties from Mozarabic Toledans during the archiepiscopate of Celebruno, and records of a few sales by them suggest that there may be even more transactions to their credit that have since been lost.[72] While it is difficult to parse the ethnicities of canons based solely on the onomastic evidence of their subscriptions, a full roster of the cathedral canons survives in the confirmation of Celebruno's reform of the number of canons in the chapter.[73]

Of the forty canons subscribing the text of Celebruno's reform, we can sort out the following. Ten of the canons had Castilian/Leonese names, like Diego or Rodrigo, or used patronymics with the *-ius/-ez* typical of Iberian middling sorts; nine had names of Mozarabic origin, had mixed names like Domingo Negro or Salvetus, or were prominent enough in the chapter that we can identify them (like Nicolás or Domingo ben Abdallah); and twelve had decidedly "non-Iberian" names, like Gautier, Robert, or William.[74] Nine canons had names like "Johannes," "Paulus," or "Petrus," ubiquitous because of their connections to early Christianity.[75] As Diego Olstein has shown, the patterns of naming were undergoing considerable changes in this period, and hybridized names make it more difficult to trace the origins of canons without prominent markers of family lineage.[76] The makeup of the chapter was a critical part of the settlement of the diocese's economic problems, given Toledo's historically cosmopolitan population and the attraction of a number of scholarly clergy, some of whom were present for the reform to forty canons. Balancing the interests of different sociocultural groups (Castilians, Mozarabs, *ultra montanes*, etc.) was tricky business, and just two years after his reform of the number of canons, Celebruno needed a further mechanism to relieve the pressure from the chapter.

On 2 March 1176, the curia of Alexander III issued a letter to Celebruno granting the archbishop the license to grant partial prebends to "suitable clerics."[77] By granting partial prebends to clerics (who would subsequently be called *portionarios*), Celebruno would be able to subdivide the revenues of churches among canons of the cathedral and supplement their incomes, which appear to have been too meagerly supported by the archiepiscopal fisc—though this was hardly a permanent fix. Issuing partial prebends to outsiders also added a mechanism by which Celebruno could supplement the work of those clerics within his administration who were able to shoulder more of the work of the archdiocese, in a fashion that is better in evidence elsewhere in contemporary Europe.[78] What makes this privilege even more remarkable is the fact that Alexander had condemned exactly this kind of practice only thirteen years earlier, at the Council of Tours, in language definitive enough to find its way into both the *Compilatio prima* and the *Liber Extra*.[79] Nevertheless, the ability to issue *portionarios* did not solve Celebruno's problems, as a poorly preserved letter from Alexander III attests. The letter, dated to 4 July 1177, suggests that a conflict had arisen over the division of revenues in the archdeaconate of Toledo and that Celebruno sought confirmation of his rights to assign them according to the customs of his predecessors.[80] Preserving his authority to decide how to divide the shares of the archdeaconate's revenues was a key part of the financial regulation of the diocese, and balancing the interests of different groups would likely have created the kinds of conflicts witnessed by Celebruno's successors in 1180, when a similar innovation reached the papal court and returned a result that upheld precedent from Celebruno's time and before.[81] Clearly, the financial health of the canons' prebends was less than ideal.

The reform of the cathedral chapter of Toledo was no small affair, and it commanded a significant amount of Celebruno's attention, judging from the charters. When the historical lens pans out to include the deposition of Bernardo of Osma, we can see Celebruno hard at work to effect positive and meaningful change in the church while abiding by the traditions and norms of his office. Further still, we can see the extension of this same interest in settling and controlling the outcomes of important practices in the ways in which Celebruno employed the tools of municipal lordship vis-à-vis the juridical tools inherent in the *fuero* that he issued for Belinchón. While other prelates would later be lauded for the many sweaty exertions (*sudores*) they undertook on Alfonso VIII's behalf, the same would surely have been said of the Orphan King's *padrino*. Managing the affairs of the archdiocese was salty work, given the legal, political, and economic purviews of the Primate of the Spains. Managing the requirements of the Roman pontiff and the Castilian king was difficult work, but bringing the two spheres into closer harmony made Celebruno's work as archbishop more manageable, and on a number of occasions we can witness him toeing just that line.

An Archbishop for an Age of Transitions

When Celebruno was elected to the episcopal throne of Sigüenza, it was an age of empire and dazzling courtly display. Emperor Alfonso VII counted renegade *amirs* as his friends and vassals, and kings and counts were numerous among those confirming his decrees.[82] By Celebruno's last earthly days, the world of the Orphan King was much different from that of his namesake, but much remained the same. It was the job of the archbishop of Toledo to manage—influence, comment on, react to, or provoke—the changes that were shaping the church in Christendom on the regional level to which his jurisdiction pertained while maintaining the confidence and patronage of the king. In this regard, Celebruno was a typical and traditional archbishop, though his archiepiscopal reign also betrays two trends that would shape the long-term development of his successors and suffragans, present and future. First, it shows that the archbishops of Toledo linked their fortunes to the success of the Castilian kingdom and its monarchs. Second, it shows the increasingly holistic involvement of the archbishops in the affairs of their province, suggesting that scholars must reevaluate the roles played by the archbishops of Toledo in light of the nuances of their involvement in the work of the archdiocese and their metropolitan province. Effectively, they were balancing fidelities to the king and to the bishop of Rome, trying to bring their respective agendas into greater harmony—but with mixed success.

While this chapter has already plumbed a number of topics, it bears repeating that the special relationship between Celebruno and Alfonso VIII shaped the development of both men, both with respect to each other and to the papacy. For Celebruno, the close relationship with the Castilian king during his most vulnerable years molded the archbishop's approach to envisioning himself as the ecclesiastical leader of the kingdom—hardly a stretch—but did so in terms of leading the church in favor of the Castilian kingdom. This leadership was likely in evidence as early as the Synod of Segovia in 1166, at which Celebruno must have been an able participant to have merited promotion to Toledo by the end of the same year. For the Orphan King, the relationship with his godfather was emblematic of the ways in which he sought the church's participation and cooperation and would set the tone for its cooperative engagement in the early days of the reign. Alfonso's own cooperation is easily demonstrated by the frequency with which he rewarded his loyal ecclesiastical subjects—notably in Celebruno's reign at Sigüenza and at Toledo—and remunerated them for their efforts on his behalf, both before and long after Celebruno's tenure.[83] These two trends suggest that for Celebruno, involvement in "the whole church of the Kingdom of Alfonso," borrowing the phrase of the Synod of Segovia, was at the core of his archiepiscopal office.

Celebruno, however, was just the first of many clerics who provide a window onto developing trends in the kingdom of Castile. His written records evince a careful balancing of papal policy and support for the royal orphan, suggesting that he was, in many ways, a model prelate for his age. During Alfonso VIII's long minority, Celebruno reinforced the royal dignity by marshalling the efforts of Castilian aristocrats, and he gave them political cover by deploying contemporary papal policy strategically. He worked to keep his diocese calm, in terms of its internal administration, so that it could weather the variety of storms that plagued the period of his tenure, first in his decade as bishop of Sigüenza and then his fifteen years at Toledo. In this regard, the excerpt from Diego de Castejón y Fonseca that began this chapter would seem to ring true: "he alone could fill up the great emptiness that would result in Spain from the lack of such a great man."

3

HOMO IGNARUS OR *REPARATOR REGNI*?
The Curious Case of Ramón II de Minerva of Palencia

But on one side, or on the other, he was of the royal blood of France and of Castile. He took the habit of Saint Benedict in San Zoilo de Carrión. . . . Growing up, Reymundo was discovering his gifts, and he had talent to occupy him in letters and charges of religion.
    —Gregorio de Argaíz, *La soledad laureada por San Benito* (1675)

There are few characters in the history of the twelfth-century Iberian Church that are as universally lamented within scholarship as Ramón II de Minerva, bishop of Palencia from 1148 until 1184. For Peter Linehan, he was an archetypal example of the corruption that reformers in the twelfth and thirteenth centuries sought to expose and render obsolete.[1] In the estimation of Derek Lomax, Ramón was pastorally incompetent; by the end of his early stay in the cathedral of Palencia, he had outlived the political utility that made him a pivotal character in the drama that was the minority of Alfonso VIII of Castile.[2] Later estimations of Ramón have largely followed this line of thinking. Even the most competent and measured analyses prefer to treat Ramón as a relic whose traditionally "feudal" utility was superseded by the increasingly legal and bureaucratic forms of governance and rulership that came to the fore in the thirteenth-century church.[3] Given the scope of Ramón's activities, such a portrait is seductive but unfair. It is more accurate to read Ramón's activities within the framework established by his peers, both chronological and geographical, in order to better sketch the portrait of a man whose clerical career was anything but ordinary, one whose activities should hardly be reduced to simple descriptions of a cleric "born half an age too late."

Ramón de Minerva's early life is easy to place within a broad context, but many concrete details are difficult to find. He appears to have perhaps been a younger (half?) brother of Ramón Berenguer IV and of Berengaria, first wife of Alfonso VII "the Emperor," given that he is acclaimed by both of Alfonso VII's sons, Fernando II of León and Sancho III of Castile, as their uncle.[4] Problematically, neither branch of the maternal line that produced Fernando II of León and Sancho III of Castile mentions Ramón, suggesting that he may have been a younger, perhaps illegitimate, son in one of the branches. The traditional supposition—that he was one of the last sons of Ramón Berenguer III—is based in part on his tutelage of Alfonso VIII and the fact that he pressed no claim of his own in the conflicts between León and Castile, suggesting that he was an outsider to the Leonese-Castilian imbroglio.[5] The elimination of the Leonese side of the marriage is further supported by the absence of any special language used by Alfonso VII or his sister, Infanta Sancha, to describe Ramón de Minerva in the charters made between Ramón and the two Leonese royals.[6] If he was unable to press a claim on the Leonese or Castilian crown and was called "uncle" by both the Leonese and Castilian kings, then it stands to reason that he was the maternal uncle of both, making him the brother of Empress Berengaria of León, Alfonso VII's first wife. Since we have no records of any brothers of Berengaria or Ramón Berenguer IV, it seems most likely that Bishop Ramón of Palencia, who occasionally styled himself "Raimundus de Minerva," was related to Ponce de Minerva, who arrived in León-Castile in the entourage of Empress Berengaria.[7] Berengaria apparently considered Ramón her kin, since Alfonso VII included the notation that a donation to Palencia in 1154 was because of the "closeness of his blood" (pro sanguinis propinquitate).[8] (Ponce de Minerva may have been an illegitimate son of Ramón Berenguer III, but there are no records of any other illegitimate children to suggest this as a more likely possibility.) Because he was bishop from 1150 well into the 1180s, we may suspect that Bishop Ramón de Minerva was born in or around the 1120s, which would place him well within the chronology of the children of Ramón Berenguer III, perhaps suggesting that he was an illegitimate son of the count of Barcelona, thus unable to inherit part of the family lands but still fortunate enough in his birth to merit a clerical post.[9] In short, exactly who Ramón de Minerva *was* is a mess. Luckily, the quality of his relationship to the Leonese royal family is not, since his appellations attest to his kinship to Empress Berengaria.

He must have been appointed because of his closeness to the royal family and because his monastic vows at San Zoilo de Carrión (and thus to Cluny, as Carlos Reglero de la Fuente has shown) afforded him a clerical status with some prestige that recommended him to a high-ranking ecclesiastical post.[10] He first appears as the bishop of Palencia in 1148, when Alfonso VII and the canons of Palencia appointed him to fill a vacancy there, and the earliest charters from the emperor to Ramón suggest that theirs was already a familiar relationship, even after the death of Berengaria in 1149.[11] Alfonso the Emperor and Ramón de Minerva worked alongside one another for nine years, during which there are several charters of donations to the diocese of Palencia whose patronage attests to an cordial relationship. Among the most significant of these, one 1154 donation gave half of the *portazgo* tax in Palencia to the church, which amounted to conceding the whole of that tax to the bishops, since they had already received half of the *portazgo* according to a 1084 charter that confirmed the possessions of the diocese and the episcopal patrimony.[12] Holding both lordship over the city and controlling major revenues in the city made the bishops of Palencia formidable and wealthy, and Ramón's connection to the royal family made him both powerful and influential.

The end of the reign of Alfonso the Emperor initiated the onset of a period of considerable difficulty for Ramón de Minerva. The emperor's two sons, Fernando II and Sancho III, were allotted the two traditional halves of the kingdom; the elder Sancho received Castile and Toledo and the younger Fernando got Galicia and León.[13] To prevent the outbreak of the war that seemed inevitable as the two grappled for peninsular hegemony, the brothers came together to formalize a treaty at Sahagún in 1157.[14] Although that treaty was a point of considerable attention for later Castilian chroniclers, Leonese authors shrugged the treaty off because of an event that was unfortunate for the Castilians: the untimely death of Sancho III in early 1158.[15] Fernando II, the king that Arabic chroniclers called *al-babuš*, "the slobberer," swept in and asserted his right, as the now-orphaned Alfonso VIII of Castile's only surviving male relative, to protect and nurture his nephew and assert Leonese hegemony in Christian Iberia.[16] It was that gesture that spurred several high-ranking Castilians into action.

"My Dearest Uncle"

Alfonso VIII was made an orphan by his mother's death in childbirth and his father's equally untimely demise, but he was not alone.[17] There was a clamor for custody of the Castilian king, and the nobility of Castile strove to assert themselves in the aftermath of Sancho III's death.[18] Rodrigo Ximénez de Rada (wrongly) records, on numerous occasions, that Toledo languished under Fernando II's dominion for nearly twelve years—the length of time required for the boy king to reach his majority—suggesting that the memory of the Leonese king's actions in Castile during the period were remembered with not a little disapproval.[19] Even with an episcopal godfather, the Leonese occupation of the heart of Castilian territory presented numerous challenges for the party of Castilian loyalists, not least of whom was the king's uncle.

From the time of Alfonso's inheritance of the kingdom of Castile in 1158 to the Cortes of Burgos that asserted his majority in 1169, the bishops were key collaborators in the *negotium regni*, and on a number of occasions, the prelates were major factors in the preservation of the kingdom.[20] However, the sources for the early period of Alfonso VIII's minority lack the kind of plentiful detail that could fill in gaps in the larger narrative. We know that Alfonso's godfather was the bishop of Sigüenza, Celebruno, who was elevated to Toledo during the Orphan King's minority.[21] What remains curious is the fact that Ramón's role is much more nebulous in this period than that of the Lara clan, whose multiple attempts to dislodge the king of León as the *tutor regis* were frustrated by the Leonese monarch.[22] Among other things, we know that Sancho III had instructed Gutierre Fernández de Castro to serve as tutor while Manrique Pérez de Lara took the role of regent, thus forcing cooperation between the two great noble families of Castile and hoping to foil any ulterior motives that Fernando II might have had.[23] We also know that the bishop of Palencia appears in a great number of charters with both the Leonese and Castilian kings, a fact that suggests that he was part of a close circle of clerics working to prevent anything unfortunate from happening to the kingdom and anything sinister from happening to the boy king.

"The course of events during the royal minority is obscure," comments Peter Linehan. "When not merely sparse, the testimony of the chroniclers of the next century is demonstrably wrong."[24] Yet despite such confusion, a special shred of evidence suggests that Ramón de Minerva was by his nephew's side from the start of his troubled minority and was steadfast until the king took his throne. Two days before the Ides of November in 1169, Alfonso VIII offered a charter that provided for a fair, one of the first *feria* celebrated in Castile, to the monastery of San Zoilo de Carrión—Ramón's own favored abbey—in recognition of his own particular connection to that house.[25] The charter includes a notation from Alfonso that it was given, in addition to the usual spiritual reasons, "to [San Zoilo] because I took my first knightly arms from the altar of Blessed Zoilo."[26] Although self-armament was more the norm than the exception in Western Iberia, as Teofilo Ruiz and Julio González have shown, the moment of Alfonso's knighthood was replete with symbolic importance.[27] The bond formed by such an act was potent, and Alfonso's patronage of the house of San Zoilo did not stop with his granting a fair.[28] By choosing (or being convinced to choose) San Zoilo in Carrión, Alfonso VIII was recognizing his uncle's influence and nodding at his special relationship to the bishop of Palencia. That relationship, although familial, must have been more than a mere dynastic bond, given that there were many other ecclesiastical houses closely related to the dynastic interests of his ancestors: San Isidoro of León held the remains of several of the boy king's maternal relatives, his mother was buried close to her homeland in Santa María de Nájera, and the cathedral of Toledo was his father's final resting place.[29] Electing San Zoilo for the ceremony of his knighthood was a symbolic recognition of the almost paternal relationship between Alfonso VIII and his "dearest uncle." Janna Bianchini has demonstrated that the relationship between the participants in the ceremony for self-knighting in Castile had incredible symbolic significance.[30] The monks of San Zoilo later reinforced their bond with Ramón with a donation from the prior to fund an anniversary mass for Ramón's own cathedral of Palencia in 1173, a gesture that was likely linked to the growing prestige of the monastery's hosting a royal knighting some four years earlier.[31] The bond between the bishop and the king, made evident by the knighting at the bishop's favorite monastery, found the third leg of its triangle with the monastery's gift in honor of its former brother.

Other testimonials also suggest the closeness between Alfonso VIII and Ramón de Minerva. During Ramón's episcopate, Alfonso VIII gave numerous substantial gifts to the diocese of Palencia. (While his simple financial and legal grants may be less evocative than the act of taking his first arms and armor from the altar of the favored house of his episcopal uncle, they had much greater impact on the long-term health of the diocesan fisc.) These donations contributed, in some cases, to the dramatic expansion of the episcopal patrimony—which one charter actually restored, turning back the clock on a number of earlier episcopal alienations and quitclaims—and were part of the wholesale growth of the resources attached to the diocese run by Ramón de Minerva. They deserve special attention here.

The earliest donation from Alfonso to Palencia comes from the time the king was only seven years old; it seems unlikely that it was the king's "own will," as the charter claims. That 1162 text granted the villages of Pedraza,

Villaniel, and Maladones to Palencia. A subsequent 1175 charter regranted those same towns but managed to give only half of Pedraza, perhaps as a result of necessary clarification (the whole-cloth rights to the town were not in the king's possession).[32] Only six weeks before his eleventh birthday, the young king confirmed Count Pedro Ansurez de Lara's bequest to Palencia of the ownership of the house of Santa María de Valladolid.[33] That gift represented a major extension of Palencia's episcopal jurisdiction into the Tierra de Campos, where the wealthy border towns between León and Castile were often formed into the *Infantazgo* lands held by royal sisters and aunts as part of their own share of the royal patrimony.[34] As if these major gifts during his minority were not significant enough, Alfonso ceded his royal jurisdiction over the *judería* and *mudéjaria* of Palencia, as well as the right to name and dismiss the *aljama* of Palencia, to the bishops of Palencia in perpetuity in 1177.[35] Maya Soifer Irish has quite rightly called this charter one of the most significant episcopal grants from Alfonso's reign, and it remains a donation of considerable interest for scholarship.[36] The impact of these gifts underlines the financial contributions that Alfonso made to the diocese during his uncle's tenure, but there were significant legal alterations made on Ramón's behalf that also elevated the position of the bishops of Palencia.

The bishops had been the lords of their city since the earliest days of the diocese.[37] Lordship on this scale meant the right (barring any royal objection) to issue *fueros* to the towns under the bishop's lordship. We know of several instances where Ramón did just that. In 1162, Ramón issued a *fuero* to the town of Villamuriel and a *fuero* to his diocesan see of Palencia in 1180. These two grants are, fortunately, instructive of not only the phenomenon of granting *fueros* but also of the variety of towns that could receive *fueros*: Villamuriel was then, as it is now, a very small town; Palencia was much larger. The *fuero* for Villamuriel was relatively brief, compared to other contemporary *fueros*, but contained a number of provisions that may provide clues about Ramón's major concerns for his practice of lordship in his jurisdiction. First, Ramón gave the *fuero* an explicitly ecclesiastical censure as its ultimate provision, noting that those who violated the terms of the *fuero* were to be immediately "cursed and excommunicated." Second, Ramón only required the people of Villamuriel to pay one current *solidus* for each house and plot of farmland. The very few items included in the Villamuriel *fuero* still included the kind of endorsements of episcopal power and of the financial health of the diocese, in the form of a regular tax; both provisions reinforced the stability that bishops often sought to cultivate in their dioceses.[38] For a small town, most of the issues that might arise were left to the townsfolk or appellate jurisdiction to deal with, and only the episcopal tax was a point of any substantive description.

Though the *fuero* granted to Villamuriel was relatively brief and appeared to require very little from the town other than certain financial obligations, the *fuero* for Palencia was anything but brief and financial. Before Ramón granted his own *fuero* to the city, Alfonso VIII had restored the bishops of Palencia to full lordship there, citing Ramón's concern for the young king and his unfortunately necessary abnegation of many lordly rights in the city to reallocate resources to support the Orphan King.[39] This 1179 charter is particularly telling because the long *narratio* lavishes extensive praise on Ramón while disparaging those who served him less faithfully during a period of his greatest need:

> Among [my vassals], Ramón, bishop of Palencia, my dearest uncle, stood out resplendent, with every kind of devotion, with watchful power and daily exertions, he who battled for me out of faithfulness and for God for his order. Omitting nothing from what was committed to him by his office, he seemed to spend it all for the sake of royal services, so that he should not only be acclaimed as a shepherd but even as the repairer of my kingdom. In order that he who exhibited for me such devoted service, nearly all of the incomes and inheritances of the Palencian see (in part having been obliged to pawn, in part having sold) having been led away by necessity, wanting in no way to withdraw his hand from my services, because of the benefit of which the aforementioned church has for the most part sustained down from antiquity has had for them, he sold and tried to sell the customs and *fueros* of the Church of Palencia, as much as he was able, to the *concejo* of Palencia.[40]

The restoration of the diocese's rights and privileges surely irked the *concejo* and leading townsmen, who must have benefitted from the alienations that Ramón made during Alfonso's minority. Despite the closeness of the bishop and the king, there were still many legal questions to be sorted out because of these restorations and their impact on the economic life of the episcopal city of Palencia. Granting a *fuero* to the city only six months after this restoration helped Ramón diffuse any lasting tension and ensure that he was able to make the most of his newly reaffirmed position as the city's lord. Because *fueros* were often the result of a negotiated process over obligations between lords and subjects, we may suspect that the negotiations began almost as soon as the ink was dry on the charter of restoration, perhaps even as a tacit condition of its issuance.

In March 1180, "with good spirit and spontaneous will, with the consent and will of all his allied canons in the chapter of San Antolín and with the consent of our lord, King Alfonso ... [Ramón] made a charter of *fuero* for the whole *concejo* of Palencia."[41] The text of the *fuero* runs more than seven pages in the modern printed edition and it includes a great number of fines and fees for a variety of crimes as well as specific notes about taxation for those who held land in the city.[42] A few examples serve to illustrate the extent of these provisions. The bishops were to have half of the judicial fines for homicides and all of the judicial fines for theft.[43] No knights ("milites armatus de senior") or their still un-remarried widows were required to pay tax for their farms.[44] Whoever disrupted the market or a fair in Palencia should pay sixty *sueldos*.[45] Some provisions were more colorful: "Anyone who throws excrement [*merdam*] into the mouth of another should pay 300 *sueldos*."[46] Those who dunked the heads of others into the river for an evil purpose should pay that same fine—an unfortunate commentary on medieval rivers' uses.[47] The specificity of the crimes and the amounts of their fees demonstrate, collectively, that the episcopal administrators of the city were focused on preserving order and collecting substantial revenues in the process.

Ramón undertook a wide variety of activities for his royal nephew. Their relationship was surely close enough to merit considerable trust between the two men. Alfonso knighted himself from the altar of Ramón's own favorite monastic community. The king granted properties and revenues to the diocese of Palencia because of that close relationship. Even those properties and rights that Ramón had to alienate or sell to preserve Alfonso during his minority were restored by the king, in large part because he felt that Ramón was one of the few vassals who did not desert him when he was in need. *Fueros* granted by Ramón demonstrated the kinds of interests that he had to cultivate to preserve the kingdom and kingship of his nephew. Perhaps no such service was as great as that rendered to Alfonso when he was trying to recover some of the territories that Fernando of León poached during the Orphan King's minority just a few years earlier.

The Infantazgo War and the Bishop "Who Lived in a Hut"

The papacy may have objected to the nepotism and political engagement of Ramón's episcopate, but those same characteristics are likely what made him such an integral part of the Castilian court.[48] The same instincts that made Ramón so well placed in the Castilian court also made him a keen collaborator in military affairs. The best example of these collaborations may, unfortunately for historical inquiry, be the one that has the most confused record in the sources.

According to Luciano Serrano, Ramón and his colleague Pedro Pérez (bishop of Burgos, r. 1156–81) were the major organizers of an offensive campaign designed to dislodge Leonese occupiers from Castilian holdings in the Tierra de Campos.[49] This conflict is sometimes called the Infantazgo War, after the region in dispute, but exactly who participated and why is unclear. The Infantazgo region lay in the wealthy Tierra de Campos, on the borderlands between the kingdoms of León and Castile, and was often allotted to royal aunts and sisters as a share of the kingdom from which they could support themselves in a fashion worthy of their position.[50] Both Palencia and its subject city of Valladolid were on the eastern and southeastern edges of the region, and so any conflict in the Infantazgo would have encroached on Palencia's territory. For this reason, we might safely suspect that the bishops of Palencia were involved in a conflict in the Infantazgo, but exactly when and how they were involved remains to be sorted out.

Luckily, we can date the end of the Infantazgo War rather precisely. The charters of Alfonso VIII usually preserve, as part of the dating clause, the memory of events of political or military significance.[51] The most famous event in Alfonso's lifetime to be preserved was, of course, the victory of Las Navas de Tolosa, but earlier military achievements found a similar afterlife in the charters of the Orphan King.[52] The Infantazgo War must have concluded by 1178, based on the dating clauses. Rodrigo Ximénez de Rada noted that the occupation of the Infantazgo dated to Alfonso's minority; Juan of Osma noted that Alfonso "moved a great and powerful army against his uncle Fernando, the king of León, and recovered the territory which is called the *Infantazgo*" in the same years that Alfonso VIII recovered Logroño from Sanç VI of Navarra.[53] The collation of this data places the Infantazgo War to circa 1178–80, probably achieving its main objectives in 1178 and sorting things out in the two years afterward, which puts the conflict right at the end of the episcopate of Ramón, exactly the same period when Alfonso restored the rights of Palencia and in the years before Palencia was awarded additional properties and privileges.[54]

Serrano's primary evidence for the claim that Ramón and other prelates had prepared an army to help Alfonso VIII recover the Infantazgo was their presence near the army in the summer of 1179.[55] Fortunately, these charters did survive the Spanish Civil War, but they are not proof positive of the bishops' having fought or led armies. However, there are some clues that Alfonso VIII was granting Ramón privileges in return for his earlier efforts. The 1179 restoration of the rights of the diocesan see of Palencia noted that Ramón was battling ("militabat"), and a donation to Palencia from the day before described the donation as being in return for "the immense and innumerable services that he [Ramón] has done and is doing for me with the greatest devotion."[56] Earlier episodes—like the Synod of Segovia, where clerics from Castile had gathered to push back against Leonese incursions—suggest that the late 1170s were not the first instance of bishops' having raised armies against Fernando *al-babuš*, but the suggestion of lost evidence, even from the most credible scholars, cannot be substituted for evidence.[57]

There is, however, some papal evidence suggesting that Ramón de Minerva did not fit into Alexander III's vision of the ideal episcopal officer, perhaps because of his military activities. Linehan has paraphrased the problem in his usual evocative fashion:

> [Twelfth-century bishops] were members of a corps which produced a whole host of real-life churchmen in all important respects the equals of the Cid's fictionalized bishop of Valencia, Jerome, who explained that he had come from France to the frontier "because of the urge he had to kill a Moor or two" but soon lost count of his tally. Ramón of Palencia, a monk whose military vocation was so pronounced (it was reported to Alexander III) that he enfeoffed his church's possessions, let his episcopal palace go to rack and ruin and went off to live in a hut—or possibly a bunker.[58]

Luckily, the same letter that Linehan cites for Ramon's conduct was partially edited by Juan Rivera Recio and has been safely dated to 1168/69.[59] The letter's specific notation of Ramón's military commitment concerned Alexander, but the words "he has put himself forward in all military affairs" (se militaris in omnibus profesionis) are particularly indicative of the reputation that Ramón had generated by his military activities.[60] Perhaps these same qualities were those that suggested to Alexander that he was "a man ignorant of ecclesiastical sanctions" (homo ignarus ecclesiastice sanctionis), but other issues, like appointing a monastic nephew to a cathedral benefice, still dominated papal attention.[61] Even if the usage of the verb *militare* in the later 1170s or the notations of Ramón's many sweaty deeds cannot be taken as proof of military activities during the Infantazgo War on behalf of the Orphan King, a pattern of behavior emerges from the reports sent to Alexander III. It seems likely that Ramón was involved with the wars that pushed the Castilian frontier back westward into León, but this was done in service of both his royal nephew and his diocese, preserving his episcopal power and the king that vouchsafed it (which meant, in this instance, moving away from the bishop of Rome).

An additional wrinkle emerges from an unexpected place: the Romanesque cathedral of Palencia. Although it has since been replaced by the current Gothic structure, the work of building the Romanesque cathedral that preceded the present edifice took nearly a century, and Ramón's episcopate falls directly in the middle of the span.[62] Building cathedrals took enormous quantities of resources, but so did the military efforts of recapturing territory; as the bishop nearest to the Infantazgo, much of the administrative burden may well have fallen on Ramón.[63] It seems likely that the financial or administrative weight of the wars in León slowed work on the cathedral or that the episcopal palace fell into disrepair as a result of the attention that the Infantazgo War commanded from the bishop of Palencia and his clergy. Indeed, Alexander III's letters in the mid-1170s, where he repeatedly instructed Archbishop Celebruno to reform Palencia's clerical discipline, may well reflect the fact that Ramón may have relaxed the strictures of local clerical discipline in order to maximize the revenues or services extracted from the diocese.[64] Those changes would also suggest that Ramón's responsibilities on behalf of the kingdom were a substantial burden that required him to abnegate some of the tasks required of prelates by pontifical prescriptions—and that Ramón was willing to do a little wrong in his diocese to do a lot right for his nephew. Even if the pope was displeased.

At the Court of Henry Plantagenet

If this pattern of military behavior suggests that Ramón was a key functionary of the crown in its larger endeavors, examples of his activities in similar arenas should betray parallels. One example of an instructive parallel is the settlement that Alfonso VIII of Castile and Sanç VI of Navarra sought to resolve their border conflict, which resulted from the same war that preceded the conflict in the Infantazgo that recovered Logroño and a handful of other towns in the region. The two kings sought Henry Plantagenet's arbitration to resolve their dispute.

A major treaty in the medieval Latin West could reshape both the geography and politics of a kingdom, and the number of treaties between the kingdoms of medieval Iberia suggests that jockeying for position was commonplace. During the time when Ramón de Minerva was bishop of Palencia, several agreements between the kingdoms of León and Castile reveal the fractious relationship between the two kingdoms. Ramón de Minerva's subscription on the treaties between his nephew and other peninsular monarchs does not, however, demonstrate that the bishop was a negotiator in the treaty process. Fortunately for this study, one of the most important negotiations for Castile involved the bishop of Palencia as a key diplomat on an embassy to the court of Henry II in the hope of resolving a dispute with Sanç VI of Navarra.

Upon reaching his majority in 1169, Alfonso VIII set about trying to expand his kingdom and to recover the territory he had lost to Fernando II of León and to the kingdom of Navarra during his minority. The conquests of territory from León resulted, after some preparation, with the Infantazgo War discussed above. The wars against Sanç of Navarra spanned, by the best historical reconstructions, a four-year period from 1172 to 1176 and recovered a number of territories on the Ebro frontier.[65] These wars turned the territorial tide in Alfonso VIII's favor, but the final resolution of the conflict was complicated by the fact that the two kings were unable to come to a mutually agreed-upon border.

The Castilian and Basque kings' inability to come to a territorial settlement led them to reach a different kind of settlement: the two monarchs agreed to seek the judgment of the most powerful king in Europe, Henry II Plantagenet. A treaty signed between them stated that the monarchs would have six years to find a solution, during which two cities (one on either side) were placed in a kind of hostageship to ensure the monarchs' cooperation.[66] A series of records first compiled by Julio González and Derek Lomax allow us to reconstruct the timetable of the embassies to Henry's court, which puts a series of diplomats (and thereby their personas) in historical play.

The records of the pleas at the court of Henry II Plantagenet preserve both the names and the positions of the clerics involved in the arbitration. The litigants from Castile were a formidable group of royal allies; Ramón, interestingly, was the only clergyman in the party of Castilians, although he was accompanied by the royal *merino* and a handful of powerful noblemen. Fernando Corral's research has uncovered additional nuggets about the process—including the presence of two champions, should Henry have decided on an ordeal of combat—and suggests that the arbitration was a considerable affair.[67] The seriousness with which Henry approached his role as an arbiter is made clear by the fact that the Angevin sovereign convoked

Parliament, including the bishops and the barons of the realm, to hear the arbitration and confirm his judgment.[68]

The decision made by Henry II for the two monarchs was an attempt to cool tempers and manage a complicated geopolitical arrangement. The internecine wars between the Iberian Christian kingdoms were a fact of life in the Iberian Peninsula, and a number of complicated treaty arrangements were fashioned by peninsular potentates to keep further conflict at bay.[69] Ramón served, according to English historical accounts, as the lead negotiator for the Castilian party, and the treaty crafted by Henry's court effectively confirmed those claims that neither party contradicted in their petitions to the court.[70] The arbitration attempted to come to a reasonable settlement, one that neither king would go back on and that would still allow the monarchs to save face.

Yet it seems most likely that, for Alfonso, the arbitration before Henry II was, above all, a political stunt designed to break the will of Sanç VI through an imposed recognition of Alfonso VIII's prestige. Corral writes that the arbitration shows "that once Alfonso VIII had his hands free after the victory in Cuenca [in 1177], which put a halt to the Almohad offensive, he solved the conflict with Navarre using the normal recourses in this feudalized society: the imposition of his political interests backed by a military force that gave him sufficient support to guarantee the submission of other monarchs and territories through the personal link that made these other kings recognize the superiority of Alfonso VIII."[71] Sending Ramón to London before Henry II moved the wily old prelate into play for the Castilian monarch; the Castilian king's bishop put the Navarrese king in check at the court of the most powerful king in Europe.

Although parts of the gathering of Parliament must have been unfamiliar, Ramón was, by the end of his third decade as a bishop, more than experienced enough to understand the intricacies of that kind of occasion. He had attended Alexander III's Council of Tours, had been present at the Synod of Segovia, had seen a number of councils held by cardinals-legate, and would even journey to Lateran III in just a few short years.[72] Gatherings of clerics, both local and international, were no small occasions in the long twelfth century, and councils and synods of all kinds have been recognized as a symbol of growing papal authority and clerical engagement to control suffragan clergy, much as meetings of the *curia regis* did between kings and their counts.[73] Ramón's position as the lone cleric in the Castilian party—matched by his opposite number from Pamplona among the Navarrese—may appear to be a token appointment, a cleric sent to ensure that Henry II understood that the king of Castile had the support of his bishops, but Ramón was no meager political force. After all, the Castilian monarch had called his dearest uncle no less than the repairer of the kingdom of Castile.

Repairer of the Kingdom or an Ignorant Man?

The reputation of Ramón de Minerva, according to scholars, was that of an anachronism—a tenth-century comital politico in a twelfth-century reformation theologian's world. When he was appointed, the church in Iberia was engaged in markedly different kinds of projects and was an organ of considerably different objectives. During the reign of Alfonso the Emperor, the aggressive expansion of the Leonese empire surely shifted the priorities of the church.[74] In his study of the life and career of Diego Gelmírez, Fletcher showed just such a prelate in the variety of exercises of his power that were possible, shoring up his lordship and aggressively expanding his influence in the regions.[75] An example of the reach of this world's political fortunes is also visible in the actions of clerics who are otherwise mysterious figures: we know that Mozarabic bishops, fleeing the Almohads' expanding influence in Islamic al-Andalus, sought refuge in Toledo in the early twelfth century.[76] That same impetus that encouraged the gallantry recorded in the *Poema de Almería* surely also encouraged the clerics of the realm to seek the expansion of ecclesiastical patrimonies and the restoration of episcopal sees in reconquered territory.[77] In this respect, the age of Alfonso VIII was much the same as that of his grandfather and namesake, with clergy who were closely aligned with the objectives of the monarchy and closely connected to its ambitions. This is the fact that makes the appointment of Ramón significant—he was a prelate steeped in the traditions of the age in which he was appointed, not in which he died.

In the late eleventh and early twelfth centuries, bishops on the frontiers of Latin Christendom operated under a different set of norms than clerics closer to the normative papal center did. Placing the papal curia in the position of deciding the norms by which the church might operate was much more complicated than it might first appear. Rome operated as an appellate jurisdiction for legal and theological matters, and the connection between canon law, theology, and the social pressures that dictated the proper operation of the Latin West (and the church in particular) rendered the papal curia the most active and effective arbiter of those norms. Effectively, the papacy was the normative center to which clerics and clerical entities were bound.

For clerics on the frontiers, some of the concerns of papal reforms must have seemed less important than more immediate concerns. Bernard Hamilton long ago noted that the clergy in the Crusader States were frequently at the heads of military forces, and the presence of warrior-bishops in the early Anglo-Norman Church was so considerable that Craig Nakashian and Daniel Garrard have recently devoted entire volumes to unpacking the nuances of their legacies.[78] Beyond even military concerns, the presence of primatial sees in regions more distant from Rome suggests that while the operations of cardinals-legate and judges-delegate lessened some of the more combustible cases' intensity, a certain amount of local autonomy provided more direct leadership in provinces where rapid responses were more necessary.[79] Even with an archbishop like Celebruno, the challenges of managing the relationships among kings and popes and prelates meant that some clerics chose kings over churchmen. We must also keep in mind the kind of background from which Ramón came. Like many churchmen of his day, Ramón was of the high nobility and was likely destined for a clerical career at an early age. He was appointed bishop in 1148 and died in 1184, so we may well suspect that he became a bishop at around the age of thirty, meaning that he had been born in the time of Queen Urraca, who often relied on the church for a variety of forms of support.[80] As a result, discerning what was remarkable, reproachful, or even remote from the norms of his era means evaluating him according to what was expected of Urraca's or Alfonso VII's clergy, not of their descendants; anything else smacks of anachronism.

Evaluating whether Ramón deserved the kind of reputation he has earned in scholarship means examining the kinds of activities that defined his episcopate. It seems more likely that, given the challenges of frontier life, Ramón and his colleagues were expected to concern themselves first with the well-being of their dioceses and with the functions proper to the cathedral chapters who were their agents. Although there was surely a spiritual angle to that well-being—fighting spiritual warfare in the tradition of Saint Anthony—and the prelates *were* responsible for that front, there was a direct physical component, too. It may well be that Ramón's concern for the physical safety of his nephew's kingdom, for its prosperity, simply took precedence over the spiritual. Although it was less likely in a medieval world, this kind of quasi-modern *Realpolitik* fits the kind of reputation that Ramón has generated in scholarship. It must be contextualized, however: given the dangers plaguing the kingdom of Castile, Ramón's behavior is hardly unexpected, demonstrating a kind of avuncular preservation instinct that would humanize an otherwise paper character. Reevaluating him as a person of considerable depth and quality makes him a more historically valid figure for investigation and helps us fit him into the larger portrait of the clergy in the kingdom of Alfonso VIII. For Ramón's episcopate, the point is that he was neither a *homo ignarus*, as Alexander III might have heard, or a *reparator regni*, by Alfonso VIII's reckoning; rather, he was both and neither. In the balancing act between Rome and Castile, Ramón clearly favored his nephew's cause, but this in turn proves that balancing the two was very hard work indeed. Alexander's critique was fair (since Ramón was no *magister artium*), but so was Alfonso's praise (since he seems to have labored considerably on behalf of the kingdom), and this is entirely the historical point. While there may be so few characters as universally lamented as Ramón de Minerva in the historical scholarship, he does not deserve his reputation.

4

A MILANESE LAWYER AT THE CASTILIAN COURT

Alderico di Palacio of Sigüenza and Palencia

The Eighth Bishop of Palencia was Don Enrico . . . he was a holy man in the time of King Alonso the 8th; . . . Many times I have seen them take earth from his tomb; they say that it is to heal infirmities, and in the boxes of the relics of this church is a little leather shoe with a scrap of paper that reads "Sandal of San Arderico."
—Alonso Fernández de Madrid, *Silva Palentina* (1536–39)

Holy sandals are not easy to come by in Latin Christendom; nor are they attached to holy men of any meager qualifications. In the case of Alderico di Palacio, bishop of Sigüenza (r. 1178–84) and later bishop of Palencia (r. 1184–1208), the historical path that might elevate his sandal to the status of a relic was curious. Two such paths were possible: first, he could have been a genuine living "holy man" whose charisma and good works attracted a following of devoted adherents; second, he could have been so important to the dioceses where he served as bishop that medieval logic and early modern memory would reckon him divinely favored.[1] Although he may have been charismatic and a holy man, the extant records argue that the second option more adequately summarizes Alderico's career, given that the chapel that was supposed to be named for him was absorbed and that his name is not officially registered by Rome. Investigating how a bishop could be so important and how that translated to his being remembered as such gives us an excellent opportunity to evaluate what being a "successful bishop" meant in medieval Iberia. Whether he favored papal policy or royal writ or some harmonizing *via media*, whether he was engaged in the work of fighting wars to the south or west or east of Castile, or whether he helped shore up the interior life of his diocese—all these questions help uncover much of what Alderico did and why he was remembered. This affords us better context to consider the ways in which clerical life could be approached in medieval Christendom writ large.

We do not know precisely where Alderico di Palacio was born, but we know that he was not from an old Castilian family. His given name—rendered variously as "Ardericus," "Aldericus" or "Andericus"—is not a typical Castilian appellation, although his seals suggest "Aldericus" may have been his preferred spelling.[2] He had been an archdeacon at Burgos for at least a decade before his promotion to the episcopate, and that Burgalese chapter's necrology records his family: his grandfather and namesake died in Milan and was listed under the date of 4 January, his brother Lanfranco was entered in the obituary under 24 April, and Jacopo di Palacio, Alderico's father, was remembered on 6 June.[3] Even without the notation of the place of his grandfather's death, the names of Alderico, his brother, and his father strongly suggested northern Italian origins, but the connection of the aristocratic name "Palacio" suggests that Alderico's father, Jacopo di Palacio, had travelled to northern Castile as a young man, settled in Burgos, and was successful enough to ensure that Alderico was able to enter the clergy in the competitive diocese of Burgos.[4] (Migrations of this type were somewhat frequent in the late eleventh and early twelfth centuries, but the majority of cases about which there is a great deal of evidence are for the upper nobility and monastic clergy.[5]) A relocation of that magnitude and success would have required a great deal of ambition, a trait Alderico seems to have acquired as part of his patrimonial inheritance.

Alderico first appears as an archdeacon of Burgos in the 1150s, subscribing documents as a witness but not acting on his own.[6] If Alderico was around the canonical age by the standards later set in 1179 at Lateran III, we can place his birth in the 1120s, meaning that by his death in 1208, he had lived to eighty years or more.[7] The many notations of his family members in the Burgalese obituaries strongly suggests that he was of local origins, likely a second-generation immigrant; his father, Jacopo, had emigrated at a time well before the 1140s.[8] What makes any of these connections significant is the great advancement achieved by Alderico (and to a lesser extent his brother, whose career Alderico seems to have supported[9]) within the larger sphere of the Castilian church: most cathedrals had sixty full canons or more, along with perhaps forty or more *portionarios*, so to advance to the rank of archdeacon and climb still further required skill, ambition, luck, and not a little perseverance.

Bishop of Sigüenza, Most of the Time

Although several consecration oaths survive in twelfth-century copies in Toledo, we do not know on what day Alderico di Palacio was elevated to the episcopate of Sigüenza.[10] By mid-January 1179, he begins to subscribe documents as the bishop of Sigüenza, where he served nearly five years before being transferred to Palencia.[11] During that half decade, Alderico's career seems to have been increasingly fruitful, a fact that reflects (in a cyclical fashion) both the increasing patronage he received from the king and the increasing engagement of the bishop of Sigüenza with larger affairs that required the attention of his colleagues and the papacy. Balancing these difficult challenges while gaining the prestige necessary to merit a future promotion suggests that, in hindsight, Alderico was a competent and capable cleric whose star was on the rise.

As we have already seen in the career of Archbishop Celebruno, Sigüenza's border position with Aragon and proximity to rich salt deposits at Belinchón and Medinaceli made it a key part of the Castilian economic and political strategy in the twelfth century.[12] Only one episcopate fell between Celebruno and Alderico, and the death of Bishop Joscelmo of Sigüenza seems to have been untimely enough to have spurred local legends that he died *en route* to the papal curia.[13] Whether it was a moment of crisis or an opportunity is unknowable, but an aging Archbishop Celebruno seems to have taken the opportunity to fill his old episcopal chair with a promising young Burgalese cleric—Alderico di Palacio.[14]

The importance of Sigüenza to both Toledan and Castilian agendas notwithstanding, Alderico's early episcopal *acta* are rather quiet. In 1180, he purchased a villa from the kinswoman of one of his distant predecessors for 550 maravedíes.[15] In 1181, King Alfonso VIII traded properties with Alderico, and "for the greatest and many services that [he rendered] to [the King] devotedly and faithfully," Alfonso also gave Alderico and his successors 10 percent of all his royal revenues and rights in the episcopate of Sigüenza.[16] By the early 1180s, Alderico had also begun to be held in high regard by his peers, whose nominations earned him an appointment as a papal judge-delegate on at least four cases.[17] Each of these cases involved a bishop from Alfonso's kingdom and each could have become a considerable conflict, provoking the kind of violence witnessed between Osma and Sigüenza in the 1160s or the violence seen in the intradiocesan conflict as Sigüenza sought to assert influence over Medinaceli.[18] Given these possibilities, Alderico's service as a judge-delegate may well have catapulted him onto the larger Castilian stage and recommended him to the episcopate of Palencia.

Alderico was appointed to a trio of panels as a judge-delegate in 1182, beginning with a case that pitted two exempt bishops from two different kingdoms against each other: Rodrigo of Oviedo against Pedro Pérez of Burgos. The second of these cases matched the archbishop of Toledo against the orders of Santiago and Calatrava. The third squared a property dispute between the bishops of Segovia and Ávila. A fourth case, some three years later, investigated the disputes between the bishop of Ávila and the *concejo* of that same city. Serving on so many and such substantial panels of judges-delegate may have even been what recommended Alderico to fill a more unusual position, albeit some 220 km away in Palencia. It thus appears that the combination of royal and papal favor propelled Alderico to his new position, in part because he had served both parties well during his short tenure at Sigüenza.

During part of his time as bishop of Sigüenza, one of Alderico's colleagues, Ramón de Minerva, took ill.[19] Exactly what Ramón's infirmity was is uncertain, but Alderico appears to have been the most suitable candidate to step in for his episcopal confrere. At first glance, Alderico appears to be a rather odd choice. Both Segovia and Burgos were much closer to Palencia (150 km and 90 km, respectively), and the prestige of both those episcopal sees would have recommended them for the task of administering the important diocese of Palencia on the Leonese borderlands. In the case of Burgos, Marino Mathé, whose clan's activities in Burgos may well have reshaped the history of that diocese, had only just come to power in 1181 and so was busy with the complicated affairs of the exempt diocese, especially in pressing his claims against the neighboring see of Oviedo.[20] As for Gonzalo Gutiérrez Girón of Segovia (r. 1177–94), the reasons for his absence are unclear but may be related to his pressing a suit against Ávila.[21] (Interestingly, Gonzalo was one of the clerics tasked with resolving the case of Bernardo of Osma's simoniacal election, but the case was entirely cleaned up by the time of Ramón's illness.[22]) It may be that the larger case between Palencia and Segovia over Portillo and Peñafiel—which had been an ongoing dispute since the 1120s—was being litigated again on a local level, although the records have been lost, since Segovia and Palencia only signed an agreement on the matter in 1190; Ramón de Minerva was probably quite reluctant to hand over jurisdiction to an adversary who had designs on territories he considered his own.[23] Alderico appears to have been the most capable candidate, as he had served in Burgos and was thus familiar with the environs of Palencia—and was not already invested in any outstanding controversies.

While he was administering the diocese of Palencia as a stand-in, Alderico still appears to have managed his own diocese of Sigüenza. In 1182, he made a rather curious donation to the chapter of Sigüenza containing two parts of a property he and the chapter had bought and subdivided among themselves, but what makes the donation interesting is that its proceeds were to pay for two sets of anniversary masses: one for Alderico's soul, and one for King Sancho III of Castile, whom Alderico may have known as a young canon in Burgos.[24] Alderico was still serving on a series of cases as a judge-delegate, but he also seems to have been engaged in settling a conflict between the aging Ramón de Minerva and the chapter of Palencia.

By the spring of 1183, the conflict between Ramón and his chapter—about, among other things, the handling of the property of deceased canons of Palencia—was boiling over. The settlement of the case of the canons has already been treated at length above, but the involvement of Alderico requires some explanation. Ramón's charter records that both Gonzalo (Pérez) of Toledo and Alderico of Sigüenza were his colleagues in the negotiated settlement with the canons of Palencia. Their involvement suggests that Alderico may have already been considered for the episcopate of Palencia, a suggestion first posited by Lomax almost a half century ago: "It looks as if, even during Ramón's lifetime, Arderico [sic] was being groomed for the succession to a bishop whose incompetence was evident, but whose royal birth and political services made him irremovable."[25] Alderico's promotion to the see of Palencia may well have its roots in the 1183 reforms of the diocese of Palencia, but it was not until early 1184, when Ramón's thirty-six-year episcopate ended with his passing, that Alderico took to Palencia.

Studium Days at Palencia

In a letter from 28 January 1184, Lucius III instructed Archbishop Gonzalo Pérez to translate Bishop Alderico of Sigüenza to the see of Palencia.[26] It was hard to see the transfer as anything other than a promotion, given the ways in which Ramón had enriched the see through the currying of favors from Alfonso VIII.[27] Of course, Palencia had been, in the mid-eleventh century, jockeying for a promotion to archiepiscopal status (in the manner that Diego Gelmírez of Santiago de Compostela would later achieve).[28] Even without such a prelate, Palencia was poised to springboard to a new level of episcopal involvement in the affairs of both Castile and the church. To do so, Alderico needed to take advantage of recent initiatives in the church as a whole and use his own skill as an administrator to advance the interests of Palencia, balancing royal and papal favor.

Nearly every Castilian bishop attended the Third Lateran Council, and we know that some of them shouldered substantial burdens to do so. We know that a cardinal paid the debts that the Toledan chapter had incurred during their stay at the council, debts owed to two Roman noblemen.[29] According to preserved lists of attendees, Alderico participated in Alexander III's Lateran Council while he was bishop of Sigüenza.[30] One of the canons from that council that had the greatest impact was the institution of masters to teach in the cathedrals to train those clergy with a responsibility for pastoral care.[31] We know that other kingdoms and regions in Latin Christendom also developed their own cathedral *studia*, and examples from the Angevin Empire, the Holy Roman Empire, or the Crusader States demonstrate that the number of masters at cathedral schools grew in the decades after Lateran III, if not as enormously as Alexander III had hoped.[32] Although the number of *magistri* in cathedral chapters increased across the kingdom of Castile, only Palencia was acclaimed for its cathedral school in the early-thirteenth-century chronicles. Rodrigo Ximénez de Rada narrated, "[King Alfonso VIII] called together wise men from the Gauls and from Italy, that the instruction of wisdom would never be absent from his kingdom, and he gathered masters of all the faculties at Palencia, to whom a great stipend was given, so that the wisdom of any faculty should flow just like manna in their mouths for all wanting to study."[33] Lucas of Túy described the foundation of Palencia with similar admiration, but he placed the foundations of the school in the episcopate of Tello Telléz de Meneses, when the school was given a royal charter and greater resources.[34] Although in both cases the narratives were linked to the royal chartering of the school more than two decades after Alderico's election, the evidence from the cathedral records nevertheless evinces his work in forming a cathedral school—usually, these were the precursors of a *studium generalis*, which later grew into a university—staffed by many clerics esteemed for their learning. Yet there was additional, anecdotal evidence for the internal popularity of the school at Palencia within Castile that may help explain the chroniclers' tone.

Some of the flowery language was certainly linked to a famous Castilian son: Dominic of Osma, founder of the Order of Preachers. According to Jordan of Saxony's *Libellus de Principiis Ordinis Praedicatorum* (ca. 1234–36),

Dominic "was sent to Palencia for instruction in the liberal sciences, which flourished there in those days. When he was satisfied that he learned them sufficiently, he abandoned them for something on which he could more profitably spend his limited time here on earth and turned to the study of theology."[35] Jordan of Saxony's note, coupled with the narratives of both Rodrigo Ximénez de Rada and Lucas of Túy, suggests that the faculty, even in the late 1180s when Dominic was studying at Palencia, must have been growing rapidly and already possessed a handful of full masters and an unknown number of otherwise untraceable junior scholars.[36] Given that *Fons sapientiae*, Gregory IX's 1234 bull canonizing Dominic (which predates both Lucas's and Rodrigo's work), described the role that Palencia played in nurturing the founder of the Order of Preachers, it seems likely that Lucas and Rodrigo were responding to a larger push to recognize Palencia's role; given the rapid pace of the early Dominicans' growth in the kingdom of Fernando III (Lucas and Rodrigo's sovereign), such a supposition seems near certain.[37] Adeline Rucquoi has shown that the impact of the later history of the school obscures the fact that it must have been vibrant by 1190/91, which suggests that by the end of the first decade of Alderico's episcopate, the school was capable of generating significant fame in the region around Palencia and having a lasting impact on the historical record.[38]

The school was not merely famous, however, for the sake of its favorite son. Alderico di Palacio's episcopate saw a dramatic increase in the number of clerics who bore the title of *magister* in their subscriptions of cathedral documents. The two masters recruited at the end of Ramón de Minerva's term as bishop may have been encouraged by Alderico, but the two men—Guillermo de Peñafiel, a canon, and a royal notary, Giraldo di Lombardo—were nevertheless figures of considerable longevity in the chapter.[39] During Alderico's tenure as a prelate, however, there were many, many more clerics recruited to the chapter, but even this gets ahead of the real historical importance of the *studium* at Palencia.

Clerics had come to the Iberian Peninsula for generations to advance their careers, seek adventure, and (least cynically of all) to serve God on the frontiers of Christendom. The recruitment of Cluniacs by Alfonso VI and Urraca has been long noted to have shifted the internal discourse of the Leonese, Galician, and Castilian churches and to have brought a number of important trends and innovations to those same kingdoms.[40] There were already, by the time of Lateran III's mandate for episcopal administrations to provide for cathedral schools, a number of important monastic *studia* and *scriptoria* in León and Castile. For example, the monastery of San Millán de la Cogolla was a vibrant monastic community with a library and scriptorium that was significant enough to have supported research for canonists and an archbishop of Toledo in the late twelfth and early thirteenth centuries.[41] Even beyond these examples, we know that Santiago de Compostela had a capable collection of clerics during the time of Diego Gelmírez, and his influence in that arena seems to have persisted after his demise, even if some were still forced to go to Francia for advanced studies.[42] Yet even in those instances where monasteries were surrounded by a dependent town, episcopal sees were almost always larger in terms of their resources and populations, recommending them even further for the development of schools. In the case of the former deacon of Burgos, the growth of the *studium* at Palencia was stimulated by both its bishop's closeness to the royal court and the diocese's proximity to some of the kingdom's wealthier holdings. Enforcing papal mandates with substantial royal endowments served both causes: improved pastoral care, and a better-educated clergy, was a win for the papal program of reform, and a greater body of educated subjects was a boon for the circle of notaries around the king.

During the time Alderico di Palacio was bishop of Palencia, we know of at least four new *magistri* that were brought in to teach and to enhance the reputation of the *studium* at Palencia. Rucquoi long ago noted that, as a group, their specialty was most likely in law, both canon and Roman, given the prevalence of these subjects in other cathedral schools and episcopal *familia* in the period.[43] Although we have nothing akin to syllabi for the courses taught at Palencia, other schools across the medieval Latin West did dictate what lessons would be taught, by whom, and by what time of year; it seems unlikely that similar, if less formal or wholly unwritten, regulations did not exist at Palencia in the same period.[44] Later Dominican accounts suggest that Dominic studied theology at Palencia, which would not have been possible without a faculty licensed to teach those studies.[45] (Dominic apparently favored, in particular, the *Collationes patrum* of John Cassian, a relatively infrequent text in preserved cathedral inventories, which suggests Palencia's library holdings were extensive, despite their current state.[46]) The exact number of clerics and teachers at the cathedral school is almost impossible to detect for the period, but the number of masters who subscribe charters does suggest that there were at least a handful of masters teaching upper-level courses with perhaps a small cadre of advanced students teaching introductory lessons.

During the time of Alderico's episcopate, the number of clerics using the title *magister* increased considerably. In some cases, their identities and activities are well known to scholars. Six names have been preserved in the cathedral sources: Parens (fl. 1190),[47] Guillermo de Peñafiel (fl. 1183–90),[48]

Ponç (fl. 1190),[49] Sares (fl. 1190),[50] Alderico's brother, Lanfranco (fl. 1200–1213),[51] and his cousin Giraldo (fl. 1200–1203).[52] All appear connected to the cathedral school, based on their positions as prebendaries or their close personal relationships with Alderico. Rucquoi has suggested that these men seem to be connected to the teaching of Roman and canon law, the former being recently reintroduced into Iberia and the latter always of great utility in the litigious would of cathedral chapters in the Latin West.[53] Her suggestion is especially well supported not only by the masters in attendance at the chapter but also by the considerable likelihood (posited by Maffei and reexamined by Martínez Díez and Rucquoi herself) that the Italian jurist Ugolino da Sasso had worked in Palencia sometime between the 1180s and '90s.[54] In addition to these men (about whom more below), the case of Domingo González, the archdeacon of Cuéllar for Segovia and a translator connected to the so-called School of Toledo, would also suggest that members of other cathedral chapters or monastic *studia* may have participated in the scholarly pursuits of the budding school of Palencia.[55]

The kind of advanced studies cultivated in the school of Palencia were most likely oriented, according to the best reconstructions of scholars, toward Roman law, canon law, and theology—all subjects that would need prerequisite instruction in the preliminary fields of the *trivium* and *quadrivium*.[56] The provision of *magistri* at other diocesan sees attests to the widespread cultivation of cathedral schools in Castile during the period, but what makes this group of clergy significant is that they appear in the same short period, revealing a nascent scholarly nexus in Palencia. Other diocesan schools may have been developing in the same period, but Palencia was second only to Toledo in the amount of scholarly activity, and even Toledo's reputation may have been skewed as a result of its reputation for translations.[57] Even this number of *magistri* (who were likely the most prestigious members of the chapter) is surely an impressionist portrait of the *studium* of Palencia rather than a realist one.

In order to support the school's Lateran III mandate of "educating the poor clerics," then, there may have several "part-time" faculty among the clergy of the cathedral chapter who taught basic lessons in between their other duties, but no evidence survives to support such a hypothesis. The incomes of the chapter, estimated five years after Alderico's death, could surely have supported several clerics to teach on a short-term basis, but exactly how many were active prior to the official royal chartering of the university in the 1210s—and the increase in patronage that accompanied that charter—is unknown. Early Dominican sources suggest that Dominic was sent to his uncle to learn basic letters before he moved to Palencia for advanced lessons.[58] Contemporary diplomatic evidence demonstrates that even clerics who did not sign their names using the title *magister* were nevertheless well educated. Pedro, the treasurer of Toledo and a prebendary at Ávila, gave his copies of the *Decretum* (*mea decreta*) to the chapter of Ávila, even though he never signed his name as a *magister* in the extant Toledan diplomatics.[59] Gifts of texts become more frequent in the thirteenth century, but the bequest of a book is not what makes Pedro's gift important; the fact that he gave copies of the *Decretum* is. While one may well expect a cathedral chapter's treasurer to have some legal knowledge, the fact that he possessed the text and considered it valuable enough to give to Ávila suggests that he valued it highly enough to make the gift a useful marker of his piety—facts that underscore that he not only owned the book but used it.[60] For a cleric who never subscribed charters as *magister*, Pedro seems to have been well, if informally, educated. How many clergy fit the same mold at Palencia, where the number of *magistri* was on par with Toledo's is unknowable, but we suspect that the number of well-educated clerics under the *magistri*'s direction at least matched one *magister* to every "untitled" cleric.

Despite the role played by the cathedral canons of Palencia in the running of the diocese and its burgeoning school, Alderico was not a serene, pacific cleric all the time. We know that he had quarreled with an archdeacon of Segovia when he was bishop of Sigüenza and had excommunicated the archdeacon, and the conflict was unresolved by the time Alderico was translated to Palencia. Lucius III promptly directed the archbishop of Toledo (then Gonzalo Pérez) to resolve the dispute between them. Whatever had enraged Alderico earned the archdeacon of Segovia his excommunication, and the use of the adverb "irrationabiliter" from the papal chancery suggests that Alderico's wrath was based on more than a minor grievance on the bishop's part.[61] Another case followed a similar pattern, except it was Alfonso VIII who was enraged. It appears that Ponç, archdeacon of Palencia and a *magister* at the *studium,* had so irritated King Alfonso VIII—the letter from Clement III describing the case fails to mention why—that a panel of judges-delegate, composed of Toledo, Osma, and Cuenca, was dispatched to cool the king's wrath and resolve whatever dispute had been provoked. Alfonso VIII's ire was so great that Ponç was, according to the pope, hiding out in a monastery, having been deprived of his benefice and fearing for his personal safety.[62] Settling the dispute was a tricky business, given the parties involved, and the fact that Master Ponç was hiding out in a monastery near Ávila suggests that he was trying to stay far from the major royal residences.

These two disputes suggest that handling the business of a cathedral school in Castile (and managing the array of clerics working there) was as fraught with conflict and complications as it was beyond the Pyrenees.[63] The balancing of episcopal power, papal influence, and royal wrath was difficult, but Alderico sits at the fulcrum of both conflicts. The importance of the chapter to the diocese of Palencia is clear in these incidents.

While the presence of *magistri* and their increasingly frequent appearances in the cathedral documents of the chapter of Palencia offer one way of demonstrating the expansion of the cathedral school, an alternative metric for the same phenomenon is the increasingly frequent presence of Palencia's clerics among the ranks of the judges-delegate in the period. Alderico was asked to serve on at least six cases, including the settlements for the annulment of the marriage of Alfonso IX and Berenguela of Castile.[64] As Bianchini has patiently uncovered, the separation of the two spouses involved the terribly complicated knot of the *arras* castles granted to Berenguela by Alfonso as marital income; they represented a power base that was recognized for more than three decades after the couple's separation.[65] Given the significance of the judge-delegate position and Alderico's caseload, we must unpack Alderico's role to understand how he might be emblematic of Alfonso VIII's third and fourth decades as king of Castile.

Several of the cases involved the bishop of Burgos in cases against two powerful abbeys in the exempt diocese of Burgos. Bishop Marino Mathé's quarrels against the abbots of San Salvador de Oña and San Juan de Burgos were separated by some three years, but the cases were very similar. Both involved, according to the papal *narratio*'s summations of Marino's claims, the usurpation of episcopal rights and privileges by the abbots in lands and parishes belonging to their monasteries.[66] If the claims of Marino were supported by the facts, they would suggest that the abbots were contravening the dictates of Lateran III and sowing discord among the high clergy in Castile, *causae* that would provoke the ire of the Roman pontiff and Castilian monarch, respectively.[67] In a similar case, the bishop of Burgos—again, Marino Mathé—was sued by Rodrigo of Oviedo for having taken possession of a number of churches that, Rodrigo alleged, lay on his side of the border (the Río Deva).[68] A compromise between the two bishops led to the settlement of the case, but the fact that it was settled at all attests to the skills of Alderico and his colleague Bishop Alfonso of Ourense.[69] Both Oviedo and Burgos were powerful dioceses exempt from archiepiscopal authority, and they lay on either side of the charged political border between León and Castile. Arriving at a compromise would have been a considerable challenge, given the economic and political forces at work, and it suggests that Alfonso of Ourense and Alderico of Palencia were esteemed for their good judgment.

During the flurry of these cases, however, Alderico himself was involved in a case brought against him by one of his own clerics. According to a letter from Innocent III dated 11 May 1207, the master of the school at Palencia, a certain I., had accused Alderico of "various excesses," including simony, dilapidation of churches, preventing legitimate appeals, and leaving benefices vacant for his own profit.[70] Although Innocent's tone and procedure suggest that the Roman pontiff was skeptical of the veracity of the charges, he nevertheless dispatched three bishops to investigate: Martín of Zamora, Gonzalo of Segovia, and Pedro Instancio of Ávila. There are no documents that removed Alderico, nor any that censured him, so we are left to presume that there was more smoke than fire in the accusations. However, the growing closeness between Alderico, the king, and Rome does appear, at least in this instance, to have shielded Alderico from a more hostile panel of judges, since two of the men tasked with the case were men with whom Alderico had had frequent contact at the court.

The selection of Alderico as a judge-delegate is significant enough—judges-delegate were selected by their peers to act as arbitrators, and their selection had to be approved by the papacy—but the fact that his canons were held in high enough esteem to serve as judges-delegate suggests that Alderico had a talented cathedral chapter. Three members of the cathedral chapter—Alderico's brother, Lanfranco, Archdeacon Giraldo di Lombardo, and Archdeacon Juan—served as judges-delegate, including as negotiators in the frequent jurisdictional disputes between Palencia and Valladolid.[71] His brother's service suggests that Alderico's power as a bishop may have gotten his brother a benefice, while his reputation for fair dealing helped advance his brother's reputation in the eyes of his fellows. These measures of the prestige of the chapter suggest that the bishop was probably also held in high regard. No wonder, then, that Alderico might be considered a saint by later generations of Palencian chroniclers, if only because he was so adept at balancing royal and papal policy that his episcopate was marked as a resounding success.

Remembering Episcopal Slippers

Alderico's diocese was reminded of his impact long after his death in 1208. Alonso Fernández de Madrid, an archdeacon writing in the early sixteenth century, noted that Alderico's tomb was a site of miracles and that the cathedral treasury held a relic belonging to the remains of Alderico. As pedestrian as the idea of preserving episcopal sandals may seem to modern readers, to the medieval clergy and their medieval parishioners, sandals were a logical, if uncommon, choice for a relic connected to an important bishop. Unfortunately, the relic and the reliquary that likely contained it are not known to have survived, but the mere mention of such a relic raises fascinating questions about the way in which Alderico was remembered.

Several eleventh- and twelfth-century authors connected *sandalia*—a term for liturgical footwear intended for use by clerics of episcopal dignity or higher—to the ceremonial regalia of the episcopate.[72] Their emphasis was certainly rooted in contemporary practice, but that *praxis* had Gospel *doxa* behind it; Christ commanded the apostles to go forth shod in sandals (Mark 6:7–9). The increasing emphasis on apostolic models of living in the twelfth century, long ago noted by Marie-Dominique Chenu, parallels the greater prevalence of the word *sandalia* in connection to prelates of episcopal or abbatial dignity (the latter being afforded the privilege of sandals by virtue of their conspicuous prestige).[73] Nor are reliquary *sandalia* the only examples of preserved episcopal slippers—and the quality of the surviving examples of *sandalia* suggest that they were a prized possession for medieval clerics of high rank.[74] Beyond even their historical preservation and theologically driven value, Miller has shown that "shoe money" (*calciamentum*) was important income for clerics and that the significance of the high clergy's regalia as a visual sign of their official power cannot be underestimated in the long twelfth century.[75]

So if the *sandalia Sancti Alderici* were a symbolically and historically significant choice for preservation *qua* relics, the question remains as to why Alderico's sandal should be preserved as the most useful object of memory. The most obvious answer for why his reputation remained strong was his connection to Palencia and to the school in its various later incarnations, but sandals also implied an episcopate remembered in evangelical and apostolic tones. The capitular *acta* from 1527 recorded the translation of his remains from their previous resting place, near the Romanesque structure's high altar, to their current resting place in the chapel of the Santa Cruz (now dedicated to the Immaculate Conception), but there were few additional details provided by the notation other than a transcription and translation of his epitaph.[76] An inventory from 1501 notes a reliquary containing "a shoe or a sandal from Saint Anderico or Enrico who was a bishop of Palencia" (un çapato o sandalia de sant anderico o henrico que obispo de Palencia) under the reliquaries listed for "santos confesores pontifices."[77] The connection to that translation and the veneration of Alderico as a saint may well have been what provoked the outpouring of devotion to Alderico and the reports of miracles, a phenomenon also noticeable in the veneration of San Julián of Cuenca in the early seventeenth century.[78] There were many episcopal saints venerated in the twelfth and thirteenth centuries, which suggests that the veneration of Alderico as a saint may have predated the translation of his remains even if the translation spurred greater attention to Alderico's memory.[79] The impact of this memorialization is twofold. First, it suggests that Alderico, far from being just an accomplished prelate in legal or economic terms, encouraged the kind of apostolic life that was becoming more prevalent in the Latin West in the long twelfth century. Second, it argues for reinterpreting the legacy of Alderico di Palacio as one of the more important prelates in the early history of Palencia.

We have no reason to suspect that it was solely because of Dominic of Osma's later sanctity that Alderico was venerated, since the usual connection (in historical texts) to the *studium* of Palencia was erroneously made to Tello Téllez de Meneses, Alderico's successor.[80] Although some early scholars believed that Alderico may have founded a *studium* at Úcles, it seems unlikely that the school was the source of the reputation that supported Alderico's sanctity.[81] One tradition suggests that Alderico was the uncle of Pedro González Telmo, an early recruit to the Dominican order, and that sanctity was a family trait.[82] The location of Alderico's tomb in the cathedral may better explain his position in the memory of the diocese. The epigraphical evidence for his tomb suggests that he was near the heart of the old cathedral, and the modest inscription on his tomb—"Here lies Don Alderico I, bishop of Palencia; he died III Ides August (11 August) in the Era 1245, the Year of the True Lord 1207"—garnered him some attention, if of the kind that usually underlined a local saint.[83] That his sanctity only appears to have become popular after he was translated is particularly noteworthy, since it fits the style of an *inventio* narrative rather than a long-standing memorialization within the larger genre of hagiography.[84]

Unfortunately, the reliquary that held Alderico's sandal must have been lost sometime between the mid-sixteenth and the early eighteenth century. Inventories from the later sixteenth and early eighteenth centuries focused on individual chapels that were then undergoing restoration, but none of them include the reliquary of Alderico di Palacio's *sandalia*.[85] An inventory taken for the Capilla de las Reliquias in the early eighteenth century does not list any relics belonging to Alderico or to any reasonable corruption/permutation of his name.[86] Even the unidentified *arquetas* held in the Museo Diocesano of

Palencia, which might have been candidates for storing Alderico's relics, are either of foreign origins or craftsmanship (especially those containing Italian or French relics) or contain relics unconnected to Alderico, as in the case of a tenth-century reliquary *arqueta* from San Salvador de Campo Muga.[87] As a result, it seems most likely that Alderico's relics were either (a) reinterred with him at some date that has been lost or (b) taken as plunder in one of the wars (Bourbon or Napoleonic) that crisscrossed the peninsula in the early modern period.[88] In either case, it seems likely that the tradition of Alderico's relics attests to a complex process of memorialization in the cathedral, which is a mostly unrecoverable phenomenon, given presently available sources.

The location of his original tomb near the high altar was a sign of his importance to the diocese, but the translation of his remains to the chapel of Santa Cruz (according to Gíl González Dávila) does not indicate that his memory had diminished in the sixteenth century.[89] Rather, the centrality of that original burial position in the cathedral suggests that Alderico would have been a presence at moments of great liturgical and social importance in the cathedral during the centuries after his death. While there are no markers of substantial cult activity from his death until the first notation of a reliquary that may have held Alderico's *sandalia* in 1481 and was named as such in 1501, we cannot conclude that his memory simply lay dormant in the cathedral. As the new Gothic edifice was being constructed, the core of the old cathedral—the high altar—would have remained intact until it could be expanded. It stands to reason, then, that during a time of great change in the physical landscape of the cathedral, the memorial fabric was also undergoing considerable, if oral and ephemeral, renovation.

So should we read the account of Alonso Fernández de Madrid as a kind of early modern spin on the Carolingian practice of reification via forgery, in which the story in the *Silva Palentina* connected the *sandalia* of 1481 to the bishop who lay near the high altar, and in so doing made him a saint? This suggests that Fernández had a desire to amplify devotion to the cult of Alderico, folding into the cathedral's observances a local saint worthy of votive offerings to support the *fábrica* of the new Gothic cathedral.[90] Worship at Alderico's tomb in the chapel of Santa Cruz would imply that there was a need to enhance the larger sacred geography of the cathedral, but there are no records of any cult activity to suggest any momentum for Alderico's veneration save that added by the *Silva Palentina*. Even if it was not an outright forgery, the memory of Alderico at the cathedral of Palencia does appear to have been particularly potent, and for good reason. His balancing of papal and royal agendas during his episcopate made his tenure as a major official in the Tierra de Campos an important period of market expansion. For all his possible sanctity—which would have seemed in short supply in the early sixteenth century—Alderico was and remained a twelfth-century saint, one whose episcopate was fairly typical of a cleric working during the reign of Alfonso VIII of Castile rather than that of a saint being worshipped in the days of Carlos I of Spain and the Habsburg Empire.

Conclusions

Alderico's episcopate serves as a proof for a number of important transitions in the middle part of the reign of Alfonso VIII. As a cleric appointed from a family with roots outside the peninsula, he was very much of an age where Burgundian adventurers and Cluniac clerics commanded outsized influence. Yet he was not an appointed politico, unlike his Palencian predecessor; rather, he seems to have been genuinely elected because of his capabilities as an administrator. He fits the model of a deacon-to-bishop *cursus honorum* that became more prevalent in the latter half of the twelfth century and was more common on the frontiers of Christendom, where practicality dominated.[91] Alderico was a character that fit the show, although his success may be the reason such an impression persists.

The career of a prelate with the wide-ranging activities that Alderico took up during his episcopate cannot be written on bronze tablets, but it would nevertheless resemble a *res gestae* from a different world. From his days at Burgos, he was active on one of the key axes of power in Castile, but his time as an archdeacon coincided with perilous days for the kingdom of Castile. His eventual election to the see of Sigüenza almost certainly came because of his work in Burgos and favor by those close to the king. Inheriting Sigüenza in those days was no easy business, as it was close to the border with both Aragon and the Almohads. His election came in the years of the Infantazgo War, in which Ramón de Minerva and Pedro Pérez (bishop of Burgos) played a major role, which may well suggest that Alderico was one of the canons responsible for moving resources and materiel into play to effect a Castilian victory there. In any case, his career at Burgos surely propelled him toward Sigüenza, where he lost neither time nor momentum.

Within the first year of his episcopate at Sigüenza, Alderico was in Rome, attending the Third Lateran Council. The increased number of clerics using the title *magister* in the cathedral records of Palencia in the years after the council demonstrates that the implementation of the program of canon

3 had teeth in the dioceses of Castile. Although there is no evidence for any implementation at Sigüenza until the tenure of Alderico's successor Rodrigo de Finojosa, the dramatic growth in the number of personnel in Palencia from the mid-1180s onward shows that Alderico recognized the value of such a measure and sought to implement it. Indeed, it seems that this kind of pragmatism was one of the common elements of Alderico's episcopate, and it was one of the strengths that helped propel him forward.

The frequency with which Alderico was selected as a judge-delegate and the strong personalities involved in the cases to which he was assigned suggest that he had a reputation for good judgment and practical wisdom. However, we know that Alderico was also capable of wrath whose impact was felt even by the appellate jurisdiction of Rome, when his unresolved quarrel with an archdeacon of Segovia prompted papal instructions to Toledo for a swift resolution before the case boiled over again. Yet that early case does not seem to have much tainted the opinions of his colleagues in the episcopate— perhaps because they were familiar with this archdeacon or perhaps because they had had similar experiences with other prelates' subordinates—and Alderico was tasked with resolving a number of cases involving the bishops of Burgos and her local competitors for property and prestige. These were the very kinds of administrative and economic questions whose pertinent details were handled locally, and the increasing frequency of judges-delegate in property questions in Castile in the late twelfth and early thirteenth centuries is as much a marker of their utility as a papal tool as it is a product of the increasing survival of the evidence. Among all the cases on his docket, Alderico's most high-profile case was the separation of Alfonso IX of León and Berenguela. The pleas that the marriage was *pro bono pacis* failed to sway papal opinion, and the number of treaties and compromises (and recompromises) attests to how monumental an effort would be required of the clerical judges-delegate responsible for dividing the properties given to Berneguela as part of her *arras* endowment.[92] The fact that Alderico was selected as a judge demonstrates the influence of two factors: first, the majority of Berneguela's holdings were within the territory of Alderico's diocese or directly bordering on it (in the Infantazgo region of the Tierra de Campos), and second, Alderico's previous service as judge-delegate ensured his credibility as an arbiter in a case of such demonstrable magnitude. The whole, then, of his service as a judge-delegate suggests that Alderico was a respected legal and administrative mind with a habit of playing fairer than most.

But what of the picture of his whole tenure? Certainly, there are few examples of any conduct that would merit the hagiographical tones that opened this chapter. In fact, Alderico seems to have been a model cleric for a period where papal and royal interests were in tension—he was a prelate who went about his business and did it well; he spotted, cultivated, and employed talent where he could; he served when he was asked; he did what he was supposed to do. For that, he may well have earned a reputation for sanctity above and beyond the evidence of his sandal, if for no other reason than that he served king, countrymen, and Christendom in a fashion that would, by the early sixteenth century, seem all too rare. While he was not the only cleric with a reputation for sanctity from the reign of Alfonso VIII, the fact that Alderico is the only saintly bishop from that period who does not now find his name in the rolls of the saints speaks volumes about how effective but unexceptional his episcopate was. In any event, his legal experience and his administrative prowess seem to have imprinted his memory on the diocese of Palencia, and the fact that he served in the same place as Ramón de Minerva—a cleric of wholly different qualities—marks his career as a kind of case study in the diverse characteristics and interests typical of ecclesiastical potentates in the period.

5

A REFORMER AND A GENTLEMAN
Martín Bazán of Osma

Don Martín Bazán. He was a monk of Saint Benedict of the monastery of San Millán de la Cogolla and went from monk to bishop, without being made abbot it seems, because in the catalog of the famous sons of that convent is this: Martín Monk Bishop.
—Gregorio de Argaíz, *La soledad laureada por San Benito* (1675)

Martín Bazán, bishop of Osma from 1188 to 1201, is usually only mentioned by modern scholars in connection with his recruitment of Dominic of Osma to the reformed cathedral chapter of Osma sometime in the 1190s.[1] However, the career of a mentor for Dominic of Osma deserves a more complete treatment than the usual stub biographies afforded by scholars working on the early Dominican movement, especially because Martín Bazán was far more nuanced a figure than the short few lines describing him in the early histories and hagiographies penned by Dominican friars in the thirteenth century. While this is itself significant, Martín Bazán was also a papal and royal servant for much of his career, balancing the two power bases with model aplomb.[2] Fortunately, modern scholarship has much more historical data with which to uncover Martín Bazán's episcopate and its important intersections with larger European trends, and doing so demonstrates that Martín was correctly remembered but incorrectly named (here, conflated with Diego d'Acebo) by early Dominican histories and hagiographies as having "worldly nobility of his birth . . . crowned by his knowledge of sacred letters and by a signal integrity of virtue."[3]

Unfortunately, we know very little about Martín's early life. However, some evidence indicates that his background was similar to that of several of his episcopal peers.[4] His surname of "Bazán"—preserved in several charters and confirmed by epigraphical evidence—demonstrates that he was of noble Navarrese stock.[5] The early modern chronicler Gregorio de Argaíz notes that he was a member of the famous Cluniac "Suso" community of the twin monasteries of San Millán de la Cogolla.[6] This community, according to Ignacio Alvárez Borge, was one of the most powerful in the Ebro River valley, renowned for its comprehensive agricultural wealth in the late medieval warm period.[7] That same wealth made the region a zone where military and economic strategic interests converged—but also surely influenced the growth of the Suso community and may be one of the major factors behind the considerable collections there and for its monks' reputation for learning. That learning likely helped retrench the influence of the prior of the community, especially in litigation against neighboring communities.[8] The cultivation of monastic power at San Millán made its monks a kind of farm system for many of the other monastic and clerical communities in the wider region.

The presence of a Bazán at a monastic establishment in the Rioja by the 1180s would suggest that his family was part of the larger movement of Navarrese into the border region, perhaps coincident with much of Sanç VI's attempts to capture the border territory during the rocky minority of Alfonso VIII.[9] A similar trend is observable in the early life of Rodrigo Ximénez de Rada, and his family's connections to the Orphan King may serve as a model by which we might imagine a similar relationship between Martín's family and Alfonso VIII. San Millán's Cluniac affiliation suggests that an older, but still vibrant, ethic of Gregorian-era reform would have been well attested in the ranks of the brothers, and Martín would have been accustomed to papal and reform-movement languages of power from the earliest period of his activity.[10] Cluny was still substantial in those days, even if the early Cisterican movement was hot on its heels, and the impact of the Cluniac order in Iberia was so considerable that it might be credited with reestablishing the links between Castile-León and the Roman curia in the eleventh century.[11] These few data points are as reliable a sketch of the background of Martín's early career as can be given, owing to the paucity of evidence regarding this period of his life.

An examination of the episcopate of Martín Bazán, however, could provide considerable detail about the origins of the Dominican Order and crucial insights into the process of reform—in the twelfth-century ecclesiastical sense—in the province of Toledo at the turn of the thirteenth century.[12] The very act of electing Martín Bazán suggests that, after considerable effort, several latent problems in the cathedral chapter of Osma were finally coming to their resolutions. The story of his election, then, begins not in 1188 but in 1176.

As discussed in chapter 2, the election of Bernardo of Osma was a major case in the archiepiscopate of Celebruno, but it was also (quite naturally) an explosive event in the diocese of Osma.[13] With Bernardo's removal, a new bishop was needed for the diocese of Osma, and recent turmoil would have likely suggested the need for a steady hand. The chapter, perhaps with considerable prodding by the archbishop, settled on the abbot of the powerful Cluniac house of San Pedro de Arlanza, Miguel.[14] The abbey of San Pedro de Arlanza was one of the great adversaries of the bishops of Burgos in frequent land disputes, but the house was near enough to Osma that the abbot may have been well known to the canons of the cathedral chapter.[15] In any case, there are so few records of Miguel as bishop of Osma—he served as a judge-delegate on one case and there are a few royal confirmations of the properties of Osma—that we know little about any efforts undertaken by Miguel to reform the chapter.[16] His successor, García, is even more mysterious: we know that he was most likely the prior of the chapter and archdeacon of Soria—coincidentally, the same posts held by Bernardo—prior to his election, but his short tenure of two years suggests that he may have just been a senior member of the chapter and a known quantity whom the canons expected to preserve the status quo.[17] After the nine-year term of a Benedictine Cluniac abbot and a two-year stint from the cathedral chapter's prior, the election of a monk from a Cluniac house appears to represent the continuation of earlier reform efforts. Although we know too little about the archiepiscopate of Gonzalo Pérez of Toledo to substantiate any speculation about archiepiscopally driven reform, such a hypothesis may be supported circumstantially by extant copies of papal letters preserved in Toledo reminding the archbishops to supervise the replacement of secular canons at Osma with regular canons.[18] It was, one suspects, his amenability to or zeal for a monasticizing *forma vivendi* that recommended Martín Bazán for the episcopate of a see that, by papal instruction, could use a bit of the monasticizing energy that pervaded the twelfth-century church.[19] The need to cultivate stronger ties to a papal program while maintaining strong-enough ties to a monarchy that needed diocesan support in a key border territory may have made Martín a useful choice for a diocese trying to recover its prestige.

Reforming and Reading at Osma and Elsewhere

The episcopate of Martín Bazán is bisected by the 1194 Treaty of Tordehumos, an ambitious agreement between the kings of León and Castile supervised by a cardinal-legate with the expressed purpose of enabling the two kings to make war on the Almohads to the south.[20] The enthusiasm and aggressive expansion in the period following Martín's election is exemplified by the royal establishment in 1189 of a diocese at a place Alfonso VIII's chancery initially named as Ambrosia (later renamed Plasencia), albeit on lands that were traditionally Leonese and not under the metropolitan authority of Toledo but of Santiago.[21] Nevertheless, the energetic expansion of this period put the new bishop of Osma in a position of some optimism, and the evidence suggests that he went right to work on the project of reforming his cathedral chapter, cultivating contacts and relationships at the royal court to buttress his efforts.

In 1190, only two years after his election, Martín won a case held in the court of Alfonso VIII against the city council (*concejo*) of San Esteban de Gormaz concerning the collection of revenues from some of San Esteban's surrounding villages.[22] The monastery town of San Esteban de Gormaz, now a brief stop on the bus route from Madrid to Burgo de Osma, was a major source of potential revenue, but the town itself never seems to have belonged outright to Martín or his predecessors.[23] In the 1174 confirmation of the properties and privileges of Osma, Alfonso VIII confirmed two donations to Osma that appear to have been in Martín's possession when he pleaded his case against the *concejo*: one that granted his church the revenues from the parish of San Sebastián and the other that confirmed a now-lost gift to the church of all the properties of "Miguel the Priest, *merino* of San Esteban de Gormaz."[24] It can safely be assumed that Miguel the Priest's properties in the city, thanks to his position as *merino*, were extensive and that they constituted a major source of rents in the surrounding hamlets. The parish of San Sebastián, overlooking the Duero River, must have commanded great influence in the heart of the city, given its proximity—one can see it from the present-day church—to the local river ford. Increasing the revenues of the diocese was part of the usual business of the office of the bishop, as was ensuring the obedience of those towns from whom the diocese collected revenues, but the importance of performing both of these tasks—with enough skill to secure a verdict in his favor—at the royal court must have marked a kind of "public relations" victory for Martín's early career. Having gained his footing at the royal court and ensured that at least some of the canons of his see were more inclined to follow his lead, Martín turned to more contentious, internal matters.

The first evidence of the reform of the cathedral chapter at Osma confirms what Dominican narrative sources had said about their founder from the beginning: Dominic was recruited from the cathedral school of Palencia to help reform the discipline of the chapter of Osma.[25] Dominic first appears in 1191 as a canon serving alongside his later mentor Diego, then the sacristan, in a *hermandad* agreement between the cathedral chapters of Sigüenza and Osma.[26] The signing of a *hermandad* agreement between chapters was a typical way to reinforce the spiritual health of both houses and to ensure that, when they were in need of basic necessities in each other's territories, the canons could seek them from houses with whom they shared an agreement.[27] Yet to say that Martín Bazán and Martín de Finojosa, the bishop of Sigüenza, simply signed an accord of friendship whitewashes their common history: for most of the twelfth century, the two dioceses had engaged in nearly a dozen suits and countersuits over a handful of properties on their mutual border; effectively, they had been at legal war with each other.[28] (The quarrel may have even included actual violence against clerics committed by the townsfolk loyal to either side, as a 1170 judicial pronouncement by Alfonso VIII suggests.[29]) Getting the two chapters to agree to even the most limited *hermandad* was a coup for both bishops, but the timing and provisions of the agreement, and the appearance of two men with reputations for holiness, suggest that part of the reason for the *hermandad*'s success was that Osma had begun to reshape its chapter toward a more monastic and regular observance.[30]

Despite this tendency for monasticizing endeavors, it does appear that Martín Bazán had more than just a regular observance of a reformed customary in mind for the chapter at Osma. In fact, it seems likely that he permitted Saint Dominic to continue attending to his studies at Palencia after he had taken up a post as a canon at Osma. One story consistently attested in the early Dominican hagiography tells of a famine at Palencia during Dominic's studies, a famine great enough that the laity were in grave danger of starvation; moved by the distress of the townsfolk of Palencia, Dominic sold almost everything he had, including his schoolbooks, to buy food to feed those too poor to feed themselves.[31] The story was so important to the narratives of Dominic's early career that it swayed even the most cautious of modern scholars: an entry in the *Anales Toledanos* records a famine in the region in 1193, and based on this fact, scholars concluded that that entry provided *post quem* for Dominic's recruitment into the cathedral chapter of

Osma.³² However, canon law allowed clerics in minor orders—including canons, provided they were at the level of subdeacons or lower—to retain their benefices and status in the chapter while they were studying, if they were not studying one of the topics forbidden by the same precepts (namely, medicine and secular law). Since Dominic, according to the unanimous testimony of early Domincan sources, was studying theology while at Palencia, it stands to reason that he was recruited in or before 1191 to Osma, sold his things in 1193 to alleviate the pains of local paupers during a famine, and returned to take the position of sacristan sometime between 1195 and 1199.³³ None of these scholarly activities could have taken place without permission from his bishop, which suggests that Martín Bazán encouraged Dominic's studies to help enhance the intellectual merits of his chapter and provide adequate training for the poor priests and clerics in the diocese, as commanded by canon eighteen of Lateran III. Effectively, Dominic's theological studies were supported by a bishop who helped encourage the tendencies of the young canon from Caleruega that compelled him to seek a mode of living in concert with the *vita apostolica*.³⁴ Bringing the chapter into closer alignment with papal priorities while cultivating ties to a royally supported *studium* was another example of Martín's careful development of the tripolar balancing of Rome, Castile, and the diocese of Osma.

The churches of Burgos and San Salvador de Oña were engaged in constant struggles over the rights of the bishop and the abbot and the taxes owed to either house. In an 1191 letter to Bishop Gonzalo Gutiérrez Girón of Segovia, Alderico of Palencia, and Martín Bazán, Clement III ordered the three men to hear the dispute between the abbot of Oña and the bishop of Burgos.³⁵ While the case between Marino Mathé and Pedro Ibañez has already been discussed above, what bears noting is that Martín Bazán had gained enough of a reputation for sound judgment in three short years that the bishop of Burgos and the abbot of Oña agreed to his service as a mutual arbitrator in their litigation. This was likely the first major delegated case handled by Martín Bazán, the most junior member of the panel, and therefore also represents one of the earliest recognizable estimations of his judgment. The case would not be the last judicial delegation to which he was assigned, but it does suggest that Martín was gaining a substantial reputation in his early episcopate. The process of negotiating peaceful relations between two churches and cathedral chapters that had been in conflict for most of their existence must have made an impression.

Martín Bazán could not have known the future of his actions in 1191— recruiting Dominic and Diego while serving as a papal judge-delegate—but his actions at the court of Alfonso VIII suggest that he was laying the groundwork for improving more than just the spiritual health of his diocese. King Alfonso, in 1192, provided such a significant donation to the church of Osma that, as Carlos de Ayala Martínez observed, Martín Bazán could not be anything less than a court favorite.[36] The villa of Valderón itself was a nice addition to the revenues of Osma; records about it are sparse in the second half of the twelfth century, but the affection expressed by Alfonso's chancery in the charter suggests that the feelings that motivated the gift may have been more important than the gift itself. Alfonso offered the villa to Osma "having had due consideration of your merits and the devotion that you did not bear against us."[37] The cultivation of patronage at the court of Alfonso VIII was crucial, since the 1174 inventory of the see's privileges does not suggest that Osma was ever very wealthy, and every addition would support the reform of the chapter and its ability to foster a comfortable monasticized observance.[38] It seems also likely that the merits and devotion mentioned by Alfonso VIII had not been simply "discovered" in the bishop of Osma in 1192; rather, the recognition in the privilege was the culmination of a pattern of behaviors that were rewarded in 1192. That service would expand even further in the coming years, but it was the papal curia that would require Martín's services next.

Judging and Reforming in the High *Meseta*

In the aftermath of the Castilian defeat at Alarcos in 1195, a number of regular episcopal tasks appear to have been temporarily diminished. A Leonese invasion of Toledo earned Alfonso IX of León both a papal condemnation—including a call from Celestine III to the Portuguese king for a punitive crusade against León—and a joint Castilian-Aragonese raid against, inter alia, one of León's more important Jewish towns.[39] The outbreak of hostilities with the Christian kingdoms of the north, along with the sack of a number of border towns by the Almohads, put the Castilians on the defensive.[40] These developments were resolved by a truce with the Almohads and a marriage alliance between the Castilians—in the person of Berenguela, eldest daughter of the Castilian Alfonso VIII—and the Leonese (through King Alfonso IX himself), which shifted Castilian focus toward Navarra and the kingdom of the young Sanç VII.[41] This shift toward Navarra eventually led to a series of major territorial additions to Castile and a renewed Aragonese-Castilian alliance, which would have likely improved the fortunes of border dioceses like Osma, Sigüenza, Calahorra, and (on the Aragonese side of the alliance with Peter II) Tarazona.[42] This suggests that in the period after the defeat at Alarcos, where Martín Bazán and his Toledan superior, Archbishop Martín López de Pisuerga, had lost two of their episcopal colleagues, Osma took on a renewed importance to Castile and to the work of the *cortes*.[43] In the second half of Martín Bazán's episcopate, from 1195 to 1201, there are a number of indications that Martín Bazán played a greater role both in the work of his diocese and in the kingdom as a whole.

Appellate conflict resolution was a key part of the complex of activities that constituted the political authority of the Castilian monarchy, since the Castilian crown traditionally relied on force of arms rather than sacral theory to legitimize the rule of kings.[44] Martín Bazán had already gained something of a reputation for his judicial acumen in the early 1190s. In a document dating to 1196, Martín serves as an investigator for the court of Alfonso VIII. The royal charter concerns a dispute between the houses of San Cristóbal de Ibeas and San Juan de Burgos and the city council (*concejo*) of Santa Cruz de Juarros. All three of these entities were located within the exempt diocese of Burgos and would have ended up in the papal courts without swift resolution. Alfonso's decision favored the two monastic houses, but this was only because "the privileges [of the houses] were brought forth in the court held before the king, and Martín, bishop of Osma, read them before the king, and, according to what they found in the privileges, the lord king and his *alcalde* judged that the abbot of San Cristóbal's and the prior of St. John's held the *collazos* [in question]."[45] The role played by Martín in the resolution of the case appears significant, since both the King and the *alcalde* relied upon Martín's interpretation of the text. We do not know if he repeated this work at other times but the task itself is significant as an indicator of royal confidence in the bishop of Osma. The trust implied by Martín's role in the case demonstrates that Martín was, by 1196, considered competent within the royal circles, a reputation reinforced by his earlier service to the papacy. The papal and royal services operated on the same track an enhanced Martín's reputation for prudent judgment.

In addition to his service at the *cortes*, Martín Bazán also appears to have served on several important papal judicial delegations in his later career. The first of these delegations whose records have survived—although surely not the first since his 1191 service—dates to 1198, when he was assigned a case between the monastery of Ripoll and the archbishop of Tarragona.[46] According to the letter of Innocent III assigning Martín and his colleagues, the bishops of Huesca and Tortosa, to the case, the matter was prima facie a property dispute between Ripoll and Tarragona. Ripoll claimed that Tarragona had usurped the rights to revenues in the town and territory of Centallas. The canons' case against Ripoll rested on the fact that Guillermo, as Innocent related it, "was caught red-handed in forging our bull and is held to be suspect."[47] Innocent sent Guillermo back to Catalonia and ordered Osma, Huesca, and Tortosa to establish whether the bulls were indeed false, to determine whether the monastery or Tarragona had the rights to the "villa and *honor* of Centallas," and to ensure that their edicts were upheld within the limits of the law.[48] The dispute between Ripoll and Tarragona coincided with another matter concerning claims over "the *castrum* of Analec" that Innocent commanded the delegates to resolve, although, given its positioning in the letter, the dispute over Analec does not appear connected to Guillermo's earlier fraud. The dispute was primarily a question of property rights in the province of Tarragona. Both of Martín's colleagues were diocesan bishops from the Crown of Aragon, suggesting that Martín was selected from a border region to serve as a balancing interest within the group and was sufficiently trusted by Innocent's curia to faithfully carry out the terms of his judicial appointment. This explains, in part, why the next judicial delegation to Martín Bazán was on one of the most high-profile canon legal disputes of the twelfth century, both in Iberia and throughout Latin Christendom.

There were few canon law cases as contentious in medieval Iberia as the grappling among Braga, Santiago de Compostela, and Toledo for the metropolitan rights of Zamora.[49] That three archbishops were contesting Zamora's allegiances made things difficult enough, but the added political importance of the case—the archbishops sat in three different kingdoms—made any solution very fragile and subject to great scrutiny. By the late twelfth century, the three metropolitan archbishops were vassals of three different kings: Braga was Portuguese, Santiago de Compostela was Leonese, and Toledo was Castilian. The question of Zamora's allegiances had been "settled" by five separate pontiffs.[50] The last of the answers was the solution posed by Innocent III in 1199, which, along with resolving the case itself, included an appellate panel to handle any wrangling after the decision had been issued.

The great importance of the Zamora case was cited by Innocent's letter because of Zamora's place in the kingdom of León and its proximity to both the Castilian and Portuguese borders.[51] The long-running dispute slowly edged out Toledo's claims based on her primacy, and the contest rested on whether Braga's claims to the lands as a more local metropolitan trumped Compostela's claims that Zamora's location was within the Visigothic province of Mérida, from which Compostela's metropolitan dignity was transferred.[52] In the larger scheme, the bishop of Zamora would owe at least nominal allegiance to Toledo as *primas hispaniarum,* but the question of direction jurisdiction brought with it privileges regarding synods and councils and de facto ecclesiastical capital.[53] Innocent had issued his sentence in favor of Compostela shortly before appointing Martín Bazán, Brecio of Plasencia, and Martín Rodrigues of Porto to hear any appeals made by Braga against previous decisions in favor of Compostela.[54] Concerning the appointment of this appellate panel, Fletcher notes: "Nothing further is known of [the struggle between Braga and Compostela], so it is to be presumed that Braga gave up the struggle at this point. During the thirteenth century Zamora was incorporated de facto among the suffragans of Compostela."[55]

The importance of delegating any appeals against the decision surely lifted a great weight from Innocent's shoulders but required supreme confidence in the clerics to whom the appeal of the decision was delegated, especially given the provision that the whole case could be retried from the beginning. Even if Martín was chosen simply as a geographical balance between Plasencia and Porto—suffragans of Compostela and Braga, respectively—Martín was himself a suffragan of Toledo and would have served as the "Toledan judge-delegate," given that even Toledo had a tenuous claim on Zamora. Martín's selection was a considerable endorsement of his credibility and ability to act impartially among papal circles. The clerics assigned to the panel must have been very well known at the curia to merit such an assignment. Bishop Brecio of Plasencia is a mysterious figure despite being favored by the papacy, but few facts remain that give us anything more than an impressionistic portrait of his reign at Plasencia.[56] Martín Rodrigues of Porto served nearly half a century at his post, but would fall out with King Sancho of Portugal in the late 1200s and was only restored to his see with great effort by Innocent III in 1210.[57] The three men tasked with such an important case as that of Zamora must have been trusted greatly in their respective posts by the papacy.

It is either a testament to Martín's selection of deputies or to his ability to manage multiple complex affairs at once that, while the case of Zamora was being litigated, Martín was able to successfully "complete" the reform of his cathedral chapter. Two letters from 1199, dated on two consecutive days, attest to the completion of the reforms required by Alexander III in the aftermath of the simony deposition of Bernardo of Osma decades earlier. In the intervening years, another letter from Lucius III instructed the bishop of Osma to further the cause of reform, replacing secular canons with regular canons.[58] Despite papal prodding, it was only by 1199 that Martín had completed the reforms, albeit not without some difficulty.

The text of the first letter from Innocent congratulated Martín on the reform of the chapter—it was now entirely composed of regular canons and would no longer allow new secular canons to be enrolled. The letter noted that Martín had done so with the support of Alfonso VIII of Castile and according to the instructions of the papacy, suggesting that Innocent was pleased with the king's concern for good discipline and with Martín's obedience to papal mandate.

> We are stirred by the burden our office to plant the *ordo* of religion and to foster that which was planted and thus it agrees with us to offer apostolic patronage and favor to the places of religion, because they should wish to achieve regular growth under our regimen and governance.
>
> Accordingly, we have understood . . . that you . . . ordered (having provided deliberation) that, according to the teaching of the Roman Pontiffs Alexander [III] and Lucius [III], of happy memory, in the Church of Osma the canons should be regulars henceforth and none will be received hereafter as portionary or secular canons into [the Church of Osma].
>
> You have also ordered certain other chapters [regulations] which we have seen to be contained in the same letter. Wishing therefore that the statute, through your pious consideration, is seen to enjoy due firmness, we confirm by apostolic authority these constitutions (or rather we can call them restitutions since, as you affirm, from a long time back this was prescribed for the church of Osma by the Roman pontiffs), just as they have been reasonably composed and accepted by your chapter, and we strengthen them by the written page of the present.[59]

Although we do not know which rule or customary the chapter followed after Martín's reform, the use of the Augustinian Rule by the Dominicans may have had as much to do with Lateran IV's prohibition against new rules as it did with Dominic's own preference for the rule's relatively simple traditions. The ability to shape its observance with a customary whose adoption would not be subject to the strictures of Lateran IV made the choice a sensible one, especially since it provided for the common holding of property, a popular statute for chapters at the time.[60] It is not too great a speculation to suggest that the chapter at Osma had readopted the Augustinian Rule with a newer customary, both based on the great number of cathedral chapters that used that rule and on Dominic's later preference for it.[61] Although we cannot know for certain which rule and customary the chapter at Osma adopted, we have additional clues to suggest what one of the major issues in the reform of the chapter might have been.

In a letter dated just after the congratulatory epistle from Innocent, a second answered a canon law question for Martín's chapter: whether it was acceptable for clerics to keep concubines. Even though Emil Friedberg wrongly identified the letter's recipient as the bishop of Exeter, the letter was a forceful enough statement of law by Innocent III that its text found its way into the *Compilatio tertia* and into Gregory IX's *Liber Extra*, as well as numerous tracts on the issue of clerical marriage.[62] The common teaching maxim that "laws are only passed to solve a pressing societal problem" seems particularly germane here: perhaps the canons of the chapter either wanted to keep their concubines and disobeyed Martín without a papal clarification, or perhaps there was genuine confusion about which women were allowed based on the customary or the copy of the Augustinian Rule in use by the chapter. The canons' concern is particularly telling given the reprimands of Cardinal d'Abbeville, whose legation to Iberia in the 1220s focused on the implementation of the reforms of Lateran IV and the pecuniary problems of the Iberian Church.[63] One of the issues noted with greatest frequency during that legation was the Castilian clergy's sexual improprieties—or the reports thereof.[64] Although there is no way of telling to what degree the reports were true, the fact that Martín Bazán sought a papal confirmation of the prohibition against clerics living with women in concubinage suggests it was a great enough problem for the bishop to need papal backup. Whatever the results, the reform of the chapter of Osma allowed Martín Bazán's successor Diego to undertake long-distance embassies on behalf of King Alfonso, a fact that suggests that the cathedral chapter was reliable enough at Osma that such journeys would not permit misdeeds back home.[65] Effectively, aligning himself with a papal reform program allowed Martín Bazán to develop an even stronger bond with the Castilian monarchy.

Wars against Navarra in the late 1190s resulted in several major acquisitions of territory under Alfonso VIII. Both in the greater Rioja and in Guipúzcoa and Álava, the Castilians expanded significantly north and east, both directions that should have benefitted the diocese of Osma. Problematically, there is no direct evidence that Osma benefitted from these conquests. In his 1204 will, Alfonso VIII admitted to having mistreated Osma during his minority, and he afforded the diocese five thousand maravedíes to provide pastoral care for the sake of his soul.[66] He added, too, that to marshal those funds to Osma, the diocesan fisc should incorporate the villa and the castles and the rights that pertained to them into their holdings. It seems highly likely that, just three years after Martín Bazán's death, the legacy of the service of the bishops of Osma—Martín in particular—reminded Alfonso VIII to square his affairs with the church. Even without new Navarrese territory added to its patrimony, it seems likely that *noblesse oblige* added to Osma's wealth, and the fact that Martín was able to serve the papacy in several important cases suggests that the situation at home was at least calm for him and his chapter. Cultivating ties with both Alfonso VIII and the Roman pontiffs had buoyed Osma's political and perhaps also economic fortunes considerably.

By the turn of the thirteenth century, the evidence for the bishop of Osma's service as a papal judge-delegate picks up considerably. In March 1201, only months before his death, Martín was assigned a flurry of cases in the diocese of Burgos, as Mateo Mathé seems to have pressed a trio of suits against the powerful monastic institutions in his diocesan territory. There were at least three such cases, but given the character of the disputes, there were likely several others. Burgos pressed cases against San Salvador de Oña, San Pedro de Arlanza, and San Pelayo de Labedo, all of which possessed common themes: monastic officials were allegedly usurping episcopal rights.[67] While these cases have as much to do with the overlapping exemptions—Oña and Arlanza were exempt monasteries, Burgos an exempt diocese—of the major players involved, the repetition of litigation between Burgos and powerful Benedictine houses in the diocese suggests an ongoing competition among wealthy clerical establishments, especially given the many important and wealthy towns that lined the lucrative Camino de Santiago. The facts of the cases themselves are less of interest here than the fact that Martín Bazán was selected in a battery of similar cases that promised considerable complexity, implying that Martín had a reputation for fairness and learning among his peers. Those qualities must have been what recommended him for the highest-profile canon law case in the Iberian Peninsula and what suggested, to the papal courts, that a battery of complicated cases was well within his ken.

The period spanning the second half of Martín Bazán's cases seems to indicate two things. First, his contacts with the Roman curia must have increased significantly after the legations of Cardinal Gregory of Sant'Angelo, while his *fama* among his colleagues must have risen considerably for him to merit a number of appointments.[68] Second, the reform of the cathedral chapter of Osma demonstrates that the spiritual life of the community was important to Martín, as both the early Dominican hagiographical accounts and the cartulary evidence make clear.[69] These elements suggest that Martín's focus as a bishop was on the order and discipline of the contemporary church and that his episcopate's efforts to that end were not wasted on an unwilling clergy. While we have less evidence to suggest that there was a major uptick in royal patronage for the diocese, we have fewer documents from Osma than any other diocese save Plasencia. It could well be that Martín was well rewarded for his diligent royal and papal service in a difficult era.

"He Went from Monk to Bishop"

We do not know exactly how Martín Bazán died, but the eighteenth-century historian Juan Loperráez Corvalán narrated the end of Martín's episcopate with more poetry than hard evidence:

> In the remainder of the year that he had of his life this Prelate maintained himself with quietude in the government of his Church, and he died in his Palace on the 26th of July, as is known by the annals of his Church . . . he whose body had stood for some years on the pavement of the church, was afterward translated to the epistolary side of the chapel which is today called that of Santo Christo, venerating previously Santo Domingo de Guzmán, covering [Martín's] bones with a stone with this brief epitaph of letters commonly called *abacial*: "Here lies D. Martín Bazán, Bishop of Osma."[70]

Loperráez Corvalán's narrative is quaint, but it has all the hallmarks of otherwise accurate scholarship, despite the poor preservation of sources from Osma. Although the codex cited by Loperráez Corvalán was itself a sub-citation and the original source of the information is unknown, the information's precision does fit with Martín Bazán's quiet disappearance from the witness lists of the charters of Alfonso VIII.

Sepulchers traditionally are, indeed, quiet places, especially when they lie beneath the pavement of a cathedral, but Martín's involvement in his church was anything but quiet. His judicial acumen won him a decision against the *concejo* of San Esteban de Gormaz and recovered more revenues for his diocesan see. We know that his service as a judicial interpreter at the court of Alfonso VIII was impressive enough that the chancery recorded his role as reader of the charters, and the judgment of both the king and the *alcalde* depended on that service. Those same skills were certainly those that prompted Alfonso, "having had due consideration of [Martín Bazán's] merits," to award the villa of Valderón to Osma. Although subsequent donations do not survive to indicate that the diocese of Osma benefitted from the conquest of large portions of the kingdom of Navarra in 1198 and 1199, we may reasonably conjecture that the diocese benefitted in some fashion from those conquests, too.

From a comparative perspective, Martín Bazán was hardly an unusual character in his age. Reforms of cathedral chapters, for example, were in the air at the time: Rodrigo de Finojosa, whose reforms are detailed in chapter 8, was engaged in a negotiated process that required archiepiscopal intervention in 1198; Martín's reforms were completed by 1199; and Julián ben Tauro of Cuenca pushed through a series of reforms by 1201, as chapter 7 will demonstrate.[71] Martín's service as a judge-delegate also paralleled a major feature of contemporary juridical practice, which saw the papacy's increasing involvement in the local cases of regional churches and saw local prelates resort to papal appeals with greater frequency. The complex of traditional episcopal acts in his diocese suggests that, contrary to what some of his predecessors had established as a model, it was perfectly acceptable to be a traditional prelate in Osma, even if it was less frequently the result of an Osman episcopate.

The reputation of Martín Bazán in the early printed histories from the kingdom of Spain suggests that there was, compared to some of his predecessors, little available information about him. In most cases, even capable antiquarians were unable to do more than attest to his presence. Even in the Dominican hagiographies, Diego d'Acebo figures as a more potent figure in the early story of Saint Domingo de Caleruega than the bishop who enrolled the young student in the chapter of Osma circa 1191. Martín's episcopate is worth studying, however, if for no other reason that it was exceptionally unexceptional: his royal service mirrors contemporary examples, and his papal correspondence was characterized by a cordial relationship, save when the dominant political problems of the day overshadowed his reputation. Bringing papal reform programs and royal political activities into concert with each other was a way to advance the cause of his episcopate generally. Martín helps us set an accurate baseline for the character of bishops at the turn of the thirteenth century in the kingdom of Castile.

In most senses, Martín was the last of a particular breed of bishops in Iberia, monastically trained young aristocrats who were elevated to the episcopate based on their *fama* and the nobility of their line. He was a capable reformer whose Cluniac tendencies did not prevent him from seeking a kind of Premonstratensian (customary) solution to his Augustinian (capitular) problem.[72] He was a capable scholar, able to read and judge good privileges from bad and to discern the proper decision in a number of complicated legal cases. He sought royal patronage, even while the royal focus shifted back and forth from the area of his diocese to the southern frontier. In the end, Argaíz's estimation of Martín's career seems just as good as any other four-word summary: "Monge salió por Obispo."

6

"HIS NAME WAS MARTÍN MAGNUS"

Martín López de Pisuerga and an Archiepiscopate
for the Thirteenth Century

The bishop Don Jerónimo, crowned on the head,
When tired from dealing with the Moors with both hands,
He could offer no account of how many he had killed,
Great was his share of the booty.
— Per Abbat, *The Song of My Cid* (1207)

For a younger son of a noble family in the long twelfth century, a clerical career represented stability, purpose, and a degree of safety. In 1192, Martín López de Pisuerga, the scion of a clan with holdings centered on the wealthy towns of Palencia and Valladolid, ascended to the highest post in the Iberian clergy: he became the archbishop of Toledo (r. 1192–1208).[1] Martín began his career in the clergy serving as an archdeacon in Palencia—very close to lands held by his father, Lope, in Valladolid—and likely gained his post as a result of his father's prestige and patronage.[2] By the end of his tenure in Toledo, Martín bore nearly every burden expected of an archbishop: he investigated candidates for the episcopate, negotiated settlements in legal cases, led cavalry raids, and protected his own rights and privileges against the attempted usurpations of others. In Martín's archiepiscopate, the transformation of the office of archbishop allows us to better examine what it meant to hold that office in an increasingly proactive, litigious, and energetic age. In contrast to the defensive political and administrative work of his predecessor Celebruno, Martín took a more aggressive approach. His career changed what it meant to be an archbishop of Toledo for the thirteenth century and afterward.

At the time of his election and consecration to Toledo, Martín's Castile was experiencing a period of substantial success. Alfonso VIII had added the dioceses of Cuenca and Plasencia, the former to Toledo's own ecclesiastical province, and the king's military capabilities afforded him substantial leverage over his neighbors.[3] From the early part of his archiepiscopate, Martín appears to have taken a leading role in the work of the kingdom, placing the crusade against al-Andalus at the core of his efforts in the affairs of the realm. The campaign against the Almohad caliphate was critical to the success of both the kingdom and the archdiocese of Toledo. In his first years as archbishop, Martín was thrown immediately into that same campaign by the arrival of an Italian cardinal named Gregory.

Gregory, cardinal-deacon of Sant'Angelo, took two trips to the Iberian Peninsula as the pontifical legate *ad latere* of Celestine III.[4] It was Gregory who communicated to his uncle, Celestine III, that Martín had been elected by the chapter of Toledo, and his connection to Iberia as a legate followed closely on his uncle's prepontifical legations as Cardinal Hyacinth Bobone.[5] His first legation, from 1192 to 1194, culminated in the momentous Treaty of Tordehumos, which was consecrated on the first Wednesday of Easter, 20 April 1194.[6] The terms of the treaty solidified a peace between León and Castile but used a newly favored method to ensure that the terms of the treaty were preserved. Ten towns in the border region between Castile and León, five from each kingdom, were placed in the hands of a party of neutral trustees; whichever monarch violated the peace first would forfeit the towns to the other party. In addition, the king of Portugal was folded in as an additional guarantor of the treaty, ensuring that there would be an added military cost to any violation of Cardinal Gregory's Eastertime accord.

A *Cabalgada* and a Youthful Candidate

In addition to theoretically guaranteeing that the Iberian monarchies could plan campaigns against the Almohads, the Treaty of Tordehumos also allowed magnates to plan their own efforts against al-Andalus. For Martín López de Pisuerga, son of an experienced Castilian potentate, Tordehumos provided the opportunity to engage in an age-old summer ritual for the Castilian middling sorts and their towns: the *cabalgada*, a long-distance cavalry raid that served both economic and military purposes along the Iberian frontiers.[7] In the case of Martín López de Pisuerga, the mechanism may have been familiar, but the results of the archbishop's own cavalry raid were extraordinary.

It is possible to date Martín López de Pisuerga's *cabalgada* with some accuracy. He must have left after the Treaty of Tordehumos was signed, since we know he was present, but before the end of the Hijri year 590, since Islamic sources record the *cabalgada* as taking place in that year. The span 21 April to 15 December 1194 describes the general dates available, but Martín's reappearance in royal charters later in the year suggests that the raid took place sometime from May through August, during the usual period of military activities in Castile.[8] During that period, something remarkable happened under Archbishop Martín's direction that made its way into both Christian and Islamic sources.

The earliest Christian testimony on the raid is that of Juan of Osma: "[Martín López de Pisuerga] led with him generous and strenuous men and a multitude of knights and foot-soldiers, with whom he raided a great part of the land of the Moors on this side of the sea, plundering it of much riches and an infinite multitude of cows, sheep and mules."[9] Never one to miss an opportunity to praise a Toledan, Rodrigo Ximénez de Rada elaborated on Juan's account significantly and managed to work in substantial praise for his predecessor:

> He stirred up arms against the king of Africa and provoked soon after the people of Arabia. His army went over to Baetica and its leader was the prelate of Toledo. The great men of the kingdom were in the councils of the prelate and the whole army was under the dignity of the prelate. His name was Martín the Great, and his clan was from Pisuerga. . . . His belt was his zeal for the faith and his arms he turned to the persecution of blasphemy. His whole flock turned to the will of that man [Martín] and the blood of the Arabs was in his sight. The Kingdom of Baetica was set to flames and it made the prelate prosper. He thus proceeded via the castles of Baetica, setting fire to the towns and the land.[10]

In the later thirteenth century, the Alfonsine historians would add the important detail that "the sea-side land of the Moors" and "the Kingdom of Baetica" mentioned by Juan and Rodrigo, respectively, was the Guadalquivir valley.[11] All three Christian sources attest to the scale and purpose of the *cabalgada* of Martín López de Pisuerga, but their praises would appear to ring hollow when confronted by the timing of the raid itself. Just a year later, the Castilians would be crushed at Alarcos and spend the next three years on the defensive.[12] Without corroboration, these sources might appear to be exaggerating the successes of the archbishop of Toledo to compensate for his king's failure in the following summer.

Islamic sources complicate the picture of the raid of 1194 on two fronts. In the first place, the *cabalgada* is universally described as a royal action. In the second place, descriptions of the expedition vary widely, depending on the author's style and motivation for writing. The latter point is typical of any historical source and can be dispensed with accordingly. The former is a question of considerable importance: conflating the archbishop of Toledo and the king of Toledo, as Castilian kings were styled in Arabic sources, creates some confusion, but the identification of actors is less important than the validation of the facts. While the Islamic sources are not ideal witnesses for the actions of Toledan archbishops, their commentaries on Martín's raid expand the view of the *cabalgada* considerably.

There are several Arabo-Islamic sources whose narratives record the raid. The earliest is that of Abū Muḥammad 'Abd al-Wāḥid al-Marrākušī, who finished writing around 1234 and described the raid thus: "In the Year of the Hegira 590, the treaty between [Yaq'ub al-Mansur] and Alfonso [VIII] was broken and the cavalry of that [Alfonso] crossed the land [of al-Andalus], and ran into its flanking points to cause great damage to al-Andalus."[13] A more specific record of the raids was noticed by Ambrosio Huici Miranda in a fifteenth-century commentary on the work of a Murcian poet from the early thirteenth century, which read, "[The Castilians] attacked everything in al-Andalus in the east and west at the same time. The contingent that had reached Seville advanced through its entire territory, sacked its district, and attacked one of the castles of its Ajarafe; it was on the verge of victory, had it not been for the vigilance of the Almohads, who advanced to meet the army and drove it out of those lands. They retreated after a number of them had died and God had caused their endeavor to fail."[14] The cultural memory of Martín López de Pisuerga's raids was even preserved in an echo in the Levantine author Ibn al-Athir's *Chronicle*. The defeat of the Castilians at Alarcos is portrayed as a direct result of Alfonso VIII's arrogance, and the king's military affairs were conflated with the archbishop's raid. Al-Athir records a letter allegedly sent by Alfonso VIII to Yaq'ub al-Mansur, saying that Alfonso intended to "humiliate [the Andalusi Muslims], empty the lands, enslave the offspring, mutilate the middle-aged and slay the young men."[15] Centuries later, reputable historians like Aḥmed b. al-Maqqarī still recorded the event as a matter of considerable scorn, and the Castilians' defeat at Alarcos was portrayed as the rightful restoration of the Almohad hegemony in Iberia.[16]

We know that Martín's raid was a point of considerable comment by authors on both sides of the religious borders of Iberia, but evaluating the raid as a turning point in the activities of the archbishops of Toledo is a more complicated affair. Prior to Martín López de Pisuerga, the last archbishop to organize a military effort was Celebruno, during his defense of Castile with Count Nuño de Lara and Bishop Ramón de Minerva of Palencia in 1165–67.[17] Given the presence of Count Nuño, it seems most likely that Ramón and Celebruno were enlisted to support Nuño with money, men, and materiel.[18] What differentiates these actions from the *cabalgada* of 1194, however, is their inherently *defensive* nature. While Martín's raid fits squarely into the well-established crusading context in the lead-up to the Crusade of Alarcos, the *offensive* nature of the war puts Martín in the primary position for the enterprise: the raid was his.[19] Canon law and crusading custom did not outlaw Martín's leadership of the raid; in fact, precedent was on his side in both cases.[20] After Martín's raid, Rodrigo Ximénez de Rada not only fought at Las Navas but also partnered closely with King Fernando III (r. 1217–52) in his campaigns against al-Andalus, and he even led his own campaigns to conquer several territories around Quesada in 1231.[21] Additionally, Rodrigo also secured a certification from Honorius III that canons of Toledo, when they were with the royal army, could use their benefices as though they were at Toledo personally, allowing them to use their assets to secure their release in case they were taken captive while on campaign.[22] While Martín was not alive to see Rodrigo's endeavors, it is clear that his influence on later archbishops endured. This kind of careful overlap between papal and royal policy agenda was only practical if there were clerics on the ground who could translate that careful balancing act into action.

Although it took place only two years into his career as archbishop, the *cabalgada* led by Martín López de Pisuerga was not the only major event that demonstrates the great changes occurring in the archdiocese of Toledo at the end of the century. As archbishop and therefore the metropolitan of his province, Martín was responsible for consecrating the bishops of his suffragan dioceses and certifying their election and consecration to the popes.[23] In 1195, Martín was presented with a candidate for the episcopal *cathedra* of Segovia who must have reminded him of his own early career. Succeeding his uncle Gonzalo in the post, Gutierre Rodríguez Girón was one of the younger sons of one of King Alfonso VIII's closest friends and advisors, Rodrigo Gutiérrez Girón.[24] Gutierre Rodríguez Girón had served as a canon of

Segovia, near his father's lands, and appears to have benefitted significantly from his father's influence, even after Rodrigo's death in 1193.[25] Problematically for the young canon of Segovia, there were some who questioned his qualifications. According to the Third Lateran Council, a bishop needed to be at least thirty years old.[26] The question of Gutierre's age appeared to be considerably vexing. To answer the question to his own satisfaction, Archbishop Martín conducted his own investigation of Gutierre's age and dutifully had the results recorded and sent to Rome for pontifical approval.

The letter, marked as ACT X.2.B.1.1. in Toledan archives, contains numerous clues as to Martín's investigative processes, but it is most interesting as a record of his thoroughness. In its entirety, the Latin text runs to nearly three hundred words, identifies many specific witnesses, and contains brief summaries of their testimony about Gutierre's age. Martín brought together his own panel of trusted episcopal colleagues, asking Martín Bazán and Rodrigo de Finojosa of Sigüenza to join his investigation to ensure its integrity and credibility. Martín called three witnesses from Segovia's chapter: an archdeacon named only as "G.," an archpriest named Juan de Frantia, and a priest called "S." Both the archdeacon and archpriest noted that twenty-two years and nine months had elapsed since the election of the previous bishop, Gonzalo Gutiérrez Girón, of Segovia. They added that Gutierre had been at least six and maybe a little more at the time of Gonzalo's election. The archpriest confirmed all the things that his colleagues said. Still, basic addition betrays that Gutierre was still too young by almost a year. Even allowing for the possibility that Martín's inspection took place several months after the death of Bishop Gonzalo of Segovia and that Gutierre had reached six-and-a-half years at the time of Gonzalo's election in early 1171, Gutierre would still have been too young to be elected to the episcopate.

Of course, exceptions to the canons of a council could be made, in theory, for persons of outstanding merit, and medieval clerics would have recalled that even at the age of twelve, Jesus had taught the masters in the Temple. In the case of Gutierre we have no reason to expect any sort of Christomimetic erudition, so a different explanation is required. The panel in question and the witnesses betray that the examinations recorded in the text cannot have been all that occurred in the proceedings. The erudition and judicial experience of Martín Bazán and the experience and learning of Rodrigo de Finojosa, Archbishop Martín's colleagues in the investigation, were well established in their day.[27] So, too, were their political instincts. Although the canons of Lateran III were firm in their insistence on the age of their bishop, the question of a bishop's age found its way into the *Compilatio prima*, but only included the canons of Lateran III among twenty other texts, complicating the matter substantially.[28] Although confusion is a possible explanation, it seems unlikely that a competent tribunal of bishops, with attendant clerks in tow, would not have been able to parse the important details pertaining to Gutierre's eligibility and deferred to the lasting power of his family's influence in the region.

A further wrinkle emerges from the royal charters of the 1180s and early 1190s. On a number of occasions, the charters include the designation that "Gutierre Rodriguez, serving as chancellor, wrote it" (Gutierre Roderici existente cancellarii scripsit).[29] If Archbishop Martín's investigation uncovered Gutierre's correct age, then his first appearance as chancellor was around his seventeenth year. To be fair, the position of chancellor was, according to scholarly consensus, a mostly honorific post until the early thirteenth century, but it was still a post reserved for persons close to the royal family.[30] In Gutierre's case, the position of chancellor would have been a great honor to his father—if it was not his father's influence that secured the post—and would have suggested that he was trusted in royal circles and fairly competent, even if the workload had required a thoroughly professionalized office while he served as chancellor.

Archbishop Martín would have surely known Gutierre from the royal court, and Gutierre's post as a deacon at Segovia placed him in major clerical orders. It seems unlikely, then, that some exception would not have been made for such a qualified candidate. In Gutierre's life, Martín would have seen several familiar themes from his own upbringing. Gutierre was from a noble family, had been assigned to the clergy from an early age, and had served as a deacon during his early career. The two men would have likely shared an interest in the crusades against al-Andalus, too, given the role played by Gutierre's father (in the conquests of Cuenca and its environs) and his brothers (who would later serve with distinction at Las Navas de Tolosa).[31] Toledo needed partners and colleagues in its suffragans, and Gutierre would have been a substantial ally for Martín, especially given the importance of Segovia's militia to the royal armies.[32] It seems only too obvious that Martín had approved and consecrated a cleric after his own heart, a warrior-cleric from a noble family, willing to fight Islam *verbo et exemplo*.

Sadly, the young bishop of Segovia was fated to disappoint Martín's expectations. "In the catalog of our bishops," the sixteenth-century antiquarian of Segovia, Diego de Colmenares, narrates, "it says, 'Don Gutierre, son of Ruy Girón, who died at Alarcos, the year 1195.'"[33] While the election of Gutierre came to naught, it did demonstrate that Martín López was a competent judge of both evidence and character, which provokes a corollary: if Martín was a competent legal mind, how competent of a legal mind was he?

To succeed in the long twelfth century, an archbishop needed to assure that his province and his administration were granted every possible right and privilege. For Martín, as for other archbishops of Toledo, that meant shoring up the integrity of his diocesan patrimony and its treasury. Several occasions allow us to reconstruct the ways in which Martín went about ensuring that his war chest remained ready to face whatever challenges confronted his administration. The records left from his tenure as archbishop show us how Martín sought to improve Toledo's financial and administrative footing. He pressed cases—to both the papacy and the Castilian crown—against military orders, against clerical institutions, and even against members of his own diocesan see. In the process, he demonstrated with his advocacy the same principle that underlined the prosecution of his *cabalgada*: playing offense against one's adversaries was better than playing defense.

Quarrels Foreign and Domestic

In the 1170s and 1180s, Toledan clerics had revolted against the archbishop—that much is well known.[34] By the 1190s, the absence of any documented quarrel suggests that any friction between the archbishops and the clergy of Toledo had died down. However, all was not well in Toledo. An unedited letter from May 1199 indicates that the papacy had heard that "nearly all your parish clergy had fallen into such wicked idleness they contumaciously refuse to obey you, entering upon new and detestable conspiracies and plots against you in the guise of confraternities."[35] The conspiracy against Martín appears to have had its roots in the financial difficulties suffered in the aftermath of the Crusade of Alarcos, but we cannot rule out other possibilities.[36] One of the most important contingents of the Toledan clergy was the Mozarabic communities' clerical sons, and the role of Mozarabs as both intellectual and economic powerhouses is well attested.[37] Celestine III recommended that the archbishops of Toledo should take the cause of Arabic-speaking Christians under Almohad rule seriously, sending clerics southward to al-Andalus to minister to the pastoral needs of Christians oppressed by the Almohads' strict enforcement of religious restrictions for *dhimmi* in their domains.[38] Sending trained preachers into Almohad realms was a dangerous proposition, given the Almohads' stance on non-Muslims and forcible conversion, and even pastoral care might have prompted capital cases under Almohad rule. In any case, the "detestable conspiracies" of the Toledan clerics died down enough that no further record of any conflict is preserved in Toledo. That said, control over his diocesan clergy was just one part of Martín's attempts to control the entities with whom he so frequently interacted.

In May 1197, well before the important 1199 letter backing Martín against "detestable conspiracies," Celestine III sent Martín a letter that conveyed upon Toledo a particularly exceptional privilege. Celestine III granted Martín the right "to impose or relax a canonical penalty on any laymen in the kingdoms of Iberia who had mistreated a cleric, so long as that cleric had not died or been mutilated."[39] The letter was a considerable boon to the archbishops of Toledo, but it could not have come without some Toledan prompting—the content of the letter is too specific for Celestine to have been spontaneous—and must have been a great moment in Martín's career as archbishop.[40] The terms of the privilege allowed Martín to relax canonical penalties against laity not only from the kingdom of Castile and his metropolitan province but from the other kingdoms of Iberia as well.[41] Such an expansive privilege was also a tacit endorsement of Toledo's metropolitan claims, since relaxing penalties against laymen from other kingdoms could theoretically override the penalties levied by prelates from other ecclesiastical jurisdictions. Effectively, it allowed Martín to excuse violations of which he approved, tacitly (if not explicitly) endorsing those punishments that condemned actions against the archbishop's own interests. The affairs of other dioceses was certainly the province of an archbishop of Toledo, as a metropolitan, but Martín's involvement in local affairs went beyond relaxing harsh punishments from jurisdictions that were not directly his own.

The reform of cathedral chapters could be a huge undertaking. As the previous chapter noted, the process at Osma took nearly thirty years. Martín Bazán's reform of the chapter of Osma seems to have influenced the decisions of two of his contemporaries to reform their own cathedral chapters. In 1199 and 1204, respectively, Bishop Julián ben Tauro of Cuenca and Bishop Rodrigo de Finojosa of Sigüenza took up their own cathedral chapters' reform. Rodrigo's reform is described more in the next chapter of this study, but Julián's reforms at Cuenca are particularly interesting for any study of Martín López's time as archbishop.

Prior to his election to the episcopate of Cuenca, Julián ben Tauro was the Toledan archdeacon of Calatrava and was from a wealthy Mozarabic family.[42] He had served under Archbishop Martín, and the two men seem to have had an amicable working relationship.[43] As a suffragan diocese of Toledo and one of the sees in closest proximity to the archdiocese, Archbishop

Martín had a vested interest in ensuring that the customs issued to Cuenca's canons were as good as was practicably possible. (In fact, some of Cuenca's founding canons also held prebends in Toledo, contrary to canonical norms but in keeping with frontier customs.[44]) Particularly important in the reform statutes of Cuenca were those privileges that shored up the frontier city's stability, a concern likely shared by both the metropolitan archbishop and his Cuencan suffragan.

The reformed statutes of Cuenca mention Martín only once, at the end of the document's *datum* clauses, but the influence of the same kind of conflicts that had plagued the Toledan chapter are palpable. One of the most frequently mentioned issues in Julián's customary is the problem of canons not being resident in the city of Cuenca and their subsequent absence from the liturgical functions of the cathedral chapter.[45] Martín had, just a few years prior, fixed both the number and conditions of his own canons in the cathedral chapter, defining in the customary the penalties and fines assessed on those who did not meet the conditions of residency and activity.[46] For a diocese struggling to gain financial ground, Julián's provisions imitated the practical and advantageous parts of Martín's reforms; no maximum number of canons was needed in the early chapter at Cuenca, because no abusively large number of canons had yet been enrolled.[47] By actively cultivating a sensible practice at the chapter of Toledo, Martín López encouraged the imitation of that practice among his suffragan bishops' chapters, implementing the same kind of reforms that Innocent had encouraged to resolve Martín's own cathedral chapter conundrums.

In previous chapters, the importance of pontifical judges-delegate has already been outlined in some detail, but for an archbishop, a judicial delegation not only reinforced the papacy's authority but also underscored his own position of appellate jurisdiction within his ecclesiastical province.[48] Martín served on at least four separate occasions for the papacy, but he surely served on many more ad hoc cases in his province as the chief cleric.[49] Cases assigned to Toledo necessarily had a higher profile than those assigned to local deacons, but the cases assigned to Martín were particularly serious. One case in particular stands apart as evidence of Martín's capabilities. In 1204, he was tasked with resolving the separation of the Castilian *infanta* Berenguela from her husband, King Alfonso IX of León (r. 1188–1230). The reform of the chapter and the royal separation demonstrate that Martín was both a capable resolver of conflicts and an able arbiter in diplomatically tense situations, both qualities that would be in high demand for thirteenth-century archbishops.

When they married in 1199, the eldest daughter of Alfonso VIII and the king of León were already in considerable trouble with canon law. The two were both descendants of King Alfonso VII "the Emperor" of León-Castile: Berenguela was his great-granddaughter, and Alfonso IX was his grandson. The two were thus first cousins, once removed.[50] The marriage brought an uneasy peace between two kingdoms that were intermittently at each other's throats and were hard-pressed to abide by even the expansive terms of the Treaty of Tordehumos, despite Celestine III's admonitions in the lead-up to the Crusade of Alarcos.[51] The marriage between Berenguela and Alfonso was patently illegal, but it appeared, to some contemporaries, to be the only solution that might secure a lasting truce between the two kingdoms. Despite its support by almost the entire clergy of León and Castile, the marriage was subject to the near-immediate wrath of Innocent III, and the pope ordered his own confessor to Iberia to separate the two.[52] For the five years of their marriage, Innocent sent a letter to the two kingdoms' clergy at a rate of one every nine months, admonishing them to compel the two royals to separate.[53] Before they finally parted ways, two sons, the future Fernando III and Alfonso Alfonsez de Molina, and two daughters, Constanza and Berenguela, would secure both the Castilian-Leonese succession and, theoretically, prevent the outbreak of further wars between the two kingdoms.[54] Separating the personalities was difficult enough, but resolving the division of property and separation of assets was an even more politically complicated affair.[55] Only the most capable prelates could be assigned to handle such a delicate matter as the dissolution of a royal marriage, and Martín was one of the few who were qualified.

In 1204, Innocent III wrote to the archbishop on a number of occasions to ensure that he was informed about his responsibilities in the case of Berenguela. In May, he wrote to outline the conditions under which Archbishop Martín and his colleagues might absolve Berenguela for her sins and lift the canonical penalties that had been issued.[56] In June, Innocent outlined the archbishop's role in restoring the *arras* of Berenguela in the Infantazgo de Campos region between León and Castile.[57] These two charges were significant matters to resolve, to be sure, and the results played out over a series of months.

On the matter of the absolution of Berenguela, who had returned to Castile and was under Martín's jurisdiction, Innocent III had much to say. Canon law made the penalties levied against Alfonso IX and Berenguela clear: they were both excommunicated, and their lands, by papal decree, were under interdict. Although the interdict would be lifted when the couple separated, the two monarchs were still excommunicated until they were penitent and sought absolution.[58] However, Innocent was no stranger to merciful treatment of the repentant, and Martín was granted, via a communique dating to 22 May 1204, the right to absolve Berenguela, if he was satisfied of her remorse.[59] Although there was more than enough precedent to allow Martín the right to absolve Berenguela in contemporary canon law, the emphasis laid on Martín's discretion suggests that Innocent trusted him to judge Berenguela's contrition.

The division of the *arras*, a marriage endowment given by an Iberian king to his queen to maintain her retinue and provide for her needs, was also a complicated affair. We do not know exactly how much of an income Berenguela was given by Alfonso IX, but we do know where that income came from: the Infantazgo de Campos.[60] As several scholars have shown, the Infantazgo region was an extensive and wealthy power base for royal women.[61] For Martín, the resolution of the matter of Bereneguela's *arras* territories could have presented serious complications. He needed ample political support from his fellow clergy to ensure that the ecclesiastical party in Castile, as the arm of the same hierarchy that compelled Berenguela and Alfonso IX of León to separate, closed ranks around Berenguela, unlike their opposite numbers in León.[62] The bishop of Palencia, Alderico di Palacio—who held extensive territory and commanded great influence in the same region—likely gave Archbishop Martín the local support he needed to make his solution to the case stick.[63]

While the negotiations over Berenguela's *arras* and her absolution must have been complicated, we have no record to suggest that they roused Archbishop Martín's temper. The same could not be said for a dispute with a military order occupying a church in the city of Toledo itself. According to the canons of the Third Lateran Council, military orders were forbidden to receive churches and tithes from the hands of laypersons without permission, and the canons further decreed that those who were disobedient to a bishop were to be placed under an interdict and their deeds invalidated.[64] No wonder, then, that when the Hospitallers accepted the church of Santa Cruz in the city without his consent, Martín was furious.[65] In the twelfth-century ecclesiastical sources in Castile, episcopal wrath (*ira*) is rare, but the terms expressed suggest that Alfonso VIII's "dearest and most faithful friend" was angry enough to provoke the king himself to action.[66]

Property rights in Toledo were certainly important to an archbishop, but Martín, more so than his predecessors, appears to have capitalized on the local market to enhance the archdiocese's and the archbishop's holdings in

Toledo. While there are surviving Latin records of purchases from Martín's time as archbishop, it is his commerce with the native Mozarabic population that stands out as a distinct difference from his predecessors' archiepiscopates.[67] From 1202 to 1206, Archbishop Martín López de Pisuerga purchased six properties from Toledan Mozarabs for a total of 730 *menkales*, a sum equivalent to about 209 maravedíes.[68] Considering that the income of the entire cathedral chapter of Palencia was approximately 10,000 maravedíes in 1211 and the income of Ávila was 7581.3 in 1250, Martín's real estate expenditures constituted a substantial investment.[69] The kinds of properties he purchased make his acquisitions even more intriguing. Of course, the availability of certain properties was out of Martín's control, but his purchases of one-half of a dam and a pair of inns and three shops, in 1204 and 1206, respectively, must still have been handsome additions to the archiepiscopal patrimony, especially given the tax exemptions that came with clerical status under the *fuero* of Toledo.[70] Martín's personal purchases, then, show him attempting to control more of Toledo, both through his political influence and through his real estate acquisitions.

An Archiepiscopate Transformed

This chapter has shown the ways in which Martín López de Pisuerga transformed the archiepiscopate of Toledo by taking a more aggressive approach. This transformation was not a revolutionary thing in its day, as many bishops (and the papacy itself) sought to influence the workings of increasingly larger parts of society more assertively.[71] The influence of the changing nature of lordship and proto-governmental structures in a wider European context cannot be overstated in this arena, and indeed, the transformations discussed in this chapter show congruences with broader developments in Europe as a whole. In studying the case of Adalbert of Mende (r. 1151–87), Thomas Bisson noted that similar attempts in the 1160s and 1170s to control a large territory and command political influence in a crucial region were met with considerable resistance from almost every level of society.[72] Control over territory was a part of the equation, but so was the ability to influence ecclesiastical subordinates, as Michael Burger has suggested for the English church; administrative episcopal structures added greater complexity and impeded bishops' ability to control their diocesan clergy.[73] Influence needed to come from many sources, and maximizing the contributions of each sector put archbishops on the firmest ground both in controlling their own archdioceses and in persuading their episcopal suffragans.

As an archbishop, Martín López de Pisuerga transformed the archiepiscopal example left by Gonzalo Pérez—about whom Peter Linehan said, "the modern historian of the church of Toledo is content to merely record just his election . . . and his death"—into an assertive archiepiscopal office capable of making grand actions seem second nature.[74] The influence exerted by Martín as an archbishop was considerable, not only because of the office itself but also because of the ways in which he vigorously pursued its prerogatives. As this chapter has shown, Martín actively changed the ways that the archiepiscopate interacted with the major elements of late twelfth-century Latin Christian society. This active engagement with larger themes and trends—crusades, financial controls, political settlements, judicial delegations, and legal reforms—defining the end of the long twelfth century tells us much about the reasons why Martín deserved the praises lavished on him by his successor.

Rodrigo Ximénez de Rada praised his predecessor for many of his personality traits, but especially for the way he pursued the prerogatives of his office: "His life was the honor of his clan and his stole was the crown of the Church. His wisdom was the peace of the many and his tongue was the information [which was the source] of discipline. His hand was turned to the subsidy of the poor and his heart to the compassion of the humble."[75] While Rodrigo's praises certainly fit with his larger pro-Toledan partisanship, they also fit rather neatly with what we already know about Archbishop Martín López de Pisuerga.[76] In almost every discernible episode of Martín's career as archbishop of Toledo, he was involved with the most important affairs in Castile. Investigating a candidate for the episcopate of Segovia was an important task, both because the candidate was the son of a favored royal friend and because the diocese was a favorite royal residence, and Martín pursued the case with force and vigor. The reform of the cathedral chapter of Cuenca evinces an archbishop concerned with the pastoral and financial health of a neighboring (and suffragan) diocese. The prosecution of a *cabalgada*, too, suggests that the archbishop was concerned with the security of the kingdom, particularly as an important truce with the Almohads was about to expire. Engaging in a crucial series of negotiations over the separation of a Castilian *infanta* and her royal Leonese husband was a task only fit for the highest-ranking and most-respected clergy in Castile. The tasks assigned to Martín were traditionally archiepiscopal in their scope, since his was an office concerned with the whole of Castile and its maneuvers, but the ways in which he pursued the completion of those tasks required a kind of vigor that was, according to Rodrigo, unmatched among his predecessors. Rodrigo often called Alfonso VIII "rex strenuus" and admired the king's dedication and effort for those tasks he pursued; perhaps it was their shared vigor that caused Alfonso VIII to refer to Martín López de Pisuerga as "my dearest and most faithful friend" (karissimo ac fidelissimo amico meo).[77] The two men were just that much alike, in no small part thanks to the way Martín helped shape papal policy's implementation of the royal agenda.

7

A MOZARAB? A REFORMER?
A SAINTLY PROFESSOR?
Julián ben Tauro of Cuenca

San Julián, second bishop of Cuenca, an honor for our Spain, an ornament of the Universal Church, the idea of Holy Prelates, great marvel of Grace, and one of the most brilliant lights, admirable in life, excelling in virtues, and prodigious in the miracles, he is the subject of this History.
—Bartholomé Alcázar, *Vida, virtudes, y milagros, de San Julian, segundo obispo de Cuenca* (1692)

For most of the long twelfth century, the city of Cuenca sat perched on an escarpment cut by the Huecar and the Jucar rivers, balanced at the borders between Aragon, Castile, and the *taifa* of Murcia.[1] Although it was briefly occupied by Emperor Alfonso VII, Cuenca was a strategic outpost for the legendary Muhammad ibn Saʿd ibn Mardanīsh; after the death of ibn Mardanīsh, Alfonso VIII laid siege to the city and, after minor setbacks, captured it in 1177.[2] The event was recorded by both chronicles and *datum* clauses in royal charters as a signal victory—in hindsight, the kind of "coming-of-age" conquest that set the standard for Alfonso VIII's later career.[3] After the conquest (which may have been financed by Toledo in order to add a new suffragan diocese[4]) and securing the surrounding territory, Alfonso VIII and his clerics seem to have petitioned Pope Alexander III to establish a new diocese in Cuenca.[5] The first bishop was elected from his post as archdeacon of Calatrava in the archdiocese of Toledo, and the close relationship between metropolitan and suffragan bishop continued for the earliest years of the diocese under Bishop Juan Yáñez, who saw at least seven major donations from the monarchy during his episcopate.[6]

While many bishops were elected from local cathedral chapters, Juan Yáñez's successor was also his successor in his earlier post of archdeacon of Calatrava. Sometime after June 1196, Julián ben Tauro (r. 1198–1208) was elevated to the post at Cuenca, but his appearance in the sources is delayed considerably.[7] Scholarship has identified him as a member of a wealthy Toledan Mozarabic family, elevated to a diocesan post to provide a culturally and politically mobile prelate for a diverse community on the frontier between Castile and the Almohads.[8] We know, too, from bills of sale that he was competent in Arabic.[9] This chapter will examine Julián's background, his episcopate's reform and consolidation efforts, and the way that he was remembered by later Cuencan historians as a saint and the "second founder" of the diocese of Cuenca.

"Cuencan Elected and Toledan Archdeacon"

Jorge Díaz Ibáñez has shown that while some early modern traditions associated Julián ben Tauro to the diocesan territory of Burgos, the best evidence (compiled first by Ángel González Palencia and clarified by Díaz Ibáñez) connects him to the Toledan Mozarabic community.[10] While Diego Olstein does not include Julián among the more prominent members of Toledo's Mozarabic population, the preservation of sources of Mozarabic origin is particularly poor and makes any overarching analysis limited.[11]

As to the wealth of the family, we have some circumstantial evidence. In an 1197 document, Julián ben Tauro purchased a major estate, valued at 600 *menkales*, comprising the assets of Gonzalo Pérez Garcés de Lerma in the hamlet of Azaña. After his election, and perhaps to avoid conflicts of interest or perhaps at the command of Archbishop Martín López, Julián donated all these properties to the cathedral chapter in exchange for anniversary masses and an annual stipend (of 20 *menkales*) for his brother, then serving as an archdeacon.[12] If the usual equivalence of maravedíes and *menkales* is accepted at its 5:4 ratio, then the value of 600 *menkales* is 750 Alfonsine maravedíes; by the price limits of the 1207 *cortes* of Toledo, the estates donated for Julián's anniversary masses were worth a half-dozen fine horses or nine hundred pairs of fine shoes.[13] A gift of such value for anniversary masses—even with his brother's stipend—suggests that Julián was able to support his clerical vocation without substantial support from their family. Olstein has suggested that Mozarabic men with blended names—that is, with Latin forenames and surnames demonstrating Arabic naming practices—became more frequent at the end of the twelfth century.[14] Although his forename is not significantly attested in Olstein's analysis, González Palencia's attribution of Julián ben Tauro to a Mozarabic family has been generally accepted, despite Olstein's mathematical demonstration that the influence of Mozarabic families in the real estate market of Toledo fell substantially at the end of the twelfth century.[15]

While Julián's identity as a Mozarabic Toledan of high economic status is supported but not definitively proven, his pre-episcopal employment is incontrovertible. Beginning perhaps as early as March 1189, Julián appears as a priest in the records of the cathedral chapter of Toledo.[16] While a certain "Frodericus" was archdeacon of Calatrava until 1194, Julián appears in his highest pre-episcopal post as archdeacon of Calatrava as early as 19 March 1195 in a charter where Archbishop Martín expanded the number of canons in the cathedral chapter.[17] The position of the archdeaconate in the far south of the Toledan archdiocese makes it a curious choice for a lateral movement to Cuenca—the city of Cuenca itself is closer to Toledo than Calatrava. The best explanation is one based on the common challenges of the two frontier territories. Both were on the very edge of Castilian territory and vulnerable to Almohad incursions; the two were also relatively poor, because they were comparatively underpopulated, and geographically far from central authority. During the reign of Julián's predecessor, the diocese received the rights to several fortresses, which suggests that the administration of the frontier with the Almohads was a key part of the Cuencan episcopate's administrative burden.[18] An administrative cleric—like an archdeacon—would have extensive experience in working with populations exposed to the particular pressures of the frontier between Castile and the Almohads. All of these considerations are only further underlined by the fact that Cuenca also shared borders with the independent diocese of Albarracín and with the kingdom of Aragon.[19]

The election date for Julián ben Tauro as bishop of Cuenca is not preserved in the sources. His predecessor Juan Yáñez appears in his last document in April 1196 and most likely died on 15 December 1197, based on the entries in the necrology; Julián appears as bishop in charters beginning in 1198 and was still listed as "Conchensis episcopus et Toletanus canonicus" as late as June 1198, suggesting that Juan was not well and Julián had been elected while he was still alive and had not renounced his benefice in Toledo.[20] In an 11 April 1198 donation from King Alfonso VIII, Julián is named directly in the text of the charter as the bishop of Cuenca, affirming that he may have served as a bishop-elect while Juan Yáñez was ill.[21] Even though the date of his consecration is not preserved in extant sources, it seems reasonable to suggest that Julián was elevated to the episcopate in the early months of 1198 and renounced his benefice in Toledo in 1201, where his brother was still an archdeacon.[22]

From Great Mosque to Cathedral of Santa María

Although the city of Cuenca's first bishop is recorded as having completed the consecration of the high altar on 15 August 1196, earlier cathedral records show that the cathedral must have been operating within an earlier temporary liturgical space.[23] The extant art-historical and architectural evidence shows clearly that the old Great Mosque of Cuenca in the Alcazar was converted into the early cathedral.[24] It is in this early space and at the newly restored high altar in the cathedral that Julián must have been consecrated to the episcopal order. In that same space, perhaps a decade later, Julián was interred; his remains were translated spectacularly in the early sixteenth century.

Cathedral neighborhoods were vibrant and presented many opportunities for episcopal agents to expand their political and economic influence in the episcopal see. In the earlier years of the 1190s, a canon named Gíl cornered the meat markets in the cathedral neighborhood, eventually willing all his butcher shops to the chapter for anniversary masses; the cathedral neighborhood was one of the key economic centers of the early postconquest city of Cuenca.[25] Just as Bishop Mauricio of Burgos would later work with royal and archiepiscopal support to begin the construction of a Gothic cathedral in his city, early evidence suggests that Julián was hard at work to fund the repair and construction of much of the cathedral.[26] In an 1194 charter, Juan Yáñez had negotiated with the canons of his cathedral chapter to secure the resources for the *fábrica* funds from the episcopal rents generated by part of the tithes of "some villages and hamlets" (una quaque ville et aldearum).[27] As Tom Nickson has shown, the construction of a cathedral was a long process, but one of the constants in the whole process in Iberia was a strain on the financial resources of the diocesan fisc, as other macropolitical endeavors and human factors diverted funds from the project.[28] The expansion of diocesan financial resources commanded the attention of bishops in every European kingdom, so it is not surprising that the same was true for Julián.[29] Julián's approach, though, was remarkable: he sought to restrain the growth of his canons' incomes while adding to the principal base of the cathedral patrimony. These two tactics were crucial for the success of the diocese after the death of its founding bishop, and Julián's achievement was as much the product of the kingdom's fortunes as it was of his talents.

In early 1201, Julián and the clergy of the city negotiated a compromise that the charter noted "pleased the lord Bishop."[30] The bishop and his canons were likely feeling the pinch of the post-Alarcos economic recovery melting slowly away, but the price edicts of Toledo in 1207 suggest that the fortunes of the chapter were not strong enough to shrug off the financial burdens of administering a diocese on the frontier.[31] The 1201 reform charter established the manner by which the finances of the chapter were to be administered with respect to both full canons (*canonici*) and those holding partial prebends (*mansionarii*).[32] A few examples of these provisions demonstrate the care that Julián took to ensure that the canons would receive a share without impoverishing the cathedral. Bishop Julián agreed that if they endowed an anniversary for themselves, canons would retain the use of that endowment's property until they died, after which it would become part of the church's holdings.[33] Anniversary endowments from parishioners or donors that were larger than sixty *menkales* (i.e., seventy-five maravedíes) were to be subdivided, with shares of the income going to cult provisions and to the various funds that provided for the canons' livelihood.[34] Canons who were ill and expected to die soon were allowed to designate someone to say their masses for them and would still receive their benefices, both to lessen the burdens of saying masses for their soul and to help provide for their transition to the next life.[35] This sample of provisions shows, at least in part, Cuenca's careful control of incomes and expenses in its administration of the chapter. These financial provisions may have strained some of the canons while the finances of the cathedral were reshuffled, but by 1207, the bishop and the chapter came together again to establish a new customary for the work of the chapter within the context of the civic code of the city.

Between the 1201 financial reform and the 1207 customary, Julián appears to have been hard at work cultivating the patronage of his see from both King Alfonso VIII and his countrymen. The earliest act of patronage, however, came not from a wealthy noble or the monarchy but from Julián himself, who gave his holdings in Peantes in Huete to support the work of the refectory in 1202.[36] Two gifts, in 1202 and 1203, from King Alfonso added the tithes of salt rents from Tagacete and Peñas de Peralveche along with sixty "free" (i.e. untaxed) *cahices* of salt from Medinaceli.[37] (Curiously, the next privilege for the chapter was a forged letter from Innocent III that provided the canons with a clarification that they could seek and obtain benefices.[38]

Likely, an enterprising canon was trying to ensure that the bishops would not check their efforts to subvent their prebends with additional benefices.) The last gift that predates the reform customary of 1207 is another gift from January of that same year, also from Julián himself, which handed over half of the bishops' holdings in Cañete to the support of the vestimentary accounts.[39] The vestimentary stipend afforded to clerics was an important part of the revenues that supported a cathedral chapter, as Maureen Miller has shown, and in a number of contemporary instances the vestimentary income for clerics was a flashpoint for conflict between bishops and their clerics or a place of specific patronage from lay hands.[40] Avoiding this kind of conflict was a shrewd move by an administrator, and Julián's experience as a bishop arbitrating in the case of the earlier reform of the chapter of Sigüenza may well have informed his desire to avoid similar conflicts. While earlier gifts from Alfonso VIII to Julián's predecessor, Juan Yáñez, had given the diocesan fisc a handful of castles and *portazgo* revenues, the gifts of salt and a share of the revenues from the taxes based on salt mining were a major financial boon for the diocese; Miguel Ladero Quesada has shown clearly that the rents from salt mines were a major source of royal revenue into the sixteenth century and even guaranteed the payment of Alfonso VIII's debts in his will.[41] Full details of Julián's cultivation of the diocesan fisc are hard to gather, given the absence of any inventory of the see's revenues, but it appears that his efforts bore some fruit, enough that Julián was able to negotiate with his canons to secure the first customary of the cathedral chapter in 1207.

At some point in the first years of the 1190s—James Powers thinks 1190[42] and Miguel Chamocho Cantudo has recently argued for the earliest months of the same year[43]—the city of Cuenca was given a *fuero* by Alfonso VIII.[44] Whenever the *fuero* was issued, it established the judicial and legal norms for the people living in Cuenca, although the relationship between the theoretical process in the code and practice in the law has been the subject of considerable scrutiny.[45] Powers noted that, despite the importance of clergy in medieval Christendom, it is strange that they are hardly mentioned in the *fuero*.[46] Even the bishops were only listed in their capacity to dispense clerics from the prohibition of serving as agents in lay cases and were reaffirmed in their rights to have a palace in the city.[47] In this context, clarifying the role of the *fuero* in the lives of the city's clergy was a major step toward knitting the clerical and lay populations together under a more unified legal framework that required fewer interventions. In March 1207, Julián and the *concejo* of Cuenca worked out a compromise over the rights of the clergy under the terms of the *fuero* and under the supervision of the archbishop.[48] In that charter, the bishop and the *concejo* agreed that for most smaller charges, the *concejo* would allow canons to be tried at the episcopal courts, but the canons and their houseguests would be tried in city courts for major crimes like homicide, housebreaking, rape, and theft.[49] Relinquishing the immunity enjoyed by the clergy in the medieval Latin West was no small matter: the concept of "criminous clerks" animated Henry II and Thomas Becket's disagreements, and the concept of the "libertas ecclesiae" is commonplace in the more activist reform treatises.[50] Handing over the right to try clerics in secular courts when they were accused of major cases was not a small gesture but created a workable framework between the local code and larger canon legal strictures, ensuring a smoother judicial process for the inhabitants of Cuenca. Peace within the walls of a frontier town was an essential commodity, bought and paid for with the relaxing of certain strictures and the co-opting of canons' energies to provide it. Municipal tranquility was also necessary for the city's prosperity and for the pastoral care that ensured the spiritual fortunes of town and townsfolk alike. Julián's charter was effectively a negotiation of the boundaries between secular and clerical, between the crown and the church, and it made those borders as porous as was practical without compromising the larger judicial framework.[51]

Unfortunately, the records for the diocese of Cuenca during Julián's episcopate are not as immediately useful as for other contemporary episcopates. During his tenure as bishop, economic diversification efforts seem to have made his cathedral chapter more economically stable, and the territorial reach of his diocese expanded into its hinterland. Having few literary sources or new construction projects that might attest to the lasting impact of the episcopate of Julián ben Tauro of Cuenca, the most prudent scholarly angle to pursue is how his work as a bishop was received by the generations that followed him.

Memory, Translation, and Divergence

There are no records of Julián's episcopate in the historical sources from the thirteenth, fourteenth, or fifteenth century. Effectively, Julián passed into a kind of gentle oblivion until his tomb was opened as part of his translation when a new Gothic cathedral was elaborated on the layers of older structures beneath.[52] We know the date of Julián's death; his appearance in the obituaries of Cuenca gives his position as bishop and the date of his death as 20 January, although some masses appear to have been celebrated in his honor in the late thirteenth century.[53] The 1518 observation of miracles near his tomb was the first chapter in a canonization saga that, as Sara Nalle has argued, seems to suggest that Cuenca was becoming a hotbed of Counter-Reformation activities.[54] The early fifteenth century was a period of immense change in the religious landscape of the Latin West, and the discovery of the remains of San Julián was a process that Miguel Jiménez Monteserín has described as a "typical case of the local bishop as local *patronus*."[55] It is clear that the extant records of Julián's episcopate served as a base on which to erect a larger virtue profile of the bishop as part of his cult memory's development, allowing a new set of charitable and curative miracles to obscure the careful administrative work of a frontier bishop. In short, the tripolar relationship that was key to Julián's success as a twelfth-century bishop was useless to the canonization partisans of the sixteenth century; what was important to Julián's career was eclipsed as soon as his tomb was opened.

In 1518, when the tomb was unsealed, the name "Julián" appeared infrequently, according to Nalle's examination; after the enthusiasm for a cult had begun to peak, the frequency of that name in baptismal records increased.[56] The testimony about the opening of Julián's tomb in January 1518 runs to almost 220 folios, beginning with the testimony of the local inquisitor and ending with the testimony of Anton Martínez, the son of a local butcher.[57] The array of miraculous events after the tomb's opening is itself staggering, as indicated by a short survey of people cured of infirmities: a woman with an old arm wound, an eighteen-year-old shoemaker suffering from a similar ailment, a teething child with a long-running fever, a young woman with a breast tumor the size of an orange, and a Roma man whose ear infection had made him hard of hearing.[58] These narratives show a rapid upswell of popular enthusiasm for Julián, one marked by an overwhelming number of healing miracles. Although the hundreds of accounts recorded by notaries under the direction of the inquisitor Pedro de los Ríos were full of cures for the long-suffering, there were no mentions of Julián's episcopate, save the use of the title "obispo." While this appears curious, it is worth noting that a similar trend was observed for the much less frequently lauded Alderico, who apparently never performed a miracle, despite the long-term presence of his relics in the treasury of Palencia.[59]

Perhaps the sheer number of cures registered after the opening of the tomb allowed the narrative about Julián to be based on an invented memory rather than on the extant records of his episcopate. Even Nalle—otherwise an exemplary scholar—was taken in by the early modern hagiographical narratives about Julián, wrongly identifying him as a Burgalese master at the nascent *studium generalis* at Palencia while Saint Dominic was a student there (and perhaps this was the persuasive part of the fictional biography).[60] Early modern hagiographers did claim that Julián was a master at the early university in Palencia, but there is no evidence from the cathedral of Palencia that supports anyone named Julián—or even with a J initial—holding a position of *magister*.[61] The accounts themselves are thin in other areas, too, but the dearth of evidence did not impede the larger canonization drive. A 1530 inventory, edited by Jiménez Monteserín, suggests that the efforts to canonize Julián were not only sincere but also expensive. The 17 September 1530 document compiled by Alonso Polo purports to itemize more than 2200 ducats spent by the Spanish clergy to secure the canonization.[62] The list of expenses profiled included the stipends for the clerics serving the altars, the cost of candles for processions, and even sixty ducats for the bulls themselves.[63] Such costs were substantial, but when combined with the extensive records from the investigations, they suggest an enormous local effort to ensure that the sixteenth-century inhabitants of Cuenca had the kind of inspiration necessary to maintain religious discipline in a time of great upheaval.

In the years between the canonization hearings in 1518 (and the financial outlays in 1530) and the celebrations of the feast of San Julián in 1595, the landscape of Iberia had changed, as had that of Europe. The descriptions of the feast do not recount Julián's career as a bishop with any recourse to the data and mention him only rarely.[64] The hagiographical accounts from the first century after Julián ben Tauro's canonization present a thin, sanitized version of a biography, usually focusing on the connection between his episcopacy and Alfonso VIII, whose own canonization had faltered in the sixteenth century.[65] In the decade before the first accounts of the feast of San Julián, Francisco Escudero penned one of the earliest books about Julián's life, and the 1589 treatment has five folios of invented biography without substantiation, followed by folios treating his episcopacy without any historically verifiable detail and adding various unsubstantiated miracles to Julián's reputation.[66] The 1611 account of Julián's life and miracles by the bishop of Salamanca, Juan Bautista Valenzuela y Velazquez, presented no new research and, in the expository chapter, recounted things that other authors had said about Julián's biography.[67] Juan Pablo Martir Riço's 1629 history of the city of Cuenca spent only six or seven lines recounting Julián's episcopate and life before quickly transitioning to an account of the translation and canonization in the sixteenth and seventeenth centuries.[68] A further survey of treatments of Julián seems unnecessary here. The contrast between the preserved material and the invented hagiography says more about seventeenth-century needs than about thirteenth-century realities and demonstrates how different the two periods were, underscoring the need for a new and revised historical narrative of the Castilian episcopate in the twelfth and thirteenth centuries.

The lesson to be learned from the historical bifurcation of Julián ben Tauro and San Julián is that medieval historical records are sometimes inconvenient—but they can reveal much more than has traditionally been assumed. Bishops like Julián ben Tauro could easily have gone missing from this larger study, save as a presence in the prosopographical appendix. Like the Blasquez bishops of Ávila, Joscelmo of Sigüenza (whose arm is the only imprint he has left on the cathedral of that city), or the short-serving Gutierre Rodríguez Girón in Segovia, there are many prelates like Julián whose records are sparse enough to be relegated to a footnote.[69] Even Peter Linehan was content to let one of Julián's contemporaries, Gonzalo Pérez, to simply and matter-of-factly state that he existed and that for twelfth-century historians that should be enough.[70] The question, then, has to be whether the bishop who died in 1208 matters to the bishop who was canonized in 1595.

I would answer that the two figures were important to each other only because they have such different trajectories and demonstrate that medieval prelates were very different from their manifestations in a later era. Julián ben Tauro, in the twelfth and thirteenth centuries, was not an infrequent witness in documents from the chancery of Alfonso VIII; nor was he a passive episcopal actor in the diocese he ruled. Rather, he stands out as a bishop who is difficult to get to know closely but who made a clear contribution to the incremental growth of his diocese. Sixteenth- and seventeenth-century cult hagiographies have obscured much of this story and clearly demonstrate why a revision of the available data is necessary. In the first place, an inaccurate early modern narrative is a clear candidate for replacement by careful scholarship. In addition, Julián's diocese was the product of a campaign that was suffused with the crusading imagery of the period, though it never received a formal bull. As a leader of a border diocese, it stands to reason that an experienced administrator, capable in Arabic, could find a place in the diocesan administration of Toledo and would find a promotion to the episcopal level when a post came open. What little data we have about the historical Julián ben Tauro validate his position as a frontier bishop of the same stripe that Bernard Hamilton found ruling sees in the Latin East and that Graham Loud saw in mitred Sicilians.[71] Administrators like Julián ben Tauro rarely make good canonization causes, and so the invention of his biography and the lack of any important notation of his episcopal acts—even in a novena composed in the late seventeenth or early eighteenth century, when the new cathedral towered over the city[72]—suggest that Julián's antiquity was more important than his historicity for contemporary cult worship.[73]

Julián ben Tauro is a cleric who makes clear how necessary a study like the present one is. Other bishops featured here are perhaps less misremembered than Julián but are also less discussed than the second bishop of Cuenca. This chapter has suggested that, while the elaborate hagiographies of the early modern cult of Julián are interesting in their own right, the materials preserved from his episcopate still portray a fascinating prelate. Julián was a cleric from a Mozarabic family, appointed to an archdeaconate from the archiepiscopal diocese, and promoted to serve a diocese with a diverse population. As a bishop, his activities to ensure domestic prosperity and tranquility of the still-new frontier diocese are the records that are extant, but they are surely not the only records created. The complexity of the diocese and its economy, demonstrated by the case of the canon Gíl, was paralleled by the complexities of the internal workings of the cathedral chapter, as shown by Julián's customary for it. There must have been much more going on at ground level than extant documents indicate. It is, therefore, quite easy to imagine the elision of the cathedral records about Julián with the "Burgalese professor" myth, which was both a simple story to tell and remember and a convincing veneer to lay over the historical records. The variety of documents preserved from medieval cathedral records makes the study of bishops possible, but the primary-source-driven approach of historical study needs to privilege the facts and not the mythology about prelates of this period. In the case of Julián, correcting the narrative is not only possible but also provides a window onto how fortunate scholars are to have even a handful of reliable records to work from in crafting newer and more reliable accounts.

HOW TO GET AWAY WITH MURDER
Rodrigo de Finojosa, Bishop of Sigüenza

Don Rodrigo showed his valor, assisting muchly the valorous Alfonso VIII, with whom he was at the miraculous Battle of Las Navas, in the year 1212, as is affirmed in our histories and on the King's death he helped bury him.
—Diego Sánchez Portocarrero, *Nuevo catálogo de los obispos de la santa iglesia di Siguenza* (1646)

There are, occasionally, bishops who appear to have had both good and bad luck in equal measure. The case of Rodrigo de Finojosa (r. 1192–1221) is a bishop of exactly this type.[1] During the wide swings in his episcopate, Rodrigo was exposed to, engaged with, and escaped from a great number of situations that would have pushed other prelates to their limits. Like his kinsman with the same name, Archbishop Rodrigo Ximénez de Rada, Rodrigo de Finojosa served for far longer than most of his contemporaries. During the nearly three decades of his career, the church in Castile saw major political and cultural shifts in its midst that would shepherd the church from the age of one great Castilian conqueror-king into the reign of his grandson.[2] This long period as bishop in an era of considerable change also means that Rodrigo was in a position to bring long-term goals to fruition in a way that few of his predecessors or colleagues could. For a bishop most often mentioned for being acquitted of a single charge of manslaughter, it is clear beyond any doubt that Rodrigo de Finojosa's reign represented a net positive for his diocese and his successors.

An examination of Rodrigo's lengthy career could easily devolve into a catalog of his extant acts. Far more interesting is the consistency with which three themes appear. First, the disobedience of some of the people in his diocese appears to have troubled Rodrigo, a fact that suggests that he was having remarkable difficulty ensuring that his episcopate remained a stabilizing regional force. Second, the reform of the cathedral chapter of Sigüenza appears to have been a matter of considerable concern for Rodrigo, both at the macro level of its customary and on the micro level of the affairs of individual canons. Lastly, the controversies that plagued Rodrigo in the second half of his episcopate suggest that he took considerable measures to ensure that he was able to use all of the legal and social tools at his disposal to effect the greatest possible control over his diocese. Of course, he was not the exception to the rule that clerical careers are dictated by the peculiarities of the circumstances that befall them rather than by any overarching set of principles or concerns. In Rodrigo's case, the careful cultivation of royal patronage helped secure his episcopate when he was in political trouble, and his reform efforts ensured that the Roman curia supported him when clergy tried to undermine his position as prelate of Sigüenza.

Nepotism, but in a Good Way

The election of Rodrigo de Finojosa, given the charter records from Sigüenza, appears to have been likely due to his family's influence, although it was not a complete surprise for the chapter. He first appears in the extant documentation from the cathedral chapter as its prior in 1189.[3] An unedited document from the cathedral archive in Sigüenza may register his presence as a subprior in 1180, but because it antedates his next appearance by more than a decade, we may suspect that a different "R." subscribed the agreement with a local landholder.[4] However, it seems highly unlikely that his first post in the chapter was as its prior in 1189, so it may well be that his absence as a witness in the earlier *acta* of prelates in the 1180s was not a fluke. It appears that Rodrigo's elevation to the post of prior, and thereafter to the episcopate, was that of old-fashioned nepotism: Rodrigo was his predecessor's kinsman.[5] Rodrigo's uncle, the bishop Martín de Finojosa, may well have advanced his nephew's candidacy after the death of the previous prior, Pedro.[6] This was not uncommon in the period in the Iberian Peninsula, as the examples of Esteban and his nephew Guillermo in Zamora, the Girón at Segovia, the Blasquez at Ávila, and even the Mathé at Burgos all demonstrate.[7]

Bernard Reilly has suggested that the elevation of Rodrigo de Finojosa was linked to Alfonso VIII's cultivation of a relationship with the family of Miguel Muñoz, an important regional lord in the eastern border regions, as part of a quid pro quo to advance the Castilian interest in the area.[8] While meddling with the election of a bishop in a key border region was not beyond the political maneuvering of Alfonso VIII and his court, the election of a member of a local aristocratic clan who had previously served in the cathedral chapter was so typical of the era—as previous chapters have shown[9]—that proving a conspiracy requires more than convenient timing. While Reilly's argument focuses on the later episode of Rodrigo de Finojosa being passed over for the archiepiscopal post that became vacant upon the death of Martín López de Pisuerga, sixteen years is a long gestation period for any maneuvering, and, further, very few bishops reigned so long; replacing the Pisuerga archbishop with a Finojosa candidate would require considerable fortune, even for those bold enough to so conspire.[10] In any case, Rodrigo de Finojosa was elected on All Souls' Day in 1192. If there were mildly illegal beginnings to his thirty-year reign as bishop, the results of his tenure as prelate may suggest that Rodrigo de Finojosa would stand apart as the reasonable exception to canonical ideas that what begins poorly ends the same.[11]

The first two years of Rodrigo's episcopate pass with hardly any documentary trace of new activities, but those that do survive suggest that he pursued the continuation of processes in his diocese that had begun before his episcopate. For example, an 1193 document records that a certain Arnaldo de Pozancos handed over properties to the diocesan patrimony as part of his promise to live obediently as a canon regular.[12] On several occasions since the early twelfth century, the papacy had instructed the bishops of Sigüenza to replace secular canons with regulars, a feature of cathedral chapter life that attests to the success of Giles Constable's "reformation of the twelfth century" among cathedral chapters.[13] The imposition of a rule in Sigüenza's cathedral chapter would be a continuing part of Rodrigo's episcopal prerogatives, but the early signs of shifting the makeup and comportment of the cathedral chapter suggest that, while his election may have derived from his clan ties, Rodrigo was no empty chasuble.

The mid-1190s were a harrowing era of ebbs and flows for the fortunes of the kingdom of Castile. While two of his colleagues fell in the battle of Alarcos, Rodrigo appears to have been deeply invested in the fight. In an 1195 document, the count of Molina and Rodrigo were raising money (and, one assumes, troops) to confront the Almohad caliph, issuing a charter "in the army of Lord Alfonso against the Saracens" (in exercitum contra sarracenos domini Aldefonsi).[14] In this context, we may suspect that Rodrigo—whose later presence at Las Navas is repeatedly attested—had earlier written to the papacy to ensure that his diocesan subjects all contributed their tithes to the episcopal fisc, a request that resulted in a papal rescript to that effect in 1194.[15] A second rescript to Rodrigo from Celestine also confirmed the bishop's right to exact tithes from even the smallest of sums.[16] Given the earlier timing of Martín López de Pisuerga's *cabalgada*, it seems very likely that the bishop of Sigüenza was financially preparing for war *contra sarracenos* in 1195, and perhaps even earlier.[17] In this context, the enrolling of regular canons into the chapter, mentioned above, argues for a kind of "two swords" effort in Sigüenza: spiritual warfare from prayerful canons and material warfare from well-funded aristocrats, all secured by episcopal backing. Put differently, Rodrigo de Finojosa was living the old Castilian proverb "a Dios rogando y con el mazo dando"—praying to God while striking with a hammer.

The 1190s leave much to be desired from the documentation extant at Sigüenza. There are no gifts from Alfonso VIII to the bishops, which could be read as a sign of considerable friction between the king's court and the bishop's administration. However, there are signs that Rodrigo was preparing for a major effort. In 1195, the bishop bought several houses in the Toledan barrio San Juan, which may have been used either as a residence for the bishop and his representatives at the archbishop's court or for the generation of income.[18] Yet it was not real estate investing that commanded most of the bishop's time; it was the resolution of an ancient blood feud between Sigüenza and the people of Medinaceli.

"Some of Whom Were Excommunicated Because of Their Excesses"

The conflict between Sigüenza and the clergy and townsfolk of Medinaceli was, by the time of Rodrigo de Finojosa's episcopate, generations old. Technically, the bishop's diocesan territory included Medinaceli, and the diocesan see was governed by the same *fuero* that governed Medinaceli itself.[19] At one point in the episcopate of Joscelmo (r. 1168–78), a cleric appointed by the bishop was attacked by the clerics and people of Medinaceli, his eyes were nearly gouged out, and his breviary was stolen—all this according to a papal letter prompted by the aggrieved cleric on his visit to the curia.[20] By 1196, the situation had morphed into a wholesale conflict between the bishop and the town in a way that required an extensive settlement to effect the reconciliation of the clergy of Medinaceli and, by way of an episcopal pardon, absolution for whatever crimes were committed. The compromise's provisions are so extensive that they deserve more space than the text of the charter has received from previous scholarship.

Rodrigo's recognition of the conflict between his position and Medinaceli's clergy began with a dramatic indictment of the situation: "Let it come to the attention of the present and the future that when the clergy of Medina[celi] were excommunicated because of their excesses, some of them, cognizant of their error and wanting to return to reason, swore to the mandate of the lord Rodrigo the bishop of Sigüenza, themselves promising to satisfy and obey all his instructions."[21] By framing the excesses of the clergy of Medinaceli in terms of disobedience to the will of the bishop, Rodrigo's reconciliation delineated those misdeeds that were independently worthy of excommunication from those that, under a distinct reading of canon and municipal law, were worthy only of lesser penalties. Conflating greater crimes with lesser ones under the heading of disobeying the bishop created a framework where the clerics guilty of only smaller infractions could passively pressure those accused of larger crimes.[22] According to the text, Cardinal Gregory of Sant'Angelo had already addressed all of this, but the clergy of Medinaceli refused to obey the cardinal-legate.[23] Disrespecting both a papal writ and a legate was bad enough, but the fact that Medinaceli was donated to Sigüenza by the monarchy made the situation between the bishop and Medinaceli a kind of perfect storm for the kind of tripolar balancing that prelates were usually keen to engage in the period. Having described the situation, Rodrigo described the extent of the criminal activities in detail.[24]

There were several acts that Rodrigo included in the litany of offenses committed by the clerics of Medina. The majority of the offenses were financial—depriving the episcopal fisc of funds or diverting proceeds from extortionate activities to local coffers. A few of the more peculiar examples can be afforded space here. Rodrigo noted that, despite the region's being under episcopal interdict, local clergy extorted one hundred gold *aureos* for Christian burial from anyone who did not bury their own dead.[25] The local clergy—against both episcopal rights and the will of King Alfonso VIII—also compelled the villagers to pay enormous tithes and rents in kind, noting that each citizen (*vicini*) was forced to pay two-and-a-half *cahices* of produce, with three *fañegas* from each *cahiz* going to the town.[26] Although no direct and accurate conversion is possible and the usage varies by region and period, the amount required by such a taxation scheme roughly equates to paying forty-eight acres' worth of produce, reserving twelve of those acres' produce for the town.[27] Those who lived on episcopal lands or cultivated episcopal fields or milled their grain at the episcopal mills were required to pay sixty *menkales* (equal to 0.255 kilograms of gold), and those who abided by episcopal rule were forced to pay one hundred *aureos* (a little over one kilogram of gold) and were driven from their own houses.[28] By enumerating the ways in which the clergy and townsfolk of Medinaceli had insulted Rodrigo's *pundonor* as bishop, he was also demonstrating the ways in which his authority should have extended into the town. In doing so, the charter also showed town's importance to the region and to the episcopal fisc.

Beyond even these shenanigans by the clerics and laity, additional factors suggest that Rodrigo and his predecessors had ample reason to take the conflict with Medinaceli seriously. The town itself was only a short distance away from the diocesan seat in Sigüenza, just under thirty kilometers, and conflict so near the cathedral would surely have undermined the bishop's attempts to control more distant contested territories. Additionally, there is substantial evidence to suggest that the salt mines in Medinaceli were some of the most important on the border regions between Old Castile and the Rioja region.[29] Between these profitable salt mines and the fact that the city of Medinaceli was a fortified border outpost at the southeastern edge of the kingdom of Castile, Rodrigo's reasons for interest in the town are rather obvious.[30] The confluence of these factors suggests that the town of Medinaceli represented a significant problem for the bishops of Sigüenza, illuminating Rodrigo's efforts to effect change in the relationship between the bishop and the town of Medinaceli.

In the two years after Rodrigo promulgated his decisions about the conflict between his episcopal administration and Medinaceli, several subsequent documents attest to the implementation and retrenchment of the same changes that Rodrigo deployed. Beginning with a June 1197 rescript from Celestine confirming that the conflict with Medinaceli had already received a decision in Rodrigo's favor, a series of at least four documents suggests a flurry of activity and frequent negotiations with subsets of the population of Medinaceli to secure their obedience to Rodrigo's 1196 edict. Celestine's confirmation of the earlier decision noted that Alexander III and Lucius III had already rendered judgments via a panel of judges-delegate, and that these were in favor of the bishops of Sigüenza and had ordered the obedience of the townsfolk of Medinaceli.[31] The lengthy text of Celestine's confirmation seemed to have done its job, because by November of the same year, Rodrigo and the clergy of Medinaceli penned a letter to Archbishop Martín López de Pisuerga informing him of the agreement that they had made and the peace that they were committed to enjoying under its terms.[32] The lengthy list of subscriptions from Medinaceli in the letter to Archbishop Martín must have suggested that the agreement had considerable support, but individual agreements with some remaining malcontents were still necessary. In a privilege datable only to 1198, the parishioners of the church of San Andres in Medinaceli promised that they would be obedient to the bishop regarding collection of tithes and the preservation of the parish's physical state and its cult observances.[33] It seems likely that other such agreements may have been made in the aftermath of the 1197 settlement, but no further texts survive. Rodrigo shifted his energy from the relationship between the cathedral of Sigüenza and the town of Medinaceli to a new focus: the cathedral itself.

Rodrigo was more than equipped to manage both the financial and the social affairs of his cathedral chapter, as his previous exploits have already shown. Having recently completed the pacification of Medinaceli, he was also in a position to bring his cathedral chapter in line with the reforms that he was implanting in the rest of his diocese.[34] The reforms of the chapter were considerable, but they aligned with the *vita apostolica* movement that was becoming increasingly popular in much of Latin Christendom during the same period.

According to the early twentieth-century historian-bishop Toribio Minguella y Arnedo, Bishop Rodrigo "tried to reestablish the cloister's discipline in all of its original splendor."[35] Problematically, Rodrigo required significant support—in the persons of Archbishop Martín López and Julián ben Tauro of Cuenca—to do so, and the lengthy text of his reforms suggests that the process at Sigüenza was complicated by a number of contemporary quarrels. Rodrigo had certain demands to which the canons eventually acceded, including that canons were to keep silent on most days and in most parts of the cloister; that canons who did not teach lessons could not enter the boys' cloister; that the chapter's members could not leave the church grounds without license; and that they were not allowed to sleep away from the chapter without prior approval.[36] The reforms were numerous, but perhaps most interesting is the process by which they were decided upon: the archbishop managed to settle the dispute between those canons who opposed his changes and the bishop.[37] The process was not, however, wholly one-sided.

The canons presented their own list of demands, most of which appear aimed at increasing their own stipends. Unfortunately, many are canon legal *palea* of now-lost disputes, but others partially suggest that, after a long period of quarrelling with the clerics of Medinaceli, the resources of the chapter were sorely depleted. Four property bequests were awarded to the bishop as part of his episcopal patrimony, annually totaling 1,220 *menkales* or 488 maravedíes (equivalent to nearly two kilograms of gold); the canons were placed under an archiepiscopal ban to remain silent about the properties thereafter.[38] The archpriestship of Molina was not to pay the *fonsado* tax, Archbishop Martín instructed, unless the bishop shared the revenues with the canons; clerics were exempt from paying them by the terms of the local *fuero*, but regular inhabitants of a territory were not.[39] The bishop had to allow foreigners or pilgrims to give alms to the canons for their prayers, and the bishop was also prevented from diverting gifts to the canons into his episcopal fisc.[40] However, Archbishop Martín rejected the canons' claim that Rodrigo was unfairly awarding benefices to foreigners rather than "sons of the church," and the archbishop allowed it so long as the bishop's choices were worthy of a prebend.[41] Having already done much, the archbishop deferred his judgment on a series of more complicated cases to the future and affirmed the consent of the parties to the decisions, with Bishop Julián serving as a guarantor.[42] Rodrigo received, then, the reforms that he sought, but these only came after he supplemented the incomes of the canons of the cathedral chapter enough to adequately provide for their stipends.

The reform of Rodrigo's cathedral chapter leads to some peculiar conclusions. There was a substantial reform of the *habitus* of the canons, especially with regard to their "clerical discipline," and Rodrigo secured a more monasticized and severe *forma vivendi* for the canons. However, his canons improved their financial fortunes considerably: of the many property disputes presented to the archbishop, most were won by the chapter. A wealthier and reformed cathedral chapter served the interests of the diocese better than it had before the reforms, but the context of these reforms—just after the resolution of the conflict with Medinaceli—suggests that the first seven years of the episcopate were a period of considerable difficulty for Bishop Rodrigo.[43] The challenges that confronted him in the first fifth of his episcopate seem to have paid off in the subsequent decades, when things became somewhat quieter for the bishop of Sigüenza.

The early 1200s saw Rodrigo engaged in a number of smaller cases in his diocese. An agreement in 1200 with Hospitallers in Atienza and Almazán, for example, suggests that the bishop and the brothers of the military order got along well.[44] By 1201, there were conflicts with another group of Hospitallers over a new oratory in Atienza, which Rodrigo was ordered (by Innocent III) to consecrate while the Hospitallers were ordered to be obedient in matters of excommunications and interdicts.[45] The parallels with Martín López de Pisuerga's own conflict with the military order's activities in his city are clear from that earlier case and serve as another example of the enduring impact of canon nine of Lateran III.[46] Purchases, royal gifts, and the settling of small disputes seem to have made for a regular, if quiet, period during the second fifth of Rodrigo's episcopate. Despite these small affairs and minor conflicts, a bizarre case, which broke in 1208, was about to throw Rodrigo de Finojosa into the gravest sort of trouble.

The Bishop, with His Crozier, in the Cathedral

Bishops and archbishops are more often murdered than charged with murder in the medieval Latin West.[47] While clerics were exempt from most judicial proceedings at secular courts in many kingdoms, the exception for "major cases"—rape, murder, arson, and the like—still left the door open for the prosecution of a cleric.[48] Even by the terms of most *fueros* in the kingdom of Castile, clerics were immune from secular prosecution except in the cases of *calumnia*—a word that means crime or slander, but has the connotative weight of physical offences that require remediation along the lines of the *lex talionis*.[49] Even beyond actual prosecution, either in ecclesiastical or secular courts, clerics were not immune from the proverbial court of public opinion. Slander clauses in the municipal *fueros* of Castile and León attest to the damage that mischievous words could do in a medieval town, and the punishment for slanderous speech suggests that real harm was done with enough frequency to merit demonstrative punishment.[50] So it is not surprising that, when a *calumnia* was allegedly committed by a senior cleric, the controversy surrounding both the case and the individual accused was both dangerous and damaging.

Rodrigo de Finojosa was certainly fortunate to have lived and served as bishop as long as he had, but his luck did not hold out for the whole of his episcopate. According to the *narratio* of a letter from Innocent III in 1209, Rodrigo was being accused of nothing short of murder: a young man had been murdered in the cathedral by the bishop with his crozier. The details of the case are imperfectly preserved and only recoverable from Innocent III's letter, but it is such a peculiar event that it deserves exploration here.

It appears that one day, while the bishop was saying mass, a fracas of some kind erupted in the cathedral, and the bishop was rushed by a group of youths. The bishop, in self-defense, swung his crozier and bludgeoned the young boy in the head. A series of surgeries were performed to revive the youth, but these were ineffective. The boy later died. Testimony from the diocese argued that the bishop was not at fault because the surgeon had not performed the procedures correctly—brain surgery being risky business in medieval Castile—and the boy had died as a result of the surgeries rather than the crozier's impact on his cranium. Despite the medical "facts" in the case, the bishop's reputation had taken nearly as bad a beating as the boy's skull, and there were vicious rumors impugning the *fama* of the bishop of Sigüenza. His kinsman, Rodrigo Ximénez de Rada, received a letter from the papacy almost as quickly as word must have reached Rome, requiring the archbishop-elect—indeed, Ximénez de Rada had yet to be confirmed!—to investigate immediately.[51] Rodrigo de Finojosa personally came to Rome to clear his name.[52] The case itself required the intervention of a panel of judges-delegate, including the bishops of Segovia and Palencia and an archdeacon, who were instructed by Innocent III to prevent any slandering of their colleague's reputation.[53] Beyond even that panel, the archbishop of Toledo had received a copy of the correspondence sent to Sigüenza in order that the decision not be countermanded.[54] The intervention of his metropolitan archbishop seems to have calmed things substantially, since there are no subsequent letters from Innocent III suggesting that there were any more whispers of misconduct on behalf of the bishop of Sigüenza.

But the case's litigation required extensive energy and research, even though Rodrigo de Finojosa appears to have developed a keen understanding of the legal questions at the heart of the matter and even compiled a canon law collection to support his case. His Roman sojourn also allowed Rodrigo to copy and compile a number of documents to aid in the preservation of his control of the diocese. In a text that has since become known as the *Collectio Seguntina*, Rodrigo assembled 116 canon law titles that paid specific attention to the obedience of bishops and the causality of homicides.[55] Given the stormy relationship between Rodrigo and Medinaceli, on the one hand, and between Rodrigo and his cathedral chapter, on the other, it is not hard to see Rodrigo's collection as being deeply rooted in his personal struggles as a bishop. Papal confirmation of an agreement, in 1210, between Rodrigo and his chapter about the positions of *mayordomo*, *camerero*, and *infirmero* suggests that Rodrigo aimed to shore up his legitimacy in the eyes of his cathedral chapter.[56] Another papal letter from Innocent, confirming a sentence from Archbishop Martín López requiring clerics and laymen in the city of Sigüenza to pay their required taxes, dates to the same period and suggests that Rodrigo was encountering as much hostility to his episcopate outside his cathedral as he was inside its cloister.[57] A *hermandad* between Sigüenza and Toledo, between the two kinsman-prelates Rodrigo de Finojosa and

Rodrigo Ximénez de Rada, suggests that some support came for Sigüenza's bishop from outside his diocese but that his reputation was still under considerable pressure.[58]

In May 1212, while the bishop was preparing to leave to join the royal armies at Toledo for the Crusade of Las Navas de Tolosa, Rodrigo made a donation from his episcopal patrimony to the cathedral chapter on behalf of his own soul and those of his parents. Given all that could happen on a campaign to even the savviest of prelates, his preparation for an untimely end is not surprising. Two of his episcopal colleagues had died at Alarcos in 1195, and Juan Mathé, bishop of Burgos, would soon fall at Las Navas. In Rodrigo Ximénez de Rada's famous narration, Rodrigo of Sigüenza is included among the prelates whose participation was favorably mentioned in the battle, albeit without substantial detail on their actions during the melee.[59] Early modern chroniclers like Diego Sánchez Portocarrero, whose *Nuevo catálogo* opened this chapter, equated this participation with his actually joining the fray; these assertions cannot be confirmed, although they may have been based in part on latent oral memory of Rodrigo de Finojosa's actions at Las Navas and would not be far from contemporary practice.[60]

Whatever fame his actions garnered, the victory at Las Navas bought Rodrigo little respite from the challenges of his episcopate. By November 1212, Rodrigo received yet another confirmation of the fact that Medinaceli and its clergy were supposed to obey the bishop of Sigüenza.[61] If the recurrence of the Medinaceli conflict was a nuisance, the collegiality of the bishop and cathedral chapter of Tarazona, just over the Aragonese border, was likely a comfort to some degree, as the *hermandad* of 1214 suggests.[62] Despite all these changes, life went on—Alfonso VIII died in early September 1214, after more than half a century as king, followed soon after by his wife, Leonor.[63] The minority of King Enrique was a precarious period, but the regency of his elder sister, the powerful politico Berenguela, and the support of the Castilian clergy struggled to bring a measure of stability to the kingdom while the challenge of the transition rolled onward.[64]

The business of the church, however, did not stop for the death of kings, no matter how long they had reigned or how much their exercise of monarchical power had influenced the church. By Alfonso VIII's death in 1214, the summons for the Fourth Lateran Council, *Vineam Domini Sabaoth*, had already been received in Castile, and the clergy of the kingdom were likely already making preparations for the long and dangerous trip to Rome in the Advent season of 1215.[65] We know that the party of suffragans of Toledo were gathered in the archiepiscopal city in July 1215—and that at least two of the Castilian prelates feared that they might not survive the trip.[66] Their actions at the Fourth Lateran Council and afterward have already been expertly treated by Antonio García y García, but it seems likely that the minority of Enrique I was a period where every bit of episcopal assistance was needed.[67] The death of the young king in 1217 (via an unfortunate roof tile incident) and the maneuvering of Berenguela and Fernando III in the aftermath eventually calmed the situation, but not sufficiently enough to prevent Rodrigo from seriously considering his legacy in the diocese of Sigüenza.[68] The provisions of the last five years of his episcopate suggest that Rodrigo was, after more than two decades of episcopal rule, considering afresh the gospel mandate to store up his treasures in the kingdom of heaven after the rockiness of the 1210s.

Rodrigo's predecessors had been no strangers to providing patronage to the cult activity of Sigüenza, and his close relationship with his kinsman Martín de Finojosa's monastery at Huerta was a likely reminder that bishops could, as Martín had, retire to the cloister after years of fatiguing episcopal labor. Such a move was relatively uncommon in León and Castile, but beyond the Pyrenees, several examples demonstrate that it was a feasible choice. The choice of retiring to a monastery would require a monastery, and since no trace of Rodrigo appears at Huerta, his kinsman's monastery of choice, the search for a location must have resulted in a different option, if Rodrigo retired at all.

The foundation of a monastery at Pinilla de Jadraque by a nobleman, Pedro Fernández de Atienza, and his siblings in 1218 suggests that there was interest in cultivating the same kind of reputable monastic environment in the region around Sigüenza.[69] A female Cistercian house, although a relatively recent introduction in Castile, like San Salvador de Pinilla de Jadraque would have meant greater competition for revenues in the diocesan territory. Rodrigo confirmed the charter and the nobles placed the convent under his protection, which would not have been possible without Rodrigo's having a desire to manage controversies surrounding the convent.[70] Pinilla de Jadraque sits in a fertile valley, like Huerta, but was on the opposite side of Sigüenza from Huerta. At a distance of about thirty kilometers, its position near the town of Jadraque suggests a location from which the nuns could receive assistance. Rodrigo's subsequent gift to the new convent of an exemption from tithes on a large portion of the convent's new land base demonstrates that he and his canons wanted the new Cistercian house to succeed.[71] A number of other gifts dot the end of Rodrigo's episcopate, but there are no indications that he actually sought monastic retirement.

"We Do Not Know the Day of His Death, Where It Happened, or Where He Is Buried"[72]

It is not unreasonable to expect that, after a thirty-year episcopate, the death of Rodrigo de Finojosa might have been a considerable loss in his diocese. His settling—albeit fitfully—of the Medinaceli affair, the compilation of a canon law collection, his participation at both Alarcos and Las Navas, his presence at the funerals of Alfonso VIII and Queen Leonor, his collaboration with Archbishop Rodrigo in the rocky minority of Enrique I and during the transitional reign of Berenguela and the ascension of Fernando III—all of these events suggest that Rodrigo de Finojosa lived and thrived in exciting times. For all of those elements, his death should have been something of note. Instead, there appears to have been little interruption in the business of the contemporary affairs of his diocese.

First, a brief sketch of the state of knowledge about Rodrigo's death. Neither a will nor an inscription survives in the cathedral of Sigüenza. The bombing of the cathedral by Franco's army—the cathedral was being used to shelter Republican fighters and their families—means that prewar witnesses are the best hope for epigraphic and diplomatic evidence.[73] Even Minguella y Arnedo remarked that, during his own episcopate (r. 1894–1920), he was as mystified as the modern scholar about Rodrigo's death based on the Seguntine evidence.[74] Surveys of other nearby dioceses and monasteries that would be likely candidates reveal an equally puzzling absence of evidence to suggest anything like a monastic retirement.

There is one document that may shed light on *when* Rodrigo de Finojosa resigned both his bodily form and the episcopate of Sigüenza. Dated to 6 May 1222, the text in question is the fulfillment of the will of a certain Pascasio Dominguez, who appears to belong to the *infançon* class of landholders; the will was drawn up while Rodrigo was still the bishop but was signed by his successor Lope because "indeed afterward our venerable predecessor Don Rodrigo, Seguntine bishop, with death intervening was not able to seal the present charter with his seal."[75] The internal language of the text notes that it was dated to 11 January 1221, but the authorization of the text awaited Lope's confirmation, which was not brought to fruition until 6 May 1222. The text itself is now lost—one suspects that the bombing of the cathedral of Sigüenza accounts for its absence—but Julio González's editions of the charters of Fernando III give us much greater ability to date it. The first appearance of Rodrigo's successor Lope is in a confirmation of the *terminos* of Plasencia that dates firmly to 10 November 1221, while Rodrigo's last appearance is in a 2 June 1221 mandate by the young king Fernando that all those who owned lands in episcopal towns in Segovia owed the diocese of Segovia—and its mentally ill bishop Gerardo—taxes as though they were residents in those places.[76] By 30 June, just four weeks after his last appearance, Rodrigo disappeared from the subscription lists of the charters of Fernando, even though later gifts—like that of 2 August 1221—were made to monasteries within the confines of his diocese.[77]

The last evidence of Rodrigo de Finojsa in the preserved documentation of the period, then, comes from Segovia, before the royal court headed to Valladolid and then to Burgos.[78] Given the *hermandad* signed between Sigüenza and Segovia, it is not unreasonable to suspect that Segovia may have been Rodrigo's final resting place. Unfortunately, there are no extant inscriptions from Segovia that suggest Rodrigo was buried there, either in the cathedral or the parish churches.[79] The extant inscriptions at Valladolid do not suggest that Rodrigo was buried there, either.[80] And there are no extant inscriptions attesting to Rodrigo's burial in the territory of the diocese of Burgos.[81] The road from Segovia to Sigüenza was a mountainous route, and while there were several favored royal residences and towns with prestigious monasteries, none of them appear to have any special connection to Rodrigo. Bishops were unlikely to simply be buried in a nonspecific locale, and the example of Rodrigo Ximénez de Rada, who was buried at Huerta according to the terms of the will he made out long before leaving for his school days in Paris, suggests that the choice of monastic burial still held sway, even in the era of the cathedral-building bishops of the early thirteenth century.[82] The presence of the Romanesque cathedral's core—finished in the early thirteenth century, but renovated and refaced on several occasions in later centuries—and the restoration of the cathedral cloister during Rodrigo's reign suggest that he may have been buried in the cathedral's main structure or in the cloister, but that the cover of his tomb was lost. While this seems remarkable—how does one lose a bishop?—it is not altogether unheard of. Alderico di Palacio's new tomb after his translation to his own chapel required a new inscription; the inscription on the tomb of Sigüenza's first bishop Bernardo de Agen (r. 1121–52) was reinscribed in the sixteenth century; and, while only his arm survived, even the remains of Joscelmo of Sigüenza (r. 1168–78) received a new marker after they were moved to the Capilla del Doncel.[83]

The ending of the story of Rodrigo de Finojosa, however, does not change the course of its nearly three decades. During his long tenure as a bishop, his influence in his diocese, like that of most bishops, ebbed and flowed, but the growth of his control over some of the more powerful institutions is remarkable. The conflict with Medinaceli, which had plagued even his most capable predecessors, subsided enough that mutual agreements seem to have been upheld. The cathedral chapter, which could have easily been the most persistent problem facing a prelate, received a revised customary and went from containing a mix of regular and secular canons to accepting only regular canons—an accomplishment for which some of Rodrigo's contemporaries received ample praise. Even the ability to calm the situation in his diocese after the unfortunate death of one of his young diocesan subjects is a considerable endorsement of both Rodrigo's political clout and his ability to sway public opinion. These qualities suggest that the reputation that Rodrigo's episcopate has in some early modern chronicles was more than simply the product of his longevity and the mention of his participation at Las Navas by his kinsman; rather, he made a considerable impact on his diocese in part because of the way that he balanced royal and pontifical agenda to retrench his own position.

In many ways, Rodrigo de Finojosa fits the portrait of a "reforming bishop" from the long twelfth century. His focus on clerical discipline, the obedience of his episcopal office, and the implementation of canon legal strategies to effect his goals have long stood as the hallmarks of the twelfth century's "papal reform movement"—a convenient, if occasionally nebulous catch-all—and the scholarly focus on these trends has shown that, as far as Rome was concerned, such emphases were critical elements of a strategy aimed at ameliorating the spiritual fortunes of Christendom writ large. To take one example, Bernard of Clairvaux's postulate that the Second Crusade had been defeated—in the Latin East, at least—because of the sinful conduct of European Christians could easily have played out in Rodrigo's own day. At Alarcos, the defeat of the Castilians ushered in a period of extraordinary religious tension, and the patronage of houses of regular religious and Rodrigo's focus on the reform of his diocese's clerical problem children, like Medinaceli, and of the cathedral chapter fit too neatly into the Bernardine paradigm to have been purely coincidental. As a final data point, then, Rodrigo's episcopate demonstrates that significant prelates might "show up" in high-profile historiography less frequently than they should. Thirty years is a long time to man one's post, even on the road through twelfth-century Guadalajara, and the episcopate of Rodrigo de Finojosa represented the culmination of a number of important contemporary trends.

9

PALEA, COMPARANDA, AND CONCLUSIONS

One consequence of [the drama of the *Reconquista*], though, has been that the presumably less spectacular developments behind the front line have attracted the attention of considerably fewer scholars. The history of the Church, for example, has been almost entirely neglected. Though there are hardly fewer ecclesiastical archives . . . their contents have still to be sorted and analysed.
—Peter Linehan, *The Spanish Church and the Papacy in the Thirteenth Century* (1971)

In the preceding chapters, the careers of a handful of bishops—only one-fifth or so—of the kingdom of Alfonso VIII were reconstructed from the available documentation. The bishops of Plasencia and Ávila, though they were at the court as often as their colleagues, are too poorly documented to be considered in detail.[1] Even at well-documented Segovia, the marrow seems missing from the considerable bones in the archival sources, since we know far less about the prelates from early modern collections than usual. Burgos has plentiful records, but the frequency of episcopal changeover makes any careful study of Burgalese relationships with Rome and Alfonso VIII particularly challenging.[2] In some cases, the data points that we do have inspire the kind of sadness for lost texts that is often a part of the medieval historian's enterprise. Brecio of Plasencia, for example, must have been a man of great prestige to have merited an appointment to the appellate panel for the Zamora case by Innocent III, but we know staggeringly little about Brecio.[3] It seems likely that, given the prevalence of both papal and royal influence over bishops in medieval Castile, these lesser-known prelates would have generally fit into the same pattern.

This chapter will attempt to fill in the gaps between the well-documented bishops featured in this volume and their peers. In the *palea* section, the careers of the clerics studied above and those for whom the data was too scarce to merit a chapter will be mapped onto major historiographical arguments to show where new lines of investigation have been opened up by this project.[4] In the *comparanda* section, the data surrounding the Castilian clerics' activities will be compared to similar phenomena in other kingdoms in order to demonstrate that Richard Fletcher's original point—that the history of León aligned with contemporary trends elsewhere—remains both valid and important to the history of Castile. The third section indicates new lines of investigation that should shape further discussion of a variety of medieval subjects.

The first section of this final chapter has two goals. First, it will bring together the major points from previous chapters and alloy them with the details of clerics for whom documentation is far scarcer. Of importance are those themes that, given their pan-European scope, have widespread use for historians working on other regions and periods. Specifically, this first section will consider the importance of the crusading movements, of feudal/manorial social models, and the reformation and renaissances of the twelfth century. By examining these themes, the *palea* section of this chapter will show that husks of evidence from both rich archives and underdocumented diocesan administrations accord with wider phenomena from beyond the Pyrenees.

In the second section, I argue for the validity of that connection by showing the ways in which the Castilian church participated in the same trends as their colleagues in other kingdoms and regions. The *comparanda* from the clerics in the Crusader States, the Holy Roman Empire, León, Italy, and England will show that the clergy of Castile participated in the same quotidian activities that defined their contemporaries' work. By connecting these examples with the wider church, this section indicates several avenues of investigation that might be quite fruitful.

In the final section of the chapter, I demonstrate that the historical importance of the Castilian clergy underscores their careers' being a vital source for further nuance in the larger narrative. Far from being simply an element of religious history, the careers of the bishops and canons of the cathedral chapters of Castile are connected to much larger social and cultural phenomena. In collating the available data from this study and the relevant historiography, I suggest the ways in which the cases under examination here underscore the important changes that will become necessary in the larger narrative of medieval Christendom.

Palea

The careers of the clerics sketched in the chapters above shared several similarities with their colleagues in less-well-documented dioceses of Castile. The ways in which bishops engaged with holy war, lordship and the exercise of power, the reformation of the medieval church, and the "twelfth-century renaissance" elucidate how, despite the paucity of evidence, lesser-known clerics might confirm that the actions of more historically accessible figures were congruent with contemporary norms and patterns.

Although there has been considerable historical discussion of the crusading phenomenon's linkage to Iberia, the general consensus is that the earliest parts of the crusading movement did not share a causal point but rather display the hallmarks of convergent evolution.[5] Early examples of wars against Muslim polities—particularly in the first *taifa* period—were defined more by the drive for *parias* payments than for the sacral/penitential aims of the crusading movement after the Council of Clermont in 1095.[6] Some scholars some have provocatively suggested that there were no crusades in Iberia in the twelfth century. However, the balance of evidence has shown that crusading became a discernible element of the military ethos of Iberian Christian potentates in the Leonese empire during the time of Alfonso VII, as the enduring influence of Cluniac and Burgundian clerics in the same period shaped contemporary religious language.[7] By the time of Alfonso VIII, the crusade was well enough entrenched and understood that the clergy assembled at Segovia in 1166 were willing and able to grant a crusading indulgence for those who repelled unlawful invaders of Alfonso's kingdom.[8] As a result, the framework of the crusade allows us to pin basic historical facts from the careers of clerics in the Castilian church onto a well-studied model.

The most obvious example of clerical participation in crusading comes from the two major pitched battles against the Almohads during the reign of Alfonso VIII. The fact that Rodrigo Ximénez de Rada was one of the major organizers of the Las Navas campaign argues for his identification as that war's architect, and it would be wrong to suggest that he was not invested in its outcomes.[9] Indeed, as I have noted elsewhere, the phenomenon of clerics bearing arms in battle in Castile during the period not only fit within contemporary legal norms (as Lawrence Duggan has shown) but also meshed with accepted cultural practices.[10] At least two bishops died in the battle of Alarcos in 1195. Gutierre Rodríguez Girón, the young bishop of Segovia—confirmed by Archbishop Martín López perhaps only weeks before—died at the battle, although he was not mentioned in the necrologies of Segovia, suggesting that his episcopate was so short that he had yet to make a will for masses and commemoration of his tenure.[11] The bishop of Ávila, whose militia had become somewhat famous for their exploits in the twelfth century, also died on the battlefield, as an 1195 charter by his successor confirms.[12] The loss of these two prelates in a disastrous defeat like Alarcos might suggest that the bishops were collateral damage—overkill during a rout—if the celebrated victory at Las Navas de Tolosa did not also count a Castilian bishop amongst its casualties. The bishop of Burgos, Juan Mathé, fell at Las Navas, a fact that suggests that accounts of the battle as a near disaster, averted only by a decisive royal counter-charge, may have underplayed the danger to the allied Christian forces.[13] The death of clerics in battle attests to their involvement in these conflicts and underscores that the crusading activities of the Castilian clerics fit within the models established for other ecclesiastical institutions on Christendom's borders: at the front, all were needed to hold the line.[14]

Episcopal cities were also equipped to handle their own defense, both with military forces and with defensive structures. While the city walls of Ávila are the most famous, the form of the cathedral suggests that the episcopal *cathedra* was also the military seat of the city, and a secret passage in the cathedral into the episcopal palace demonstrates the importance of the church as a link in the fortifications of the city.[15] When Celebruno of Toledo conceded a *fuero* to the town of Belinchón, he included conditions that organized the city's resources to provide for its defense and supported the raiding activities of the townsfolk.[16] At Cuenca, the famous *fuero* of that city offered a prize payment ("a Moorish slave") for those clerics who journeyed with the raiding party to serve as chaplain.[17] In the early days of Christian Cuenca, the bishop and church were granted several major fortifications around the diocesan see, a fact that connected the bishops closely to the work of defending their territory.[18] In that light, it seems no accident that the first three prelates to lead Cuenca were former archdeacons of Calatrava.[19] Plasencia's position on the frontier was so perilous that the Almohad counterattack in 1196 and 1197 sacked the city and royal charters were not issued from Plasencia until February 1199.[20] The creation of new frontier dioceses, like Cuenca and Plasencia, and the development of episcopally sanctioned tools to foster episcopal subjects' raiding capabilities supported the military organization of Castilian towns, in turn supporting royal crusading endeavors.[21]

Scholarship has established the crusading movement as one of the outgrowths of a larger expansion of Latin Christendom in the long twelfth century, and the religious importance of crusading suggests a broader link to the religious revival of that period. As Brenda Bolton noted, "The success of a crusade not only demonstrated the reinvigoration of Christendom but was also regarded as proving that mission and crusade could only succeed against a background of Christian renewal."[22] Giles Constable, too, showed that a link to what he dubbed "the reformation of the twelfth century" was part of a two-pronged approach—monasticizing the clergy and encouraging greater involvement in religious activity in the whole of society.[23] It stands to reason that the norms governing clergy were likely in flux during the period under examination in this study, and if monasticization was taking place in the wider Latin Christian world, then it should also be present in Castile. In particular, the case of cathedral chapter reforms (and the resolution of disputes about the proper exercise of clerical functions and discipline) suggests that the reformation of the twelfth century, by Constable's formulation, finds some support in the Castilian evidence.[24]

In this book's case studies, several examples of cathedral chapter reform suggest that the papally sponsored reforms of the previous half century were gaining traction in the provinces. Although they were also driven by local concerns, the bishops who pressed for reform in their chapters were responding to and participating in a wider dialogue about the proper conduct of clerics, particularly with regard to the *vita apostolica* formulations gaining traction in reformist treatises.[25] Transforming Osma from secular to regular, concurrent with eliminating *portionarios* and ensuring that clerics did not keep concubines, was part of a long process, finally completed by Martín Bazán in 1199.[26] Martín's neighbor, Rodrigo of Sigüenza, encountered a far more peculiar set of challenges, but, with the intercession of Archbishop Martín López, he was able to come to a set of financial and social compromises that moved the chapter to a much stricter form of observance.[27] Although the *nombramiento* charter enumerating the canons predated it by almost a decade and a half, Julián ben Tauro's reform of the chapter of Cuenca offered a number of instances in which chapters were guided toward a more functional *forma vivendi* when the influence of the original membership had been occluded.[28] At Cuenca, this meant an increased insistence on financial and residency requirements, likely as a result of the greater financial pressure created by levies of funds to support the *fábrica* (construction and maintenance accounts) of the cathedral.[29] There were a number of electoral reforms for subject chapters, too, such as those undertaken by Ramón de Minerva and Alderico de Palacio for the abbey of Husillos.[30] Although the connection to the physical plant may seem out of place in a question of clerical reform, an absence of clerics could be as troubling as an absence of mortar: cathedrals were physically constructed by stone but intellectually and socially constructed by the clerics who participated in their activities.[31] Reforming the chapters meant reforming, essentially, the whole of the institutional church.

Although some of the more detailed evidence describes the reform of clerical bodies as a whole, individual clergy were also the objects of reform-minded energies as well. The papal alarm at Ramón de Minerva's conduct and the deposition of Bernardo of Osma demonstrate the more "high-profile" instances of personal reform pressure, but other instances suggest that reform energies were directed toward many other clerics.[32] Additionally, examples of righted reforms suggest the potency of these themes. One instance from a letter of Lucius III—where the preserved documentation tells us too little to satisfy historical curiosity—suggests that two Toledan canons were set on dueling, and archiepiscopal intervention was needed to prevent them from doing so.[33] In another case, an 1177 letter from Alexander III to Archbishop Celebruno noted that a canon from Sigüenza had been deprived of his goods and benefice because some thought him a criminal; the canon was thought to have been innocent.[34] According to letters sent to Santiago de Compostela, the clergy of Plasencia (before Plasencia had been made a diocese of its own) had rebelled against Ávila, disrespecting and disobeying the bishop.[35] Similarly violent quarrels—Sigüenza versus Osma, Palencia versus Segovia—seem to have plagued the second half of the twelfth century; the fact that these conflicts were ever resolved attests to the staying power of a vision of a unified and (internally) peaceful clergy serving Christendom writ large.[36] Although these instances demonstrate the impact of a number of different sub-themes—among them obedience to proper authority, peaceful conduct among peers, and the rule of canon law over clerics—the larger point is that some of the reformist ideas about clerical behavior and obedience of prelates were being played out "on the ground" in the Castilian church. Unfortunately, not enough evidence survives to draw a composite narrative that would pass scholarly muster. Even if some of these battles had less to do with the "monasticization" thesis posited by Constable, the *clericalization* of clerical behavior is widely attested in the sources for the church in Castile.

In part, these behaviors were expressed in intellectual productions that were later taken up in learned tracts. The twelfth-century Castilian church had no *Book of Gomorrah* nor a Peter Damian to write it, but Charles Homer Haskins's *Renaissance of the Twelfth Century* still—despite some of its more problematic assumptions—has strong links to the abilities and productions of Castilian clerics in the period covered by this study.[37] The two most obvious examples of episcopal authors are Bishop Melendo of Osma (r. 1208–25)—a canon legal scholar who had taught at Vicenza and Bologna—and Archbishop Rodrigo Ximénez de Rada (r. 1208–47), whose chronicles are still some of the best narrative sources for twelfth and early thirteenth century Christian Iberia.[38] The *Collectio Seguntina* of Rodrigo de Finojosa of Sigüenza demonstrates that Melendo was not the only legal mind in the ranks of the Castilian clergy.[39] Pedro de Cardona (el. 1180–82), too, was acclaimed as a "doctor legum magnificus" by the Annals of Vic before he was drafted to the cardinalate.[40] Mauricio of Burgos (r. 1213–38) was called "commendable in letters" by Marc of Toledo, one of the more substantial translators of medical and theological texts in early twelfth-century Toledo.[41] While these bishops' and archbishops' activities as *literati* in their own right testify to the groundswell of intellectual activities engaged in by Castilian clerics, the impact of these trends can be seen earlier and more locally in the evidence from their cathedral chapters.

Cathedral chapters in Castile, like those in other regions, were one of the prime sources for candidates for the episcopate, so it is not surprising that their ranks contained considerable cultivated talent.[42] Among these chapters, there were a number of canons who actively pursued what might be termed an academic agenda. While evidence about the *studium* at Palencia has already been presented above, the number of canons who employed the title *magister* during the whole of the period in question is at least thirty-eight: seven at Burgos,[43] two at Segovia,[4] thirteen at Palencia,[45] two at Ávila,[46] three at Sigüenza,[47] two at Osma,[48] and eight at Toledo.[49] Moreover, Cuenca had at least one, while none are attested at Plasencia, probably due to a paucity of early evidence.[50] The presence of *magistri*, while suggesting the overall intellectual acumen of the chapters, can be given much greater depth with recourse to specific examples presented by clerical authors, book collectors, and translators.

Beyond indicating increased literacy among the clerics of Castilian cathedral chapters in the period, some have argued that the presence of Ugolino da Sesso and Saint Dominic offer further evidence that, even among those who do not appear in the records from cathedral chapters as "masters," there was a pool of talent in the chapters capable of considerable intellectual achievement.[51] The career of Domingo González, Segovia's archdeacon of Cuéllar and a frequent resident in the chapter at Toledo, as a translator of metaphysical texts also suggests that the reputation of the "School of Toledo" was not undeserved.[52] Although many years his junior, Marc of Toledo was one of the more important translators at work in the first decades of the thirteenth century—providing both a revised and more literal translation of the Qur'an and the works of the Almohad founder Ibn Tumart—but he never rose above the rank of subdeacon in the chapter and never styled himself "magister."[53] In his will, preserved in the cathedral records of Ávila, the treasurer of Toledo's chapter donated his copies of Gratian to the church of Ávila, implying that he and his colleagues held the text in high enough esteem to value it as a gift worthy of prayers and masses for the treasurer's soul.[54] Other examples—Michael Scot or Gerald of Cremona—could be offered to further expand on the better-documented work being done at Toledo, but the point is rather clear: it was not just the clerics with miters and croziers who were capable of working well with pen and parchment.[55] The clergy of the cathedral chapters, both at the top and bottom of their ranks, actively participated in and helped shape the intellectual upswell characterized by Haskins's "renaissance" thesis, even though Haskins himself paid comparatively little attention to developments in Castile when they did not directly inform historical territories in which he was more comfortable working.[56]

This section's overarching goal has been to demonstrate that the thematic convergence of historiographical theses can be found in more than just the best-attested sources and the prelates who shaped them. Instead of rejecting the *palea* of evidence from these less fortunate dioceses, connecting them to more developed case studies has validated the results of these better-attested clerics. The overarching narrative of the previous chapters shows that using these *palea* of evidence can present new thematic avenues of study. In the examples above, the smaller samplings of the data have shown that in the cases of the reformations of the twelfth century, the crusades, the exercise of lordship, and the renaissance of the twelfth century, the relevant points of data support the conclusion that Castilian clergy participated actively in all these phenomena. As a whole, these less-well-attested examples show that the evidence that might have been lost in the passage of time would likely have demonstrated the same points.

Comparanda

The history of Castilian clerics appears to parallel the histories of the clerics of other kingdoms or regions in Latin Christendom, especially the history of bishops and their cathedral chapters in the kingdom of Sicily, in the Holy Roman Empire, in León, in Angevin England, and in the Crusader States. Thematically, the same elements that helped shape the Castilian episcopate were present in other kingdoms and had similar effects on the diocesan experience: the election of canons to the episcopate, the involvement of episcopal authors with the twelfth-century renaissance, and the control of chapters by bishops.

With only a few exceptions, all of the members of the Castilian episcopate elected during the reign of Alfonso VIII were members of cathedral chapters. Martín Bazán, his predecessor Miguel of San Pedro de Arlanza, Pedro de Cardona, and Martín de Finojosa were the only four clerics elected from a monastic background to serve as prelates. Most of the bishops were deacons or archdeacons, and most were based either in dioceses to which they were elected or in the diocese next door.[57] Electing a cleric with substantial administrative experience made good sense, given the number of responsibilities with which bishops were tasked.[58] In the dioceses of Norman Sicily, deans and archdeacons were elected to high posts, both because they appeared to be effective administrators and because they had close working relationships with the monarchy and high nobility; some were from monastic backgrounds, but most were cathedral canons of some stripe.[59] The same general trend is readily apparent in the Latin East, where the crusader nobility seems to have reconciled early on with the need for administratively adept clergy in posts of high authority; very few were monks and most had experience as archdeacons or deans.[60] In the diocese of Orvieto, the tendency toward improved administration was so pronounced that episcopal registers, in a notarial fashion, begin appearing in the mid-twelfth century, and the bishops themselves appear to have embraced these administrative trends substantially.[61] Verona's clergy, too, were locally derived, and their participation in the elections of the bishops of Verona is well attested.[62] In the Holy Roman Empire, similar tendencies are well represented, especially the connection between local power politics and the episcopate.[63] Similar tendencies are visible in much of the northwestern European continent.[64] In the kingdom of León, too, archdeacons and deacons were elected to the episcopate most frequently, but not without royal or aristocratic influence and approval.[65] In Lisbon, the election of the first bishops was based on royal influence but slowly became local and administrative over the first century after the creation of the diocese of Lisbon.[66] The collective evidence from Latin Christendom, as it stands, is a demonstrable attestation that the experience of the Castilian clergy prior to their election to the episcopate—administratively inclined and elected from the local chapter—was a reflection of the society of Christendom writ large, and their histories validate the historical analysis of scholars working on other regions and their local churches.

Even beyond the historical parallels between the elections of bishops from cathedral chapters, additional comparative avenues exist for studying the ways in which clergy engaged with the cultural revivals of the long twelfth century. Of course, a number of prelates beyond the Pyrenees engaged with the twelfth-century renaissance as authors and scholars. It is worth noting that even in Haskins's original monograph, the contributions of Castilian clergy to his research base were far fewer than those of northern clerics and usually served as way stations as Arabic texts moved north to scholars who used them in a fashion with which Haskins was more comfortable.[67] The activities described above of Pedro de Cardona, Mauricio of Burgos, Rodrigo Ximénez de Rada, and Melendo of Osma show clearly that the prelates of Castile were enmeshed with Haskins's renaissance; their cathedral chapters were as well. The list of bishops mentioned in Haskins's work is too long to count, but Burchard of Worms, Hugh of Amiens, Otto of Friesing, Fulcher of Chartres, and Gratian of Chiusi were all mentioned by Haskins, and their experience suggests that the episcopate was not isolated from the widespread fashion of intellectual activity Haskins described.[68] Cathedral schools in both Paris and Chartres employed *magistri* to teach and guide young clerics.[69] Individual schools also existed at important ecclesiastical houses, like that of Santa Cruz de Coimbra in Portugal, where canons taught and studied together.[70] The evidence shows that the bishops and clerics of the medieval Latin West were authors and scholars at roughly the same rate as their compatriots—individuals like William of Tyre or Otto of Friesing were not ubiquitous in ecclesiastical provinces, but they were conspicuous.[71] Bishops and their cathedral chapters were not always highly literate or hypergraphical scholars, but they could be, and when they were, they engaged with the intellectual themes and revivals of their day. In doing so, the Castilian clergy shared the experiences of their colleagues in other regions.

If the elections of bishops from local diocesan chapters in Castile and their engagement with the intellectual activities of the twelfth-century renaissance mirrored practice from Latin Christendom generally, then the interactions of prelates and canons on matters of clerical discipline form the third leg of the historical triangle. Already, the cathedral chapters of Cuenca, Osma, Toledo, and Sigüenza have demonstrated the validity of the study of cathedral chapter reform in the kingdom of Castile, which suggests that parallel experiences would further cross-validate the study's importance. The expansion of chapters of canons regular in the long twelfth century underscores the tension created by changing economic and social conditions, factors that inflected the observances of cathedral chapters to better meet the needs of their parishioners and satisfy their superiors.[72] Although no systematic study of cathedral chapter reform has been done for the whole of Latin Christendom, these patterns have long been linked to both the revival of the *vita apostolica* and the expansion of the profit economy in contemporary societies.[73]

In his groundbreaking 1960 study, Richard Fletcher began his final chapter with lines that bear repeating: "To claim that there was little that was unusual about the Leonese church in the twelfth century may seem a lame conclusion. It will appear less so to those who are acquainted with the work of Spanish ecclesiastical historians. Much of their writing has been underpinned by the assumption that there was something special or unusual about the church in Spain, an assumption explicable in part by the tendency to study it in isolation, rather than as a member of the community of western Christendom."[74] The three topics mentioned here—elections, reforms, and renaissance—suggest that the experience of the Castilian clergy was very similar to that of their brothers and colleagues across their western border. And whether in the example of obedience oaths sworn by clerics to their superiors or the death of bishops battling Islamic polities, the clergy in the kingdom of Castile engaged in practices similar to those of contemporary clergy in other regions and kingdoms.[75] Such a conclusion may seem remarkably simple, but it is a kind of Occam's razor for ecclesiastical history and all of the other historical subfields it communicates with: the church was more or less the same across Europe, even when it was inflected by local circumstances and shaped by intellectual forces that were not necessarily controlled by the church itself.

Conclusions

No book on the church in medieval Latin Christendom can be comprehensive—there are neither pages nor sufficient sources to support such a claim. The brevity of the case studies in this volume present only a fraction of the total activities of the prelates under observation because only a fraction of the sources are preserved. The clerics' lives—especially their youths—cannot be reconstructed in their entirety, but the themes that appear prevalent and important in their episcopates demonstrate that they provide a window into histories that would otherwise be lost. Historical scholarship cannot recover sources that do not exist to write a history that has yet to be compiled from the evidence. Instead, the elements of histories that would otherwise be recovered from a more extensive source base can be unlocked by using church and ecclesiastical sources.

The histories of several phenomena have already been shown to be well attested in the archival sources of the Castilian church. In the histories of the crusades, the reformation of the twelfth century, and the twelfth-century renaissance, the clergy of Castile demonstrate that the large-scale reorientation of Latin Christian society of the period was also present in Castile. Even though many of the most important scholarly contributions on the twelfth century might be nuanced considerably by the employment of Castile's sources, no project can be comprehensive. Accordingly, it has been my intention in this volume to provide future scholars working on these same themes with representative case studies that build a larger narrative. In some instances, there have even been early examples to offer the basis for correcting and enhancing future studies that offer thematic examinations. With this new foundation having been laid, more work on the history of the Castilian church will contribute to a renewed conversation about the clerics whose experiences support a more nuanced analysis of these important trends.

In the case studies here, the clerics that defined the Castilian church demonstrated that such a correction of the meager narrative (and its contributions to larger themes) is feasible. Celebruno, bishop of Sigüenza and later archbishop of Toledo, showed that a high-ranking cleric, closely connected with the monarch, had the potential to guide the course of a kingdom when it was under considerable duress. Ramón de Minerva, bishop of Palencia, showed that the reputation of clerics in scholarly estimates can be substantially skewed both by the perspective of normative sources and by the ways in which the exercise of episcopal duties on behalf of the realm could be misunderstood by reading from the center. Bishop Alderico di Palacio of Palencia, the son of northern Italian immigrants, represented the changing nature of the episcopate—experienced administrators, legally competent, and capable of playing many roles—and the ways in which Castilian clergy were representative of larger changes in Latin Christendom. As the bishop who recruited the young Saint Dominic to the chapter of Osma, Martín Bazán serves as a window onto the ways Dominic's own (well-attested) experience within the reformation of the twelfth century reflects the conditions and concerns of contemporary Castilian clergy, effectively unlocking the early history of Dominic from an ecclesiastical angle. The career of Martín

López de Pisuerga balanced royal/political, religious, and legal concerns in a fashion that left a sizable impact on the nature of the Toledan archiepiscopate in the thirteenth century. As a member of the Mozarabic population of Toledo, Julián ben Tauro of Cuenca's experiences raised the question of how episcopal histories are written and highlighted the demands on a frontier bishop in a nascent diocese during a period of aggressive expansion. Finally, Rodrigo de Finojosa showed how these same developments played out on a more local and less famous level in Sigüenza, as Rodrigo navigated the challenges of his thirty-year career as bishop. The clerics who defined the Castilian church can enlarge and correct our understanding of the larger trends important to the historiography of medieval Latin Christendom.

While the major focus of this book's research has been on the tripolar relationship of local clergies, the Roman curia, and the Castilian monarchy, there are other themes that merit further study. The analyses of the Castilian episcopate presented here will provide other scholars with a series of studies united by a common chronology and regional focus—and a fuller picture of the larger Latin Christian world in the twelfth century. Contrary to the assertions of many, there is still history to be written from the sources of the kingdom of Castile during the long twelfth century.

Appendix: Summary Profiles of the Castilian Episcopate, 1158–1214

Archbishops of Toledo

Juan de Castellmorum (Juan "de Segovia")
Dates: fl. 1148–66; pont. 1152–66
Pre-episcopal position: bishop of Segovia (1149–51); sacristan of Toledo (1146–49)[1]
Order: secular cleric (cathedral canon)
Social class: burgher
Place of birth: Burgundy[2]
Place of burial: Toledo
Conciliar attendance: Legatine Council of Valladolid (1155), Council of Tours (1163), Synod of Segovia (1166)[3]

Celebruno (Cerebruno, Cenebruno)
Dates: fl. 1143–80; pont. 1166–80
Pre-episcopal position: bishop of Sigüenza (1156–66); archdeacon of Toledo (1143–56)[4]
Order: secular cleric (cathedral canon)
Social class: burgher
Place of birth: Poitou[5]
Place of burial: Toledo
Conciliar attendance: Council of Rheims (1148), Legatine Council of Valladolid? (1155), Council of Tours (1163), Synod of Segovia (1166), Third Lateran Council (1179)[6]

Pedro de Cardona (Pere de Cardona)
Dates: fl. 1162–83; pont. 1180–81 (elect only)
Pre-episcopal position: abbot of Husillos (1178–80); royal chancellor (1178–80)[7]
Order: monk (Vic)
Social class: comital (son of Ramon Folc III de Cardona and Sibilia)[8]

Place of birth: Cardona?
Place of burial: San Lorenzo in Damaso?
Conciliar attendance: Third Lateran Council (1179)[9]

Gonzalo Pérez

Dates: fl. 1157–92; pont. 1182–92
Pre-episcopal position: archdeacon of Toledo[10]
Order: secular cleric (cathedral canon)
Social class: burgher?
Place of birth: unknown
Place of burial: Toledo
Conciliar attendance: none

Martín López de Pisuerga

Dates: fl. 1190–1208; pont. 1192–1208
Pre-episcopal position: archdeacon of Palencia[11]
Order: cathedral canon (Palencia)
Social class: comital (son of Diego López de Fitero)[12]
Place of birth: Pisuerga/Fitero
Place of burial: Toledo
Conciliar attendance: none

Rodrigo Ximénez de Rada

Dates: fl. 1200–1247; pont. 1208–47
Pre-episcopal position: bishop-elect of Osma (1208)[13]
Order: Cistercian (Santa María de Huerta)
Social class: comital (son of Ximéno de Rada)[14]
Place of birth: Rada
Place of burial: Santa María de Huerta
Conciliar attendance: Fourth Lateran Council (1215), First Council of Lyon (1245)[15]

Bishops of Burgos

Pedro Pérez

Dates: fl. 1155–84; pont. 1156–81
Pre-episcopal position: archdeacon of Burgos[16]
Order: secular cleric (cathedral canon)
Social class: burgher
Place of birth: unknown
Place of burial: Burgos
Conciliar attendance: Council of Tours (1163)[17]

Marino Mathé[18]

Dates: fl. 1165–1200; pont. 1181–1200
Pre-episcopal position: archdeacon of Burgos[19]
Order: secular cleric (cathedral canon)
Social class: burgher

Place of birth: Burgos
Place of burial: Burgos
Conciliar attendance: none

Mateo Mathé

Dates: fl. 1181–1202; pont. 1200–1202
Pre-episcopal position: dean of Burgos[20]
Order: secular cleric (cathedral canon)
Social class: burgher
Place of birth: Burgos
Place of burial: Burgos
Conciliar attendance: none

Fernando González

Dates: fl. 1200–1202; pont. 1202–5
Pre-episcopal position: scribe, chapter of Burgos[21]
Order: secular cleric (cathedral canon)
Social class: aristocratic (nephew of Alfonso VIII)[22]
Place of birth: unknown
Place of burial: Burgos
Conciliar attendance: none

García Martínez de Contreras

Dates: fl. 1200–1202; pont. 1206–11
Pre-episcopal position: none
Order: secular cleric (cathedral canon?)
Social class: aristocratic (son of Martín González de Contreras)[23]
Place of birth: unknown
Place of burial: Burgos
Conciliar attendance: none

Juan Yáñez Mathé

Dates: fl. 1200–1212; pont. 1211–12
Pre-episcopal position: archdeacon of Burgos[24]
Order: secular cleric (cathedral canon)
Social class: burgher
Place of birth: Burgos
Place of burial: Burgos
Conciliar attendance: none

Mauricio

Dates: fl. 1200–1212; pont. 1213–38
Pre-episcopal position: archdeacon of Toledo[25]
Order: secular cleric (cathedral canon)
Social class: burgher
Place of birth: Toledo
Place of burial: Burgos
Conciliar attendance: Fourth Lateran Council (1215)[26]

Bishops of Palencia

Ramón II de Minerva

Dates: fl. 1145–84; pont. 1148–84
Pre-episcopal position: monk of San Zoilo de Carrión[27]
Order: Cluniac (Santa María de Huerta)
Social class: royal? (half-brother of Empress Berengaria of Navarra)[28]
Place of birth: unknown
Place of burial: Palencia
Conciliar attendance: Third Lateran Council (1179)[29]

Alderico di Palacio (Arderico, Anderico)

Dates: fl. 1155–1208; pont. 1184–1208
Pre-episcopal position: bishop of Sigüenza (1179–84)[30]
Order: secular cleric (cathedral canon)
Social class: burgher
Place of birth: Burgos?
Place of burial: Palencia
Conciliar attendance: Third Lateran Council (1179)[31]

Tello Téllez de Meneses

Dates: fl. 1204–46; pont. 1208–46
Pre-episcopal position: canon of Segovia[32]
Order: secular cleric (cathedral canon)
Social class: aristocratic (son of Tello de Meneses)[33]
Place of birth: Segovia
Place of burial: Palencia
Conciliar attendance: none

Bishops of Osma

Juan Téllez

Dates: fl. 1147–73; pont. 1149–73
Pre-episcopal position: archdeacon of Segovia[34]
Order: secular cleric (cathedral canon)
Social class: burgher
Place of birth: Segovia?
Place of burial: Osma
Conciliar attendance: none

Bernardo

Dates: fl. 1176–81; pont. 1176–78 (deposed)
Pre-episcopal position: prior of Osma[35]
Order: secular cleric (cathedral canon)
Social class: burgher
Place of birth: Burgos
Place of burial: Burgos
Conciliar attendance: none

Miguel
Dates: fl. 1158–85; pont. 1178–85
Pre-episcopal position: abbot of San Pedro de Arlanza[36]
Order: Cluniac (San Pedro de Arlanza)
Social class: unknown
Place of birth: unknown
Place of burial: Osma
Conciliar attendance: Third Lateran Council (1179)[37]

García
Dates: fl. 1185–88; pont. 1186–88
Pre-episcopal position: prior of Osma[38]
Order: secular cleric (cathedral canon)
Social class: unknown
Place of birth: unknown
Place of burial: Osma
Conciliar attendance: none

Martín Bazán
Dates: fl. 1188–1201; pont. 1188–1201
Pre-episcopal position: monk of San Millán de la Cogolla[39]
Order: Cluniac (San Millán de la Cogolla)
Social class: aristocrat
Place of birth: Baztán?
Place of burial: Osma
Conciliar attendance: none

Diego d'Acebo
Dates: fl. 1190–1207; pont. 1201–7
Pre-episcopal position: prior of Osma[40]
Order: Cistercian (Cîteaux, after consecration as bishop)[41]
Social class: aristocrat
Place of birth: Villaseca[42]
Place of burial: Osma
Conciliar attendance: none

Rodrigo Ximénez de Rada
Dates: fl. 1200–1247; pont.-elect. 1206–8
Pre-episcopal position: household cleric[43]
Order: Cistercian (Santa María de Huerta)
Social class: comital (son of Ximéno de Rada)[44]
Place of birth: Rada
Place of burial: Santa María de Huerta
Conciliar attendance: Fourth Lateran Council (1215), First Council of Lyon (1245)[45]

Melendo

Dates: fl. 1185–1207; pont. 1208–25
Pre-episcopal position: dean of Burgos[46]
Order: Benedictine (Santa Cruz de Coimbra)[47]
Social class: burgher
Place of birth: Coimbra?
Place of burial: Osma
Conciliar attendance: Fourth Lateran Council (1215)[48]

Bishops of Segovia

Guillermo

Dates: fl. 1121–70; pont. 1158–70
Pre-episcopal position: archdeacon of Toledo[49]
Order: secular cleric (cathedral canon)
Social class: unknown
Place of birth: unknown
Place of burial: Segovia
Conciliar attendance: Council of Tours (1163)[50]

Gonzalo Gutiérrez Girón

Dates: fl. 1177–94; pont. 1177–94
Pre-episcopal position: unknown, probably deacon[51]
Order: unknown
Social class: aristocrat (brother of Rodrigo Gutiérrez Girón)[52]
Place of birth: unknown
Place of burial: unknown
Conciliar attendance: Third Lateran Council (1179)[53]

Gutierre Rodríguez Girón

Dates: fl. 1182–95; pont. 1195
Pre-episcopal position: archdeacon of Segovia; royal chancellor[54]
Order: secular cleric (cathedral canon)
Social class: aristocrat (son of Rodrigo Gutiérrez Girón)[55]
Place of birth: Segovia
Place of burial: Segovia
Conciliar attendance: none

Gonzalo Miguel

Dates: fl. 1190–1211; pont. 1196–1211
Pre-episcopal position: canon of Toledo?[56]
Order: unknown
Social class: aristocrat (son of Gutierre Miguel)[57]
Place of birth: Segovia
Place of burial: Segovia
Conciliar attendance: none

Gerardo

Dates: fl. 1211–24; pont. 1211–24
Pre-episcopal position: unknown[58]
Order: unknown
Social class: unknown
Place of birth: unknown
Place of burial: unknown
Conciliar attendance: Fourth Lateran Council (1215)[59]

Bishops of Sigüenza

Celebruno (Cerebruno, Cenebruno)

Dates: fl. 1143–80; pont. 1156–66
Pre-episcopal position: archdeacon of Toledo (1143–56)[60]
Order: secular cleric (cathedral canon)
Social class: burgher
Place of birth: Poitou
Place of burial: Toledo
Conciliar attendance: Council of Rheims (1148), Legatine Council of Valladolid? (1155), Council of Tours (1163), Synod of Segovia (1166), Third Lateran Council (1179)[61]

Joscelmo (Joscelino)

Dates: fl. 1161–78; pont. 1168–78
Pre-episcopal position: canon of Segovia (1143–56)[62]
Order: secular cleric (cathedral canon)
Social class: unknown
Place of birth: unknown
Place of burial: Sigüenza (partial[63])
Conciliar attendance: none

Alderico di Palacio (Arderico, Anderico)

Dates: fl. 1155–1208; pont. 1179–84
Pre-episcopal position: archdeacon of Burgos[64]
Order: secular cleric (cathedral canon)
Social class: burgher
Place of birth: Burgos?
Place of burial: Palencia
Conciliar attendance: Third Lateran Council (1179)[65]

Gonzalo

Dates: fl. 1185; pont. 1185
Pre-episcopal position: unknown
Order: unknown
Social class: burgher
Place of birth: Atienza?[66]
Place of burial: Sigüenza
Conciliar attendance: none

Martín de Finojosa

Dates: fl. 1158–96; pont. 1185–92 (retired)
Pre-episcopal position: abbot of Santa María de Huerta (1179–84)[67]
Order: Cistercian (Santa María de Huerta)
Social class: aristocrat (son of Miguel Muñoz Finojosa de Campos)[68]
Place of birth: Finojosa
Place of burial: Santa María de Huerta[69]
Conciliar attendance: none

Rodrigo de Finojosa

Dates: fl. 1190–1221; pont. 1192–1221
Pre-episcopal position: prior of Sigüenza[70]
Order: secular cleric (cathedral canon)
Social class: aristocrat (nephew of Miguel Muñoz Finojosa de Campos)
Place of birth: Verdejo?[71]
Place of burial: Sigüenza
Conciliar attendance: Fourth Lateran Council (1215)[72]

Bishops of Ávila

Sancho Blasquez

Dates: fl. 1150–81; pont. 1160–81
Pre-episcopal position: priest of Ávila[73]
Order: secular cleric (cathedral canon)
Social class: burgher
Place of birth: Ávila?
Place of burial: Ávila
Conciliar attendance: Council of Tours (1163), Third Lateran Council (1179)[74]

Domingo I

Dates: fl. 1176–87; pont. 1182–87
Pre-episcopal position: deacon of Ávila[75]
Order: secular cleric (cathedral canon)
Social class: unknown
Place of birth: Ávila?
Place of burial: Ávila
Conciliar attendance: none

Domingo II Blasquez

Dates: fl. 1181–90; pont. 1187–90
Pre-episcopal position: deacon of Ávila[76]
Order: secular cleric (cathedral canon)
Social class: burgher
Place of birth: Ávila?
Place of burial: Ávila
Conciliar attendance: none

Juan II

Dates: fl. 1181–95; pont. 1191–95
Pre-episcopal position: deacon of Ávila[77]
Order: secular cleric (cathedral canon)
Social class: unknown
Place of birth: Ávila?
Place of burial: Ávila
Conciliar attendance: none

Yagüe

Dates: fl. 1191–1203; pont. 1195–1203
Pre-episcopal position: deacon of Ávila[78]
Order: secular cleric (cathedral canon)
Social class: burgher
Place of birth: Ávila?
Place of burial: Ávila
Conciliar attendance: none

Pedro Instancio

Dates: fl. 1191–1212; pont. 1203–12
Pre-episcopal position: archpriest of Ávila and treasurer of Segovia[79]
Order: secular cleric (cathedral canon)
Social class: burgher
Place of birth: unknown
Place of burial: Ávila
Conciliar attendance: none

Domingo III Blasquez

Dates: fl. 1210–27; pont. 1213–27
Pre-episcopal position: prior of Ávila[80]
Order: secular cleric (cathedral canon)
Social class: burgher
Place of birth: Ávila?
Place of burial: Ávila
Conciliar attendance: Fourth Lateran Council (1215)[81]

Bishops of Cuenca

Juan Yáñez

Dates: fl. 1176–97; pont. 1183–97
Pre-episcopal position: archdeacon of Toledo[82]
Order: secular cleric (cathedral canon)
Social class: burgher
Place of birth: Toledo?
Place of burial: Cuenca
Conciliar attendance: none

Julián ben Tauro

Dates: fl. 1173–1208; pont. 1197–1208
Pre-episcopal position: archdeacon of Toledo[83]
Order: secular cleric (cathedral canon)
Social class: burgher
Place of birth: Toledo?
Place of burial: Cuenca
Conciliar attendance: none

García Ruíz

Dates: fl. 1193–1225; pont. 1208–25
Pre-episcopal position: archdeacon of Toledo[84]
Order: secular cleric (cathedral canon)
Social class: burgher
Place of birth: Toledo?
Place of burial: Cuenca
Conciliar attendance: none

Bishops of Plasencia

Brecio

Dates: fl. 1180–1212; pont. 1190–1212
Pre-episcopal position: sacristan of Valladolid[85]
Order: Benedictine (Santa María de Valladolid)
Social class: unknown
Place of birth: unknown
Place of burial: Plasencia
Conciliar attendance: none

Domingo

Dates: fl. 1171–1232; pont. 1212–32
Pre-episcopal position: abbot of Valladolid[86]
Order: Benedictine (Santa María de Valladolid)
Social class: unknown
Place of birth: unknown
Place of burial: Plasencia
Conciliar attendance: none

Notes

Abbreviations

ACC   Archivo Catedralicio de Cuenca
ACT   Archivo Catedralicio de Toledo
BNE   Biblioteca Nacional de España
DRH   *De Rebus Hispaniae*
PL   *Patrologia Latina*

Chapter 1

This chapter's epigraph is drawn from Fletcher, *Episcopate*, 27.

1. Reilly, *León-Castilla Under Alfonso VII*, 267.
2. No full articles about Gonzalo Gutiérrez Girón exist. For his biographical data, see the appendix to this volume.
3. Bianchini, *Queen's Hand*, 7.
4. Julian-Jones, review, 497.
5. Fancy has argued for the importance of recentering religious histories. Fancy, *Mercenary Mediterranean*, 140–51.
6. Bisson disputes this, preferring to call it an effort "to remodel lord-kingship, not replace it": Bisson, *Crisis*, 524–29.
7. Giebfried, "Crusader Constantinople's 1205 'Magna Carta.'"
8. Suárez Fernández, *León en torno a las Cortes*.
9. The classic study of the archbishops of Toledo is Rivera Recio, but the most instructive chapter is that on the provinces themselves and their internecine squabbling. See Rivera Recio, *La Iglesia de Toledo*, 1:245–93.
10. The best modern study of the development of Toledo's province is that of Holndonner, but see his collation of the primatial privileges: Holndonner, *Kommunikation*, 565–70, 571–89.
11. Garrido Garrido, *Documentación*, 1:129–30.
12. Fletcher, *Saint James's Catapult*, 107, 196–97.
13. In Barber's 1992 textbook, Castile is mentioned far fewer times than France or England; a similar absence is noticeable in Rosenwein's more recent medieval textbook. See Barber,

Two Cities, 39, 49, 50, 78, 94, 161–62, 329, 343–48, 351–64, 391; Rosenwein, *Short History*; Cole and Symes, *Western Civilizations*. Larger examinations in macro-theses, like Constable's "reformation" (where Castile and Iberia are not mentioned) or Bisson's "crisis" (where there are only nine mentions), still underserve Castilian history. See Constable, *Reformation*; Bisson, *Crisis*, 31, 96, 97, 101, 102, 248, 296, 540, 541.

14. The exceptions that prove the rule are, inter alia: Linehan and Hernández Sánchez, *Mozarabic Cardinal*; Pick, *Conflict and Coexistence*; Ayala Martínez, "Los obispos."
15. Reilly, *León-Castilla Under Alfonso VII*, 44–48.
16. Krasner Balbale, "Between Kings and Caliphs," 173–218; Catlos, *Kingdoms of Faith*, 275–76; Kennedy, *Muslim Spain and Portugal*, 209–23.
17. Fernando seems to have styled himself as "rex Hispaniarum" from around 1162 to at least 1175. González, *Fernando II*, 251–89.
18. Barton, *Aristocracy*, 17–27.
19. Honeycutt's bibliographic essay for *Medieval Feminist Forum* offers an excellent "jumping-off point" for the study of queenship and corporate monarchies: Honeycutt, "Queenship Studies."
20. The adapting of Kantorowicz's "two bodies" model has changed dramatically since its first publication but remains resonant. Kantorowicz, *King's Two Bodies*.
21. For the details of these two clerics, see their respective chapters below.
22. Barton, *Aristocracy*, 18–20; Doubleday, *Lara Family*, 35–40.
23. "Quicumque honorem infra regnum regis Aldefonsi tenet sit eius vasallus." Linehan, "Synod of Segovia," 42.
24. "Et quicumque tunc vocatus ad servicium eius venerit tantum de iniuncta sibi penitentia remittimus quantum si Iherosolimam visitaret." Ibid.

25. Riley-Smith only notes the campaigns of 1197 by Henry VI as being of a similar vintage. Riley-Smith, *Crusades*, 187–88.
26. "Item generali capitulo de decreto addimus ut nullus decetero guerram in regno regis Aldefonsi facere presumat, quod si facere presumpserit et ammonitus ab episcopo suo desistere noluerit extunc sit excommunicatus et maledictus et sepultura Christianorum ei denegetur si in guerra illa mortuus fuerit." Linehan, "Synod of Segovia," 42.
27. Linehan, *Spain, 1157–1300*, 24–32; Linehan, *History and the Historians*, 297–300.
28. The role of Burgos is well attested in the period. Linehan, *History and the Historians*, 450, 481; Estepa Díez, Álvarez Borge, and Santamarta Luengos, *Poder real y sociedad*, 336–45; Ruiz, *Crisis and Continuity*, 196–34; Dalché, *Historia urbana*, 246–55.
29. On Alfonso's self-knighting from the altar of San Zoilo, see Todesca, "Selling Castile," 34; Martínez Díez, *Alfonso VIII*, 38–39; González, *Alfonso VIII*, 1:142, 180; 2:211–13. Shadis, Bianchini, and I have all separately affirmed the magnitude of the marriage. Bianchini, *Queen's Hand*, 46–47; Shadis, "Happier in Daughters," 81–82, 95–96; Lincoln, "*Una cum Uxore Mea*," 13–27. The increased importance that scholars attribute to Leonor is clear, even in the rediscovery of a singular document from Leonor's chancery. Cerda Costabal and Martínez Llorente, "Un documento inédito."
30. "Pro eo quod desuper altare beati Zoyli primus arma milicie sumpsi." González, *Reino de Castilla*, 2:211–13. On the importance of this fair to the economic history of Castile, see Todesca, "Selling Castile," 34; Ladero Quesada, *Las ferias de Castilla*, 22.
31. E.g., Barton, *Aristocracy*, 18–20; Lourie, *Curia and Cortes*, 73–74. Miriam Shadis and I have both argued that the marriage itself was also the start of a major shift in the royal family's politics of the era:

Shadis, "Happier in Daughters," 81–82, 95–96; Lincoln, "*Una cum Uxore Mea*," 13–27.
32. Lincoln, "*Mihi pro fidelitate militabat*," 29–33.
33. García Fitz, *Relaciones políticas y guerra*, 121–34.
34. Corral, "Alfonso VIII."
35. Powers, *Society Organized for War*, 48–50; Holt, "*In eo tempore*"; Bianchini, "*Infantazgo*," 68; Nieto Soria, "La fundación del obispado"; Díaz Ibáñez, "La iglesia de Cuenca," 31–38.
36. Smith, "Iberian Legations," 101–9; Nieto Soria, "La fundación del obispado," 131.
37. Holndonner has made a similar argument about the political impact that the growing diocese had on the work of the archbishops on their province. Linehan, *History and the Historians*, 290, 343; Holndonner, *Kommunikation*, 459–61.
38. Walker, "Leonor of England"; Shadis, "Happier in Daughters," 92–95; McKiernan Gonzalez, "Monastery and Monarchy," 214–36; Palacios Martín, "Alfonso VIII y . . . Plasencia."
39. Shadis, "Happier in Daughters," 89–92; Lincoln, "*Una cum Uxore Mea*," 13–16.
40. Palacios Martín, "Alfonso VIII . . . en Extremadura," 158–61; Palacios Martín, "Alfonso VIII y . . . Plasencia," 82–84, 86–90; Powers, *Society Organized for War*, 57.
41. Bianchini, *Queen's Hand*, 28–35; Lourie, *Curia and Cortes*, 74–76; O'Callaghan, *Cortes of Castile-León*, 16–17, 82, 96; Linehan, *History and the Historians*, 325; Holt, "*In eo tempore*," 7–8.
42. The birth of Fernando is recorded in the *Anales Toledanos*: Porres Martín-Cleto, *Los Anales Toledanos*, 158. The exact dating of the truce is uncertain, but Almohad sources noted that the king broke the truce with the archiepiscopal raids of 1194, about which see Minguella y Arnedo, *Historia de Sigüenza*, 1:481–82; Gómez and Lincoln, "'Sins'"; Gómez, "Alfonso VIII and the Battle," 144–45; Ayala Martínez, "Holy War and Crusade," 128–30; Lincoln, "Beating Swords into Croziers," 96. On the war of Alarcos in general: O'Callaghan, *Reconquest and Crusade*, 61–62; Izquierdo Benito and Ruiz Gómez, *Alarcos 1195*.
43. Smith, "Iberian Legations," 96–109.
44. Lincoln, "'Holding the Place,'" 498–500.
45. Ibid., 486–89.
46. Ayala Martínez, "Breve semblanza"; Lincoln, "Beating Swords into Croziers," 92–95; Lincoln, "*Mihi pro fidelitate militabat*," 31.
47. Minguella y Arnedo, *Historia de Sigüenza*, 1:481–82; Gómez and Lincoln, "'Sins'"; Gómez, "Alfonso VIII and the Battle," 144–45; Ayala Martínez, "Holy War and Crusade," 128–30; Lincoln, "Beating Swords into Croziers," 96. See also, on the war of Alarcos, O'Callaghan, *Reconquest and Crusade*, 61–62, and Izquierdo Benito and Ruiz Gómez, *Alarcos 1195*.
48. O'Callaghan, *Reconquest and Crusade*, 62–64; García Fitz, *Castilla y León*, 201–3, 448–49; Lincoln, "*Mihi pro fidelitate militabat*," 24–26; Alvira Cabrer, "*Si Possides Amicum*," 188–90.
49. Conedera, *Ecclesiastical Knights*, 119.
50. Fortún Pérez de Ciriza, "La quiebra," 473–85; Lincoln, "'It Pleased the Lord Bishop.'"
51. Lincoln, "'Holding the Place,'" 492–93, esp. 493n118.
52. Shadis, "Happier in Daughters," 88, 90, 96; Lincoln, "*Una cum Uxore Mea*," 13–20.
53. Cerda Costabal, "La dot gasconne," 233–39; Cerda Costabal, "Leonor Plantagenet," 639–42; Alvira Cabrer and Buresi, "'Alphonse,'" 219–27.
54. On the Aragonese influence over the region and conflicts with Angevins and Capetians: Bisson, *Crisis*, 371–72; Smith, *Crusade, Heresy*, 31–35.
55. González, *Alfonso VIII*, 3:335–36. See also Shadis, "Happier in Daughters," 89–92; Lincoln, "*Una cum Uxore Mea*," 13–16. It is likely also during this campaign that Diego d'Acebo and Saint Dominic of

Osma were first exposed to the heretical tendencies of the "Good Men" in the Toulousain: Mandonnet, *St. Dominic*, 21–29; Vicaire, *Saint Dominic*, 46–60; Tugwell, "Notes," 42–47.
56. Lincoln, "Prosopography," 212–14.
57. González, *Alfonso VIII*, 3:341–47.
58. Alvira Cabrer, "Prendiendo el fuego," 174, 180–86.
59. Ayala Martínez, *Las Cruzadas*, 312–14; O'Callaghan, *Reconquest and Crusade*, 66–74; Gómez, "Alfonso VIII and the Battle," 144–51; Ayala Martínez, "Holy War and Crusade," 131–33; Alvira Cabrer, *Las Navas de Tolosa 1212*, 71–74; García Fitz, *Castilla y León*, 211–12; García Fitz, *Relaciones políticas y guerra*, 141–44.
60. Ximénez de Rada, *De Rebus Hispaniae* (hereafter *DRH*), 257–58; *Crónica Latina Regum Castellae* (hereafter *CLRC*), 55; Alvira Cabrer, *Las Navas de Tolosa 1212*, 82, 325–87; Ayala Martínez, *Las Cruzadas*, 312–14; O'Callaghan, *Reconquest and Crusade*, 70–76; Gómez, "Alfonso VIII and the Battle," 151–60; Ayala Martínez, "Holy War and Crusade," 132–34; García Fitz, *Castilla y León*, 335–44, 361–66; García Fitz, *Relaciones políticas y guerra*, 142–47.
61. Lincoln, "Beating Swords into Croziers," 98.
62. Linehan, *History and the Historians*, 295–97; Alvira Cabrer, *Las Navas de Tolosa 1212*, 467–509; Fromherz, "Making 'Great Battles' Great"; García Fitz, "Las Navas." In the sixteenth century, canonization efforts for Alfonso VIII saw even these crusading successes as an important sign of his royal sanctity: Ariazaleta and Jean-Marie, "En el umbral de santidad," 1–16.
63. Shadis, "Happier in Daughters," 84–85.
64. Lincoln, "Prosopography," 210–12.
65. Barrios García, *Documentos*, 75.
66. Powers, *Society Organized for War*, 42–43, 56–58.
67. Engel and Martín Martín, *Provincia Compostellana*, 4:42–43.
68. Palacios Martín, "Alfonso VIII y . . . Plasencia."
69. The archives of Plasencia are not extant before 1238, and there are no "capellanus hostis" or similarly named figures mentioned in the archival documents of Ávila: Barrios García, *Documentos*, 23–126. The clerics of Osma and Sigüenza had occupied each other's churches (violently) and it had taken the intervention of Alfonso VII to resolve the case some years before: Linehan, "Synod of Segovia," 38n29.
70. Linehan, "Synod of Segovia," 38n30, edited a short text from the court of Alfonso VIII that betrayed the tension between Osma and Sigüenza, which was sorted out by Celebruno.
71. On the role of Pedro "el Castellano" and his conflicts with Alfonso VIII, see Barton, *Aristocracy*, 115–16.
72. Barrios García, *Documentos*, 23–91.
73. I have surveyed this in the prosopographical appendix to this volume as well as in a separate essay, but have come to different conclusions than traditionalist local historiography from Ávila: Lincoln, "Prosopography," 212; Heras Hernández, *Los obispos de Ávila*, 76–92.
74. Morales y Tercero, "Inventario general," 258.
75. There are only ten from Osma: Loperráez Corvalán, *Descripción histórica*, 3:9–51; Riaño Rodríguez and Gutiérrez Aja, "Documentos," 217–82.
76. Desprèe, *La batalla de Sigüenza*, 177–227; Manrique García, *Sangre en La Alcarria*, 77–87.
77. Garrido Garrido, *Documentación*, vols. 1 and 2; Hernández Sánchez, *Los cartularios*; Abajo Martín, *Documentación de Palencia*; Villar García, *Documentación*.
78. Brown, *Body and Society*, 446–47.
79. "To claim that there was little that was unusual about the Leonese church in the twelfth century may seem a lame conclusion. It will appear less so to those who are acquainted with the work of Spanish ecclesiastical historians. Much of their writing has been underpinned

by the assumption that there was something special or unusual about the church in Spain, an assumption explicable in part by the tendency to study it in isolation, rather than as a member of the community of western Christendom." Fletcher, *Episcopate*, 221.
80. Ayala Martínez, "Los obispos," and Ayala Martínez, "Alfonso VIII y la Iglesia."
81. Reilly, *León-Castilla Under Alfonso VII*, 267.
82. Linehan, *Spanish Church*, 323:

> Could one fail to discern the intervention of the Almighty, the action of the divine hand in all this? The foregoing pages have been devoted to the experiences of a group who would surely have answered such a question in the negative: Fernando's own ecclesiastical contemporaries to whom so much of the cost of Christendom's successes was charged. In so far as the Roman Church spoke for Christendom, Christendom's debt to Fernando and his house was freely acknowledged; and it was paid by allowing the king to reimburse himself from the national church. To the pope it seemed perfectly equitable that the monarch who was responsible for smoking out "the filthy pagans" from the south of Spain should be given a fairly free hand in the frontier church and also further north.

83. The royal archive is the exception: González, *Alfonso VIII*, vols. 2 and 3, with corrections by Estepa Díez, Álvarez Borge, and Santamarta Luengos, *Poder real y sociedad*, 271–308.
84. González noted the value of Alfonso's reign as a period of Castilian independence, where the sources could be examined distinctly from neighboring kingdoms and where answers about the history of medieval León-Castile might be extracted: González, *Alfonso VIII*, 1:64–68.
85. A recent volume has begun to fill this gap: Gómez, Lincoln, and Smith, *King Alfonso VIII of Castile*.
86. Linehan, *Spanish Church*, 323–30.
87. Fletcher, *Episcopate*, 221–28.
88. Fletcher, *Saint James's Catapult*, 296–300.
89. Carl, *Bishopric*, 265–72.
90. See, inter alia, these works by Ayala Martínez: "Los obispos"; "Alfonso VIII y la Iglesia;" "Los obispos leoneses y las guerras santas de Fernando II," 1:91–105; "Breve semblanza."
91. Rucquoi, "Gundisalvus"; Rucquoi, "La double vie." The recent popular volume about Dominic of Osma shows the long-standing interest Rucquoi has had in Dominic's religious and cultural background: Rucquoi, *Dominicus Hispanus*.
92. Holndonner, *Kommunikation*, 37–108.
93. Foote, *Lordship*, 161–92; Miller, *Formation*, 3–14, 176–77; Freedman, *Diocese of Vic*, 145–49; Loud, *Latin Church*, 521–24; B. Hamilton, *Latin Church*, passim, e.g., 50, 84, 111, 113–14; Sayers, *Papal Judges Delegate*, 276–77.
94. Barton, *Aristocracy*, 6–7, 221–24; Doubleday, *Lara Family*, 3–4; Bianchini, *Queen's Hand*, 3–4, 257–61; Soifer Irish, *Jews and Christians*, 7–9, 11–12; Ruiz, *From Heaven to Earth*, 1–5, 8–11, 37–53.
95. I have recently laid out this method of "history from the middle": Lincoln, "About Three Clerics," 1–30.
96. On Gutierre Rodríguez Girón's death, the early modern (but usually reliable) testimony of Diego de Colmenares noted: "El catálogo de nuestros obispos, dice: Don Gutierre, hijo de Rui Girón, que murió en la batalla de Alarcos, año 1195." Colmenares, *Historia*, chap. XVIII.11.
97. Al-Ḥimyarī records the capture of the governor of Plasencia, referring either to Bishop Brecio or his archdeacon-turned-*alcalde* Pedro de Taiaborch, in the aftermath of 1195: al-Ḥimyarī, *Kitab ar-Rawd al Mi'tar*, 63. The only document in the archives when an inventory was taken

in the late eighteenth century was a papal bull dating to 1218: Morales y Tercero, "Inventario general," 258. Even in the late sixteenth century, when an antiquarian searched the see of Plasencia to compile the "anales" of the church, there was no known original of the foundational documents in Plasencia's archives. The composer of that chronicle noted that "[la] bula original de la erección de la dicha iglesia [de Plasencia] no se halla sino inserta en la del papa Honorio I, en el año quinto de su pontificado, que fue 1221 de la natividad del Señor, en la cual confirma la dicha erección a pedimento del rey don Fernando el Santo, tercero desde nombre": Correa y Roldán, "Anales," 45–46.

98. The approach of Bianchini's thoughtful work on Queen Berenguela demonstrates that it is possible to reconstruct the work of singular figures and situate them in their historical and historiographical context thoroughly enough to recolor the picture of both the historical persons in question and the world in which they lived. Effectively, scholars of medieval queenship like Bianchini have not only made women more historical but have turned the whole of medieval history inside out and made it more widely suitable for study. Bianchini, *Queen's Hand*, 3.

Chapter 2

This chapter's epigraph is drawn from de Castejón y Fonseca, *Primacia de la Santa Iglesia de Toledo*, 3:705: "Por la muerte de don Juan, de la persona de Cerebruno, sujeto tal, que pudo llenar el gran vacio que causò en España la falta de un varon tan grande. Fue Cerebruno Noble, i en el sentimiento de algunos, Frances de nación, i en virtud, letras, i prudencia tal, que mereció ser Maestro del niño Rei don Alonso."

1. Martínez Díez, *Alfonso VIII*, 25–40; González, *Alfonso VIII*, 1:673–85, 785–91; Barton, *Aristocracy*, 19; Doubleday, *Lara Family*, 35–43; Linehan, *History and the Historians*, 279–90; O'Callaghan, *Reconquest and Crusade*, 51.

2. The trend was most evident in the buildup to the Synod of Segovia and the ill-fated crusade against Fernando II's occupying forces: Vann, "Town Council," 49–50; Linehan, "Synod of Segovia," 42–43; Linehan, *History and the Historians*, 286–87; Lincoln, "Beating Swords into Croziers," 88–89; O'Callaghan, *Reconquest and Crusade*, 51.

3. Reeves, "Education and Religious Instruction," 106–7; S. Hamilton, *Church and People*, 182–88; Spinks, *Early and Medieval Rituals*, 134–43.

4. Jussen, *Spiritual Kinship*, 15–43; Baucells i Reig, *Vivir en la Edad Media*, 611–18. In addition to late medieval work, there is significant evidence of this trend in early modern Italy, and much of it suggests continuity from the late medieval period: Alfani, *Fathers and Godfathers*, 1–26; Alfani, Gourdon, and Vitali, "Social Customs." It is worth noting that Alfonso also had a chaplain from an early period, although his being mentioned in only a single charter makes it difficult to determine at what age Gutierre began his service: Garrido Garrido, *Documentación*, 1:252.

5. *Patrologia Latina* (hereafter PL), vol. 170, col. 1145C-D; *Historia Compostellana*, ed. Falque, 396–97.

6. Minguella y Arnedo, *Historia de Sigüenza*, 1:423.

7. On Celebruno's Poitevin heritage: ibid., 1:106–14; Rivera Recio, *La Iglesia de Toledo*, 1:199–200. Raimond of Toledo's role as a patron of arts and culture has garnered some attention: González Palencia, *El Arzobispo Don Raimundo*; Rivera Recio, *La Iglesia de Toledo*, 1:197–98, 2:296–98; Haskins, *Renaissance of the Twelfth Century*, 285–86; Linehan, *History and the Historians*, 269–78; Gonzálvez Ruiz, *Hombres y libros*, 66; Jacquart, "La Escuela de Traductores," 183–93. Celebruno first appears as a canon of Toledo in 1147 and did so

until his election to Sigüenza in 1155: Hernández Sánchez, *Los cartularios*, 63–103.

8. Hernández Sánchez, *Los cartularios*, 103–5; Peces Rata, *Paleografía y epigrafía*, 96–97; Minguella y Arnedo, *Historia de Sigüenza*, 1:397–405. On the number of foreign bishops in the twelfth century in Sigüenza, see González, *Alfonso VIII*, 1:418–19; Peces Rata, *Los obispos*, 38–47. A parallel can be charted in the bishops of Segovia during the same period: Bartolomé Herrero, "Obispos extranjeros."

9. The two sons of Alfonso VII appear as cadet-kings while they were still mere boys.

10. Reilly, "On Getting to Be a Bishop," 37–68; Reilly, "Court Bishops"; Reilly, *León-Castilla Under Alfonso VII*, 144–45.

11. Peces Rata, *Los obispos*, 40; Peces Rata, *Paleografía y epigrafía*, 96–97; Minguella y Arnedo, *Historia de Sigüenza*, 1:400.

12. Porres Martín-Cleto, *Los Anales Toledanos*, 131–32.

13. Nickson, *Toledo Cathedral*, 158–59, 162, 164; Linehan, *History and the Historians*, 278.

14. The examples of Anglo-Norman England to this effect are most prevalent: Brooke, *Churches and Churchmen*, 111–15.

15. This tendency to favor the "imported" clerics from beyond the Pyrenees is well worn in the accounts of Alfonso VII's reign, as well as those of his mother and grandfather: Reilly, *León-Castilla Under Alfonso VI*, 136–60; Reilly, *León-Castilla Under Urraca*, 225–50; Reilly, *León-Castilla Under Alfonso VII*, 240–73.

16. Hernández Sánchez, *Los cartularios*, 174.

17. Minguella y Arnedo, *Historia de Sigüenza*, 1:400; Estepa Díez, Álvarez Borge, and Santamarta Luengos, *Poder real y sociedad*, 314–16.

18. Minguella y Arnedo, *Historia de Sigüenza*, 1:401. Bianchini has noted that the role of Sancha Raimúndez was a stabilizing one in the border region between León and Castile as well as in the whole of her brother Alfonso VII's empire: Bianchini, "*Infantazgo*," 59–65; Bianchini, "Daughters, Wives."

19. Holndonner's catalog of the letters has missed several letters lost to the ravages of time, but his careful scholarship nevertheless uncovered several that coincided quite neatly with Celebruno's trip to the Council of Tours, discussed in greater detail below. See Holndonner, *Kommunikation*, 606–25, esp. 615–17; Somerville, *Pope Alexander III*, 22–32.

20. Erdmann, "Das Papsttum und Portugal," 55–58; Smith, "Iberian Legations," 91–97.

21. Smith, "Iberian Legations," 91–97; Reilly, *León-Castilla Under Alfonso VII*, 124–26; Lay, *Reconquest Kings*, 122–23.

22. A. Duggan, "Conciliar Law," 328–41.

23. Somerville, *Pope Alexander III*, 28.

24. Somerville's edition of the list of attending bishops does not mention Osma, and the early modern chronicler of the diocese does not mention the bishop's attending the council. It is also possible that Juan refused to journey to the council because his recent violent occupation of the border towns in question would earn him the rebuke of Alexander III, who later would uphold Celebruno's excommunication of Juan of Osma. See ibid., 28–29; Loperráez Corvalán, *Descripción histórica*, 1:137–43; Holndonner, *Kommunikation*, 412–15, 416–21, 608–12.

25. Holndonner, *Kommunikation*, 416–21.

26. Somerville, *Pope Alexander III*, 28–29.

27. "El 25 de octubre de 1166, el rey Alfonso VIII 'el Bueno' o 'el de las Navas de Tolosa,' hace donación a la Iglesia de Sigüenza, a su Obispo Don Cerebruno y sucesores en la misma . . . haciendo grandes elogios de su padrino Don Cerebruno, y de la Iglesia de Sigüenza que le había prestado grandes servicios." Peces Rata, *Los obispos*, 42.

28. "Decet regiam potestatem aliquem sibi bonum et fideliter servientem donis remunerare et de bonis

possessionibus suis in dominum et usum deo servientium, intuitu pietatis et misericordie transferre." Minguella y Arnedo, *Historia de Sigüenza*, 1:423.
29. "Dono inquam vobis patrino meo et ecclesie vestre predictam villam cum dictis pertinentiis pro servicio quod mihi devote et fideliter exhibuistis pro pluribus etiam dampnis que pro me ecclesia segontina sustinuit, ut libere et quiete pacificeque vos et successores vestri in perpetuum habeatis et possideatis." Ibid.
30. On this clerical allegiance, see Linehan, *History and the Historians*, 278–81, and Powers, *Society Organized for War*, 48–50, but also the earlier work of Luciano Serrano, *El obispado de Burgos*, 2:71–72. It is telling that, as Alfonso emerged from his minority in 1217, Fernando III and Queen Mother Berenguela rallied support from the clerics, towns, and nobility in a similar fashion to repulse the Leonese: see Bianchini, *Queen's Hand*, 141–53.
31. Linehan, "Synod of Segovia," 34.
32. Ibid.
33. Barton, *Aristocracy*, 191–94; Ayala Martínez, "Los obispos," 166–72, 180; Ayala Martínez, "Alfonso VIII: Cruzada y cristiandad," 79–80, 92–93; Ayala Martínez, "La Iglesia en tiempos de Alfonso VIII," 253n46; González, *Alfonso VIII*, 1:451–63.
34. I have outlined these similarities in a comparative table in my dissertation: Lincoln, "Episcopate," 76. I plan to treat these similarities in a future study.
35. "Celebrata est sinodus apud Secobiam a domino Johanne Toletano archiepiscopo et Hispaniarum primate et ab omnibus episcopis regni regis Aldefonsi, et quantum ad honorem Dei et exaltationem domini pape et ad pacem regni domini nostri Aldefonsi reformandam convenimus." Linehan, "Synod of Segovia," 42.
36. Cerda Costabal, "Leonor Plantagenet," 630–47; Lincoln, "*Una cum Uxore Mea*," 13–16; Barton, *Aristocracy*, 19.

37. Hernández Sánchez, *Los cartularios*, 516–21; Linehan, *History and the Historians*, 287–89; Holndonner, *Kommunikation*, 451–57, 585–87.
38. Rivera Recio, *La Iglesia de Toledo*, 2:102–6; Hernández Sánchez, *Los cartularios*, 152–55. On the process behind the issuing a *fuero*, see Clemente Ramos, "Buenos y malos fueros," 117–26; García-Gallo de Diego, "Aportación al estudio," 398–408. The history of Toledo's own *fuero* betrays the complexities that belie even the most well-studied of *fueros*: García-Gallo de Diego, "Los fueros de Toledo," 407–50.
39. Ladero Quesada, "La renta de sal," 822–23; Estepa Díez, Álvarez Borge, and Santamarta Luengos, *Poder real y sociedad*, 79–80; O'Callaghan, *Cortes of Castile-León*, 183–85.
40. Rivera Recio, *La Iglesia de Toledo*, 2:106; Hernández Sánchez, *Los cartularios*, 154–55. The confirmation of the *fuero* by a number of Celebruno's cathedral clergy suggests that the *fuero* was a mostly internal matter and the subscription of Joscelmo is likely due to their shared border and the affinity between the two men.
41. The Code of Cuenca rarely includes the clergy in its provisions: Powers, *Code of Cuenca*, 3, 4, 132, 134, 174.
42. Rivera Recio first numbered the clauses, and Hernández Sánchez saw fit to preserve them. Rivera Recio, *La Iglesia de Toledo*, 2:102–6; Hernández Sánchez, *Los cartularios*, 152–55.
43. For two contrasting views of this well-worn debate: Reynolds, *Fiefs and Vassals*, 1–47; Bisson, *Crisis*, 84–181, esp. 95–104. These were the same items that Nakashian has recently noted were likely to draw the high clergy and secular lords together in mutual interest: Nakashian, *Warrior Churchmen*, 6–8.
44. Burger, *Bishops, Clerks*, 36–37, 247–49; B. Hamilton, *Latin Church*, 91–92, 95–96, 111–12, 129–32.
45. "Quando fuerit fonsado cum tota Castella admonitio vadant de vos tertia pars de

cavelleros in illo fossado et pedones nullum fonssado faciant." Rivera Recio, *La Iglesia de Toledo*, 2:102–3.
46. Ibid., 2:103: "Alia fazendera non facient."
47. Powers, *Society Organized for War*, 17, 31.
48. "Infanzones qui intrarent in termino de Belinchonde de moiones ad intro tales foros habeant quomodo alios vicinos de Belinchon." Rivera Recio, *La Iglesia de Toledo*, 2:103.
49. "Iudeos qui ad Belinchon venerint populare tale foro et tales colonias habeant quomodo alios populatores christianos. Et qui de illo occiderit, octavo pectet." Ibid.
50. Soifer Irish, *Jews and Christians*, 42.
51. "Et homines de Belinchon qui ad archiepiscopum voluerint ire contra christianos habeant moion in Toleto et in Madrid et in Buitrago et quomodo la serra tenet et a medina et a Molina. Et contra sarrazenos non vadant ad illum." Rivera Recio, *La Iglesia de Toledo*, 2:105.
52. Ibid., 2:103: "Qui hominem occiderit de CCCtos morabotinos octaviuum pectet ad palatio." Ibid., 2:105: "Nullus homo non det homicidium per bestiam que occiderit hominem aut per parietem aut per casa aut si fuerit mortuus in aqua aut in silo aut in puteo aut in fonte aut si ab arbore fuerit occisus. Per istas totas aut alias qui fuerint similes istas non det homicidium."
53. Ibid., 2:105: "Iudez et alcaldes et saion mutent eos ad caput anni."
54. The notion that the *señor* of the town (the archbishop or his tenants) would not sit in court on Fridays, as a day of judgment, suggests this fact, especially when viewed in light of the other provisions about Christians suing other Christians and the need to travel to archiepiscopal stronghold to do so. "Et senior de la villa non sedeat cum alcaldes in die veneris et si ibi sederit, non iudicet alcaldes et si iudicaverint, pectent la peticione, et in illos alcaldes sedeant iudice e merino" (ibid.).
55. Ibid., 2:102: "In primis ut non habeatis manneriam nisi ut vos hereditetis unus ad alteros usque ad septimam generationem et qui de vobis non habuerit filios aut propinquos sive gentes, ponant suos vicinos causam illius pro eius anima ubi corpus suum iacuerit vel ubi ei placuert." Ibid., 2:103: "De Ganado de Belinchon non predate montadgo in nulla terra et qui hoc fecerit duplent illud."
56. Ibid., 2:105: "Et homine qui adduxerit ad Belnichon panem aut vinum ad vender, non pectet portadgo."
57. Ibid., 2:104: "Et cavalleros qui fuerint in fonsado cum archiepiscopo aut um suo seniore una quinta dent et homines de Belinchon qui a parte de palacio fecerint culpa, suo ganado aut sua pignora pignorent et non de suo vicino." Ibid., 2:105: "Pedones qui fuerint in guardia pro quinto dent septimo. Non dent quinta nin de Ganado nin vino et mauro et maura et de aliud non dent quinta."
58. Ayala Martínez has rightly observed that the prelates of Osma in the early part of Alfonso VIII's reign are shrouded in mysteries aplenty: Ayala Martínez, "Los obispos," 161–62.
59. The scholarship on the election of Osma has shown that, while the culprit was most likely Bernardo, the case is anything from perfectly positive: C. Duggan, "Case of Bernardo of Osma"; Linehan, "Royal Influence," Holndonner, *Kommunikation*, 430–32; Rivera Recio, *La Iglesia de Toledo*, 1:266–68.
60. C. Duggan, "Case of Bernardo of Osma"; Linehan, "Royal Influence."
61. The letters requiring the reform of the cathedral canons of Osma begin soon after the period in which Bernardo's election was to have illegally taken place: Archivo Catedralicio de Toledo (ACT) X.2.C.1.6. (= *Papsturkunden in Spanien. Kastilien*, no. 221), ACT X.2.C.1.8. (= *Papsturkunden in Spanien. Kastilien*, no. 183).
62. "Quia per simoniam irrepserunt, non sunt habendi inter episcopos, et ideo, si a sedibus, quas tenere videbantur, expulsi fuerint, non possunt

restitutionem petere antequam vocentur ad causam." Gratian of Chiusi, *Concordia Discordantium Canonum*, ed. Winroth et al., 304–5 (C.3 q.1 d.p.c.6).
63. Bernardo last appears as bishop of Osma in a charter dated to July 1176: González, *Alfonso VIII*, 2:432–33.
64. The letters from Alexander III, Lucius III, and Innocent III cover a three-decade span. They all concerned, according to the pontiffs, the question of secular canons being replaced with regular canons: Vicaire, "Saint Dominique," 40; Mansilla, *La documentación pontificia*, 205.
65. The letter was rediscovered by Vicaire, who proposed several dates for it, but his supposition of 1176 or 1179 seems to fit. Given that a new prelate was already present at Osma in 1179, the most likely date is 1176: see Vicaire, "Saint Dominique," 40.
66. This letter, ACT X.2.C.1.8 (= *Papsturkunden in Spanien. Kastilien*, no. 183), has been partially edited by Holndonner: Holndonner, *Kommunikation*, 432n94. This letter undermines Linehan's argument about the identity of the deposed bishop of Osma most significantly, because restoring a cleric to a post he was not supposed to have lost would have been a moot issue.
67. On the penury of the chapter: Linehan, *Spanish Church*, 101–51; Nickson, *Toledo Cathedral*, 45–48. On the qualities of the chapter and the frequent promotion of the canons: González, *Alfonso VIII*, 1:411–34; Rivera Recio, *La Iglesia de Toledo*, 2:22–29.
68. Burger, *Bishops, Clerks*, 6–8, 43–52.
69. See Miller's comments on "shoe money" in *Clothing the Clergy*, 20–23. Julián ben Tauro of Cuenca compromised with his canons about the conditions set for them to receive their vestimentary payments. This suggests that those payments were crucial to the ongoing maintenance of the kind of "exhibited holiness" described by Miller, but the reform charter was surely negotiated, as the examination in chapter 7, below, indicates.
70. This undated and unedited privilege is still preserved at Toledo. Given the emphasis on the number of canons present in the 1174 charter, I suspect that this document belongs to roughly the same period, likely just after the enumeration of the canons, in order to limit the draws on the episcopal patrimony: ACT Z.1.G.1.9A.
71. Hernández Sánchez, *Los cartularios*, 162–80.
72. González Palencia, *Los mozárabes*, nos. 91, 124, 134A, 134B, 157, 163, 176, 183, 215, 230, 234, 235, 239, 253, 257; Hernández, "Los mozárabes en Toledo," 57–124; Hernández Sánchez, *Los cartularios*, 136–232; López Pita, "Contribución," 429–32.
73. Olstein has shown that the names of Mozarabic canons do follow some patterns of hybridization, and I have followed his suggestions to this effect, except where explicit evidence makes clear that the canons in question belonged to a particular group: Olstein, *La era mozárabe*, 127.
74. For ease of reference, I will proceed in order. I reckon the following as "Leonese/Castilian" names: Didacus, Martinus M(artínez), Didacus, Rodericus, Pedro Martínez, Lupus, Guterius, Johannes Talavera, Didacus, Pedro Flaínez, and Domingo Pérez. As for Mozarabic names: Domingo González of Cuéllar, Domingo ben Abdala al-Polincheni, Forto, Salvetus, Nicolaus, Matihas, Dominicus Niger. The "foreign" names in the chapter include: Willielmus, Bernardus, Fredicus, Christoforus, Raimundus, Stephanus, Petrus Gilberti "aliena manu scribens," Robertus, Jordanus, Guillelmus, Felix, Robertus. Hernández Sánchez, *Los cartularios*, 160–61.
75. Of these, the subscriptions record the following: Petrus, Johannes, Johannes, Martinus, Paulus, and Johannes (ibid.).

76. Olstein, *La era mozárabe*, 123–32.
77. Hernández Sánchez, *Los cartularios*, 520.
78. There is surprisingly little scholarship on the prevalence of the *portionarios*, but their frequency in the reform of cathedral chapters in the late twelfth century suggests that they were more prevalent than we may have realized: Lincoln, "'It Pleased the Lord Bishop,'" 271–75.
79. Somerville, *Pope Alexander III*, 49.
80. ACT I.9.G.1.1A. (= *Papsturkunden in Spanien. Kastilien*, no. 157). I am grateful to the archival staff at the Archivo Catedralicio de Toledo for their assistance in reading this damaged letter.
81. Hernández Sánchez, *Los cartularios*, 522.
82. Sirantoine, *Imperator Hispaniae*, 345–49.
83. González, *Alfonso VIII*, 2:164–66; Hernández Sánchez, *Los cartularios*, 141–42, 144–45, 156–57, 165–66, 178–79. I have included Queen Leonor's own patronage of the Becket shrine, probably encouraged by Alfonso as well.

Chapter 3

This chapter's epigraph is drawn from Argaíz, *La soledad laureada*, fol. 349v: "Pero sea por un costado, sea por otro, el fue de la sangre Real de Francia, y de Castilla. Tomo el Habito de San Benito en San Zoil de Carrion, Priorato que era de S. Pedro de Cluni, el año del noviciado, fue a professar a Cluni, costumbre que tenían introducida los padres Cluniacenses: y de esta profesión he visto en el Archivo de Oña un testimonio, en cierto apuntamiento de una Escritura del Archivo de Carrion, que en Oña esta copiada. Crecio en edad Reymundo, fue descubriendo prendas, y talento para ocuparle en las letras, y cargos de la Religion."

1. Linehan, *History and the Historians*, 248; Linehan, *Spain, 1157–1300*, 28–32.
2. Lomax, "Don Ramón," 291.
3. Barton, *Aristocracy*, 26; Rivera Recio, *La Iglesia de Toledo*, 1:259–61; Linehan, *History and the Historians*, 248, 272, 291.
4. Abajo Martín, *Documentación de Palencia*, 120–22, 132–36.
5. The marriages of Ramon Berenguer III have been examined by de Vajay, but no son named Ramón exists in the sources: de Vajay, "L'aspect politique."
6. Abajo Martín, *Documentación de Palencia*, 97–120. Ramón de Minerva's family was mysterious even to Holndonner, and he was forced to rely on the conventional wisdom: "Auch als Überbringer der königliche Nuntius 'R.', in dem der katalanische Adelige Raimund de Minerva, Sohn Ramon Berenguers III., Bruder oder Halbbruder Berengarias, der Gemahlin Alfons' VII. und Verwandter des königlichen 'álferez' Graf Pons de Minerva (1140–44) gesehen wird, der im März 1148 schließlich für seine Dienste mit dem Bischofsstuhl von Palencia belohnt wurde." Holndonner, *Kommunikation*, 343.
7. On Ponce de Minerva, see Barton, "Two Catalan Magnates," 248–65.
8. González, *Alfonso VIII*, 1:143.
9. Ramón Berenguer was the father of children born from the 1110s to the 1130s, which fits into the possible scheme for Ramón de Minerva's birth: de Vajay, "L'aspect politique," 73.
10. Reglero de la Fuente has shown convincingly that San Zoilo was linked to Cluny: Reglero de la Fuente, *Cluny en España*, 340–42, 732–34. The connection to San Zoilo was a lasting one for Ramón (as will be shown in this chapter) and one that was well known, as the quotation from Argaíz as the head of this chapter suggests.
11. Abajo Martín, *Documentación de Palencia*, 97–120.
12. Ibid., 33–35, 104–6.
13. The division of the kingdom was provided for by the position of the two brothers as cadet-kings during Alfonso VII's life and by his will: González, *Alfonso VIII*, 1:663–73.
14. The Treaty of Sahagún has been the subject of comment in several instances: González, *Alfonso VIII*, 1:668–71; Linehan, *Spain, 1157–1300*, 9; Martínez

Díez, *Alfonso VIII*, 22; Lincoln, "(Re)Writing a History."

15. The date of Sancho's death is recorded in, among other places, the *Anales Toledanos*: Porres Martín-Cleto, *Los Anales Toledanos*, 134.
16. Ibn Ṣāḥib al-Ṣalāh appears to be the first to call Fernando II *al-babuš*: Ibn Ṣāḥib al-Ṣalāh, *Al-Mann bil-Imāma*, 145.
17. Queen Blanca died either from complications arising from Alfonso's birth or as a result of a subsequent pregnancy and a difficult delivery (perhaps of a royal brother, called Sancho): González, *Alfonso VIII*, 1:144–47.
18. Simon Barton has detailed the actions of the nobility in the minority of Alfonso VIII, but the narrative is well attested by Linehan, González, and Martínez Díez: Barton, *Aristocracy*, 19–23; González, *Alfonso VIII*, 1:147–79; Linehan, *History and the Historians*, 279–80; Martínez Díez, *Alfonso VIII*, 25–40.
19. *DRH*, VII.16.29–31, VII.18.32–35; Linehan, *Spain, 1157–1300*, 26.
20. On the Cortes of Castile in the period, there is much scholarship: Cerda Costabal, "Assemblies of Alfonso VIII"; Cerda Costabal, "Parliamentary Calendar"; O'Callaghan, *Cortes of Castile-León*, 9–20; Procter, *Curia and Cortes*, 70–94.
21. Celebruno's relationship to Alfonso VIII is detailed in the previous chapter.
22. Barton, *Aristocracy*, 19–20, 264–65; Doubleday, *Lara Family*, 35–38.
23. Barton, *Aristocracy*, 264–65; Doubleday, *Lara Family*, 36–37; González, *Alfonso VIII*, 1:147–49; Linehan, *History and the Historians*, 279–80; Linehan, *Spain, 1157–1300*, 25–26.
24. Linehan, *Spain, 1157–1300*, 25–26.
25. On the early existence of fairs (*feria*) in León and Castile, see O'Callaghan, *History of Medieval Spain*, 297; O'Callaghan, *Cortes of Castile-León*, 187.
26. González, *Alfonso VIII*, 2:211–13.
27. On the phenomenon of self-armament and self-coronation in Portugal, León, and especially Castile: González, *Alfonso VIII*, 1:18n147; Ruiz, "Une royauté sans sacre."
28. There are at least six additional charters of donation or confirmation from the reign of Alfonso VIII: 2:263–65, 734–36, 769–70; 3:9, 154–55, 315–17, 625–27.
29. González, *Alfonso VIII*, 1:145, 145–46n37, 146, 147, 148, 148n48, 149, 149n50.
30. Although she makes these claims using and commenting on the ceremony around the self-knighting of Fernando III, it stands to reason that the court memory of the same actions by Alfonso VIII influenced the process. Bianchini, *Queen's Hand*, 146–48.
31. Abajo Martín, *Documentación de Palencia*, 147–48.
32. Ibid., 127–29, 151–53.
33. Barton, "Count, Bishop and Abbot," 89–97.
34. Abajo Martín, *Documentación de Palencia*, 143–45. The impact of the Valladolid donation was enormous and gave Palencia increased influence in the region: González, *Historia de Palencia*, 1:183–85. On the Infantazgo, see T. Martin, "Fuentes de potestad"; T. Martin, "Hacia una clarificación"; Bianchini, *Queen's Hand*, 37–68; Bianchini, "*Infantazgo*."
35. Abajo Martín, *Documentación de Palencia*, 158–60. The king had given, in 1175, forty Jewish families (presumably their worth of tax revenues) to the bishops of Palencia (ibid., 153–55).
36. See the excellent work by Maya Soifer Irish on grants of this type of lordship over Jewries in medieval Iberia: "*Tamquam domino proprio*," 534–66; *Jews and Christians*, 132–50.
37. Vaca Lorenzo, "El obispado de Palencia," 46–47, 53–70; Abajo Martín, *Documentación de Palencia*, 5–9.
38. For the text of this *fuero*, see Abajo Martín, *Documentación de Palencia*, 125–26.
39. Ibid., 167–69.
40. Ibid., 167–68:

    Inter quos, Raimundus, palentine sedis episcopus, karissimus avunculus meus, precipuus extitit, qui, cum devotione omnimoda, vigili ope et diuturnis sudoribus, Deo pro ordine, mihi pro fidelitate militabat. Qui nichil pretermittens de conmisso sibi officio totus regalibus serviciis vacare videretur ut non solum pastor set et regni reparator posset nuncupari, qui, pro tam devote michi exhibito servicio, palentine ecclesie universis fere redditibus et hereditatibus, partim pignori obligatis, partim venditis, necessitate ductus, nullatenus volens subtrahere manum meis serviciis consuetudines et foros ecclesie Palentine, de quorum emolumento iam dicta ecclesia antiquitus ex magna parte sustentabatur, soltavit et vendit, prout potuit, palentino concilio. Precium inde habitum in ipsum retorquens concilium ut ipsis palentini benigniores et pronitiores coadiutores ad guerram regni proinde existerent.

41. The specifics of each example will be detailed below, but the text of the *fuero* was edited most recently by Abajo Martín in *Documentación de Palencia*, 173–81.
42. An extensive analysis of the *fueros* of Palencia in the time of Alfonso VIII reveals a number of similarities in the kinds of provisions sought by the townsfolk in Palencia and in the rest of the kingdom: González Mínguez, "Fueros palentinos," 59–76.
43. "Habeat episcopus . . . medietatem de homicidio et totum furtum integrum et traitionem." Abajo Martín, *Documentación de Palencia*, 174.
44. "In Palentia, nullus milites armatus de seniore det solidos pro marcio vel aliquid, nec, eo mortuo, uxor eius usque nubat." Ibid.
45. "Quicumque diruperit mercatum de Palencia vel feriam pectet LX solidos." Ibid., 177.
46. "Qui miserit merdam in bocca alterius pectet CCC solidos." Ibid., 176.
47. "Qui per malam voluntatem miserit caput eius in rivo, ita ut totumcaput aqua cooperiatur, pectet CCC solidos." Ibid.
48. In one instance, Celebruno of Toledo was instructed to investigate whether, as the pontiffs had heard, Ramón had appointed a nephew to a benefice: ACT X.2.A.2.3A (= *Papsturkunden in Spanien. Kastilien*, no. 148).
49. Serrano, *El obispado de Burgos*, 2:97–98.
50. For the recent scholarship on the Infantazgo, see T. Martin, "Fuentes de potestad," 97–136; T. Martin, "Hacia una clarificación"; Bianchini, *Queen's Hand*, 37–68; Bianchini, "*Infantazgo*."
51. Estepa Díez, "Memoria y poder real," 190–91, 195n30. Holt has made a thorough study of this trend for the reign of Fernando III, where the evidence confirms Estepa Díez's thesis: Holt, "*In eo tempore*."
52. Estepa Díez, "Memoria y poder real," 189–208.
53. González, *Alfonso VIII*, 2:625–72; *DRH*, VII.18.36; *CLRC*, 43.
54. Abajo Martín, *Documentación de Palencia*, 167–86.
55. Serrano, *El obispado de Burgos*, 2:97.
56. Abajo Martín, *Documentación de Palencia*, 167: "Cum devotione omnimoda, vigili ope et diuturnis sudoribus, Deo pro ordine, mihi pro fidelitate militabat." Ibid., 165: "propter inmensa et innumerabilia servicia que mihi devotissime fecit et facit."
57. Linehan, "Synod of Segovia," 32–36; Vann, "Town Council," 48–50.
58. Linehan, *History and the Historians*, 248.
59. The letter is catalogued in Toledo as ACT X.2.A.2.11 and was partially edited by Rivera Recio: Rivera Recio, *La Iglesia de Toledo*, 1:259–60n33.
60. Ibid.
61. Lomax, "Don Ramón," 291n16, cites a number of texts. Among them is Biblioteca Nacional de España (hereafter BNE) MS 13035, a compilation of notes and texts crafted by Burriel, for one of his many ecclesiastical history

projects in the early eighteenth century. Unfortunately, the texts cited by Burriel went unedited and are accessible only in the manuscript. Berger's work has connected that text with ACT X.2.A.2.3A, a text that survives well enough to compare its contents favorably with Burriel's edition. Berger, *Provincia Toletana*, 50; *Papsturkunden in Spanien. Kastilien*, no. 148.

62. On the eclipse of Romanesque Palencia by the later Gothic cathedral begun in 1321, see Ara Gíl and Martín González, "El arte gótico en Palencia," in J. González, *Historia de Palencia*, 1:318–19. The consecration privilege sent by Honorius III to Ramón's early thirteenth-century successor is well preserved, and the tenor of the letter suggests that it had been ongoing since the early reconquest: Salcedo Tapia, "Vida de Don Tello Téllez de Meneses," 175–76; Abajo Martín, *Documentación de Palencia*, 280–81.

63. Tom Nickson has recently offered a view of the costs of the early-thirteenth-century efforts to build in Toledo and the ways in which those costs affected construction: Nickson, *Toledo Cathedral*, 59–75.

64. There are at least four such letters suggesting that Palencia's discipline was a matter of significant concern for the papacy, and there are copies preserved still in Toledo: ACT X.2.A.2.3A (= *Papsturkunden in Spanien. Kastilien*, no. 148), ACT X.2.A.2.3B (= *Papsturkunden in Spanien. Kastilien*, no. 150), ACT A-6.D.1.12, and ACT X.2.A.2.3D (= *Papsturkunden in Spanien. Kastilien*, no. 152).

65. Álvarez Borge, "La Rioja," 206–7, 209–14, 224–30.

66. González, *Alfonso VIII*, 2:440–43; Lomax, "Don Ramón," 1:281.

67. Corral, "Alfonso VIII," 31.

68. Cerda Costabal, "Parliamentary Calendar," 8–11.

69. Mansilla, "Inocencio III," 13n16.

70. Corral, "Alfonso VIII," 32.

71. Ibid., 41.

72. On the Council of Tours: Somerville, *Pope Alexander III*. On the Synod of Segovia: Linehan, "Synod of Segovia," 31–44; Linehan, *History and the Historians*, 280–83. On the itineraries and councils of Cardinal Hyacinth Bobone, see Smith, "Iberian Legations." On Palencia's attendance at Lateran III, see Mansi, *Sacrorum Conciliorum*, 22:216.

73. On the control of clergy by the papacy and clerical attempts to harness papal ideals for their own local purposes: Robinson, *Papacy*, 209–43. For the use of assemblies to shape the relationship between monarchs and nobles: Bisson, *Crisis*, 529–72.

74. Barton, "El Cid"; Ayala Martínez, "Alfonso VII y la cruzada"; Ayala Martínez, "Iglesia y violencia."

75. Fletcher, *Saint James's Catapult*.

76. Fita, "Obispos mozárabes."

77. Lipskey, "Chronicle of Alfonso the Emperor," 163; Barton and Fletcher, *World of El Cid*, 251.

78. B. Hamilton, *Latin Church*, 113–36; Nakashian, *Warrior Churchmen*; Gerrard, *Church at War*. On the phenomenon of armsbearing clergy: L. Duggan, *Armsbearing and the Clergy*, 102–45. I have outlined this case more generally in Lincoln, "Beating Swords into Croziers," 88–91, and Lincoln, "*Mihi pro fidelitate militabat*," 19–21.

79. The papacy's development of these tools and the rise of an administrative church were two of the more important processes of the long twelfth century: Robinson, *Papacy*, 121–208; Winroth, "Legal Revolution."

80. On the church's role during Urraca's reign: Reilly, *León-Castilla Under Urraca*, 225–50.

Chapter 4

This chapter's epigraph is drawn from Fernández de Madrid, *Silva Palentina*, [1:] 221: "El VIII obispo de Palencia fue Don Enrico, que algunos llaman Santo Arderico: fue santa varon en tiempo del rey Don Alonso octavo; murió en el año de 1208, por quien dizen que nro. Señor hiço muchos milagros; yo ví muchas veces sacar tierra de su sepultura, dicen que para sanar de las enfermedades, y en las caxas de as reliquias de esta iglia. está un çapatico de cuero con un letrero que dice *Sandalia Sancti Anderici.*"

1. The contours of medieval sanctity were long ago sketched by Goodich, Bell and Weinstein, Vauchez, and Ward. While none of these authors examines Alderico in detail, they do suggest that his sanctity was within the norm: Goodich, *Vita Perfecta*, 213–41; Bell and Weinstein, *Saints and Society*, 135–37; Vauchez, *Sainthood*, 157–246; Ward, *Miracles*, 166–92.
2. His subscriptions are consistent among original charters, and see his seals, some of which survive in good condition: Fernández de Madrid, *Silva Palentina*, plates between 222 and 223.
3. Maffei offered the first evidence for Serrano's conjecture that Alderico was of Lombard origins, but Serna Serna's edition of the obituaries of Burgos makes Alderico's background incontrovertible: Serrano, *El obispado de Burgos*, 2:161–62, 2:162n11; Maffei, "Fra Cremona," 42n30; Serna Serna, *Los obituarios*, 283, 395.
4. Membership in the cathedral clergy was a significant social status marker, as Ruiz has shown for two clans: Ruiz, "Prosopografia burgalesa," 467–99.
5. This was relatively common in the late eleventh and early twelfth centuries, as Reilly, *León-Castilla Under Alfonso VI*, 72–82, and Reilly, *León-Castilla Under Urraca*, 29–34, have demonstrated.
6. Garrido Garrido, *Documentación*, 1:247, 272, 274.
7. Tanner, *Decrees*, 212.
8. The influx of immigrants from northern Italy and parts of Francia is attested by specialist scholarship, but the potential of these "Franci" was made all too clear by the success of Henri and Raymond of Burgundy: Reilly, *León-Castilla under Alfonso VI*, 72–82; Reilly, *León-Castilla Under Urraca*, 29–34.
9. On Lanfranco, who seems to have been named a canon by his brother Alderico, see Serna Serna, *Los obituarios*, 395; Abajo Martín, *Documentación de Palencia*, 231–34. I have sketched his career in Lincoln, "About Three Clerics," 13–18.
10. Similar privileges survive for Gonzalo of Segovia (r. 1177–94) and Juan Yáñez of Cuenca (r. 1183–95): ACT X.2.B.1.1B; ACT X.1.E.1.6.
11. González, *Alfonso VIII*, 2:514–15.
12. See chapter 3.
13. Minguella y Arnedo, *Historia de Sigüenza*, 1:129. Joscelmo was far enough from his see that only his arm was interred at the cathedral in the Capilla del Doncel: Peces Rata, *Paleografía y epigrafía*, 51.
14. The proximity of Toledo and Sigüenza and the archbishop's influence over his royal godson make Celebruno's influence on the decision to promote Alderico seem very great indeed. Without the royal nod, clerics would find the patronage well drying up; without archiepiscopal favor, censures and taxes would weigh far heavier on a cathedral chapter.
15. Minguella y Arnedo, *Historia de Sigüenza*, 1:442.
16. Ibid., 1:444–47, quote from 445: "Pro multis et maximis servitiis que mihi devote et fideliter hucusque ex hibuistis et cotidie exhibetis."
17. For the cases on which Alderico served: Barrios García, *Documentos*, 65–68, 69; Garrido Garrido, *Documentación*, 1:342–43; Hernández Sánchez, *Los cartularios*, 522–23. By the early thirteenth century, the procedure for nominating a judge-delegate was well established: Sayers, *Papal Judges Delegate*, 109–18.
18. Because Rodrigo de Finojosa played a major role in resolving this dispute, the conflict is described at greater length in chapter 8.
19. Ramón's career is treated at length in chapter 3.

20. The record of Marino's arbitration is preserved in the records of Ávila from early 1182, suggesting that the case began well before that: Barrios García, *Documentos*, 65–68.
21. Gonzalo is poorly known to scholarship, but Bartolomé Herrero considered him to be a local and of modest capabilities: Bartolomé Herrero, "Obispos extranjeros." The records for Gonzalo's case against Ávila are preserved in Burgos: Garrido Garrido, *Documentación*, 1:342–43.
22. Colmenares, *Historia*, 150–51; Linehan, "Royal Influence"; C. Duggan, "Case of Bernado of Osma," 77–96.
23. The dispute's history and the resolution of 1190 have been treated in detail in Herrero de la Fuente, "Los documentos."
24. Minguella y Arnedo, *Historia de Sigüenza*, 1:449.
25. Lomax, "Don Raimundo," 1:291.
26. ACT X.2.A.2.7 (= *Papsturkunden in Spanien. Kastilien*, no. 223).
27. On Ramón's impressive financial improvements to the episcopal fisc of Palencia, see chapter 3.
28. For Palencia's attempt to become an archdiocese, see Vaca Lorenzo, "El obispado de Palencia," 47–52. Regarding Diego Gelmírez and the granting of Mérida's provincial rights to Santiago, Fletcher's narrative is still standard: Fletcher, *Saint James's Catapult*, 107, 196–99.
29. ACT A.6.E.1.18 (= *Papsturkunden in Spanien. Kastilien*, no. 202).
30. The list of signatures records the presence of "Odelricus Seguntinus" among the members of Toledo's province who attended the council: Mansi, *Sacrorum Conciliorum*, 22.216.
31. Tanner, *Decrees*, 220. On the impact of this canon on Iberian cathedral schools: Guijarro González, "Las escuelas y la formación del clero"; Guijarro González, "Masters and Schools"; Kosto, "Reconquest," 103–6.
32. Barrow, *Clergy*, 208, 210–17, 226–27; Thomas, *Secular Clergy*, 112, 242; Pixton, *German Episcopacy*, 211–13. Boyle expressed some skepticism about the scale of the growth of cathedral masters, but his comments should be read as balancing the regional and happenstance quality of the development of these schools rather than negating them: see Boyle, "Constitution 'Cum ex eo,'" 342. Numbers of schools and chapters that sponsored them and the relationship to the Third Lateran Council are hard to come by, but Yolles has recently recuperated much of the church's reputation for intellectual activity in the Crusader States: Yolles, "Latin Literature," 9–169.
33. "Sapientes a Galliis et Ytalia convocavit, ut sapiencie disciplina a regno suo nunquam abesset, et magistros omnium facultatum Palencie congregavit, quibus et magna stipendia est largitus, ut omni studium cupienti quasi manna in os influeret sapiencia cuiuslibet facultatis." *DRH*, VII.xxxiiii.
34. "Eo tempore rex Adefonsus evocavit magistros teologichos et aliarum artium liberalium et Palencie scolas constituit procurante reverentissimo et nobilissimo viro Tellione eiusdem civitatis episcopo." Lucas Tudensis, *Chronicon Mundi*, IV.84, 57–60.
35. "Postmodum autem missus Palentiam, ut ibi liberalibus informaretur scientiis, quarum studium ea tempestate vigebat ibidem; postquam eas, ut sibi videbatur, satis edidict, relictis his studiis, tanquam in quibus temporis huius angustias minus fructuose vereretur expendere, ad theologie studium convolavit." Jordan of Saxony, "Libellus," 28.
36. The early history of the school of Palencia is a well-worn path, but the recent work of María Jesús Fuente Pérez has added a much-needed critique of how much water can be drawn from rocky sources: Fuente Pérez, *El estudio general*. See also Lorenzo, "Palencia," 167–69; Celada, "La enseñanza de la Teologia," 116; Martínez Diez, "La Universidad de Palencia"; Adeline

Rucquoi, "La double vie." On Dominic's school days, see Tugwell's analysis in his series for the *Archivum Fratrum Praedicatorum*: Tugwell, "Notes."

37. Walz, "Acta Canonizationis," 123–94; García-Serrano, *Preachers in the City*, 23–46.
38. Rucquoi found one text slightly later, but in such an early history of a school, the few additional months matter. The early date (1 April 1191) is found in Minguella y Arnedo, *Historia de Sigüenza*, 1:471, but Rucquoi cited a copy of the same text preserved at the monastery of San Juan de Burgos: Rucquoi, "La double vie," 725n7.
39. González, *Alfonso VIII*, 2:505–744; Abajo Martín, *Documentación de Palencia*, 194–97, 212–15, 215–18.
40. For a synthesis of these trends, see Rucquoi, "Éducation et société," 7–14.
41. Linehan, *History and the Historians*, 346.
42. Fletcher, *Saint James's Catapult*, 324–26; Fletcher, *Episcopate*, 53–61.
43. Rucquoi, "La double vie," 723–33.
44. The earlier evidence is better documented in the north, but the impact of education on young clerics is a well-studied phenomenon: Barrow, *Clergy*, 170–208.
45. For the accounts for Dominic's *studium* days at Palencia, see Jordan of Saxony, "Libellus," 28.
46. The *Collationes patrum* of Cassian was recorded as one of Dominic's favorite books as early as Jordan of Saxony: see ibid., 32–33. The inventories of Palencia, as they are at present, were certainly reduced by the predations of early modern wars and the *desamortización* programs of the nineteenth century: San Martín Payo, "Catálogo del Archivo."
47. Abajo Martín, *Documentación de Palencia*, 212–15.
48. Ibid., 194–97, 212–15, 15–18.
49. Garrido Garrido, *Documentación*, 2:266–69; Abajo Martín, *Documentación de Palencia*, 215–18.
50. Abajo Martín, *Documentación de Palencia*, 215–18.
51. Ibid., 230–31, 31–34, 38–41, 63–64.
52. Ibid., 231–34, 34–35, 37–38.
53. Rucquoi, "L'université de Palencia," 8–10.
54. See the scholarship omnibus cited above, note 36.
55. On the life and work of Domingo Gonzalez, see the work of Fidora and Rucquoi: Fidora, "La recepción de San Isidoro"; Fidora, "Dominicus Gundissalinus"; Rucquoi, "Gundisalvus." For the problematic label of a "school" at Toledo and its history during the reign of Alfonso VIII, see Benito Ruano, "Ámbito y ambiente"; Gargatagli, "La historia de la escuela"; Gonzálvez Ruiz, "La escuela de Toledo."
56. Rucquoi, "La double vie," 723–33.
57. On the reputation of Toledo as a hub for translations and the ways in which this skews the reputation of the school as a whole: Kosto, "Reconquest," 103–6. Ramón Gonzálvez Ruiz included an entire index of translators at work in Toledo, which demonstrates this point in a rather dramatic fashion, albeit not specifically for this period: Gonzálvez Ruiz, *Hombres y libros*, 475–77.
58. Jordan of Saxony, "Libellus," 28.
59. Barrios García, *Documentos*, 84; Hernández Sánchez, *Los cartularios*, 220–44.
60. Ruiz has noted that contemporary wills begin to subdivide their bequests to spread around the patronage of the deceased to a variety of monastic houses, collegiate chapters, and other ecclesiastical endowments: Ruiz, *From Heaven to Earth*, 41–53, 120–24.
61. The letter is dated 1 March 1185, which meant that the dispute had already happened in the first year of Alderico's episcopate at Palencia. ACT E.7.C.2.7 (= *Papsturkunden in Spanien. Kastilien*, no. 230).
62. Clement's letter is dated 14 April 1190 and says very little about what exactly provoked King Alfonso: ACT X.2.A.2.2. (= *Papsturkunden in Spanien. Kastilien*, no. 261).

63. The cases of unrest at Paris and Oxford suggest that cathedral schools could be messy businesses: Fumagalli Beono Brocchieri, "Intellectual," 186–87.
64. Mansilla, *La documentación pontificia*, 322–23, 335–36, 385; Garrido Garrido, *Documentación*, 2:82–83, 109–11.
65. Her lengthy discussions have shown that Berenguela's agency not only received recognition by the guarantors of the dissolution agreements but also endured until the death of Alfonso IX: Bianchini, *Queen's Hand*, 37–179.
66. Mansilla, *La documentación pontificia*, 322–23, 335–36, 385; Garrido Garrido, *Documentación*, 2:82–83, 109–11.
67. Tanner, *Decrees*, 216–17.
68. Garrido Garrido, *Documentación*, 1:343–44.
69. Ibid., 2:6–7.
70. A group of judges-delegate was dispatched to investigate "super simonia duplici, dilapidatione, absolutione incidentium in canonem sententie promulgata, quodque appellationibus ad nos interpositis deferre contempneret, nencnon quod in manibus suis, ultra tempus in concilio Lateranensi statutum, vacantem tenuierit dignitatem, et quod furtum quoddam subtraxerit instrumentum, in quo a iure canonicorum iura episcopalia dinstinguuntur." Mansilla, *La documentación pontificia*, 388.
71. Garrido Garrido, *Documentación*, 2:142–43, 143–44, 145–46, 147–48; Abajo Martín, *Documentación de Palencia*, 231–34.
72. An omnibus citation would run for pages, but see Honorius of Autun, Hugh of St. Victor, the second recension of Gratian's *Decretum*, and Lotario di Segni (Innocent III): *PL*, 172, col. 0607A–D; *PL*, 177, col. 0354A; Gratian of Chiusi, *Decretum Gratiani*, ed. Friedberg, D.96.c.14; Lotario di Segni, *De sacro altaris mysterio*, *PL* 217, 780D–781A.
73. Chenu, *Nature, Man, and Society*, 1–48, 202–38.
74. Jervis et al., "Stepping Across the Mediterranean." Also of importance is the restoration and identification of a shoe belonging to Queen Eleanor Plantagenet (r. 1170–1214) and the qualities that footwear of the highest grade in the late twelfth and early thirteenth centuries might have had: Barrigón, "Not So Royal Shoe."
75. Miller, *Clothing the Clergy*, 21–23; Hoose, "*Sabatati*," 257–73.
76. San Martín Payo, "Inscripciones," 56 and 56n70. The full text of the Acta Capitulares may be found in Archivo Catedralicio de Palencia, Acta Capitulares, 39, fol. 25or. The pertinent details have been transcribed and edited in the edition of the *Silva Palentina*: Fernández de Madrid, *Silva Palentina*, 128–29n1.
77. Archivo Catedralicio de Palencia, Armario I, Legajo 1, no. 15 (modern no. 15, 1501), fol. 9r. This may be the same reliquary mentioned in a different, earlier inventory from 1481, but the text is vague, noting that there was just "otro sin titlulo que dise isti santi reliquariae Obispo palentina." Archivo Catedralicio de Palencia, Armario IV, Legajo 8, no. 1 (modern no. 884, 1481/82).
78. For more on the way the cult memory of San Julián altered the memory of the prelate, rather than simply enhancing it, see chapter 7.
79. Vauchez, *Sainthood*, 167–73; Bell and Weinstein, *Saints and Society*, 135–37, 142–219; Goodich, *Vita Perfecta*, 26–36, 48–51, 142–47, 213–41.
80. This is the assertion made by the thirteenth-century chroniclers who made Alfonso VIII's charter of patronage for the school the foundational moment, rather than the proliferation of masters during Ramón de Minerva's and Alderico di Palacio's episcopates. The *magistri* at Palencia included at least six different individuals during Alderico's tenure as bishop: Abajo Martín, *Documentación de Palencia*, 212–15; ibid., 194–97, 212–15,

215–18; Garrido Garrido, *Documentación*, 2:266–69; Abajo Martín, *Documentación de Palencia*, 215–18; ibid., 215–18; ibid., 230–31, 231–34, 238–41, 263–64; ibid., 231–34, 234–35, 237–38.

81. Fernández de Madrid, *Silva Palentina*, 221n1; Rafael de Floranes y Encinas, *Origen de los estudios de Castilla, especialmente los de Valladolid, Palencia y Salamanca*, BNE, MS 10839, fols. 67v–94v, esp. 84v, where Floranes notes: "A diligencia, dice, de un tio suyo [i.e. de Pedro González Telmo] Obispo de aquella Ciudad (por la cuenta D. Arderico antecesor de D. Tello) fue puesto allí a los Estudios desde muy joven." In his 1633 treatment of the history of San Antolín, the patron saint of Palencia, Francisco de Sandoval noted that the bishops of Palencia had, even then, a reputation for holiness in the days of the grand reconquest: "la santidad de su Iglesia; la nobleza de sus hijos; la virtud de sus prevendados, el valor de sus mayores; la excelencia de sus Obispos, y la estimación en las Religiones mas apartadas que la veneran por la mas insigne Ciudad en todos tiempos que conoció la España Tarraconense. Escrivire también de S. Enrico Santísimo Prelado nuestro por quien hecho Dios grandísimos milagros, no me olvidado de la Universidad ilustrísima que aquí floreció, enriquezida por el Rey don Alonso el Octavo." Sandoval, *San Antonino Español*, fol. 87r–v.

82. The identification of Saint Pedro González Telmo as Alderico's nephew was attested widely in early modern accounts, although there is no contemporary notation of such a relationship: González Chantos y Ullauri, *Santa Librada*, 178–91; BNE, MS 10839, fols. 67v–94v, esp. 84v, where Floranes notes: "A diligencia, dice, de un tio suyo [i.e. de Pedro González Telmo] Obispo de aquella Ciudad (por la cuenta D. Arderico antecesor de D. Tello) fue puesto allí a los Estudios desde muy joven." García-Serrano has traced the role of Pedro González Telmo within Fernando III's court and his role as a chaplain of the king: García-Serrano, *Preachers in the City*, 15, esp. 15n44. The house where Dominic lived was transformed by the episcopate of Palencia in the sixteenth century: San Martín Payo, "Inventorio de la Catedral de Palencia," 28 (Arm. I, Leg. 3, no. 14, modern no. 56), 260 (Arm. VI, Leg. 2, no. 4, modern no. 1058).

83. San Martín Payo, "Inscripciones," 56.

84. Perry, *Sacred Plunder*, 2–6.

85. For example, the chapel of Saint Jerome: Archivo Catedralicio de Palencia, Armario I, Legajo 3, no. 48, modern no. 48 (1637).

86. This inventory is held not in the Archivo Catedralicio de Palencia but in the office of the director of the Museo Diocesano de Arte Sacro. As such, it has no formal shelf number, since it lives, tastefully framed, in his closet until the faded beauty of the parchment polychromed text can be restored. I am grateful to the curator of the Museo Diocesano de Arte Sacro de Palencia, Don José Luís Calvo Calleja, for allowing me to consult this unedited and uninventoried text.

87. José Luís Calvo Calleja investigated the contents of the reliquaries of his collections with me to determine if, by chance, any of the *arquetas* or *relicarios* in their collections might presently contain Alderico's relics. Despite our thorough efforts, none of the reliquaries that we opened contained such a find; rather, they held relics from Roman or Toledan sources.

88. Cerda Costabal and Martínez Llorente have proposed that the Napoleonic hypothesis is most suitable in "Un documento inédito," 61–62.

89. González Dávila, *Teatro eclesiástico*, 2:152.

90. Nickson has observed a similar trend for the church of Toledo's building program: Nickson, *Toledo Cathedral*, 131–56.

91. On this pattern generally in Castile as compared to other frontier regions, see the final chapter of this volume.
92. On the *arras* lands awarded to Leonese and Castilian queens, see Bianchini, *Queen's Hand*, 59–61.

Chapter 5

This chapter's epigraph is drawn from Argaíz, *La soledad laureada*, fol. 295r: "D[on] Martín Bazán. Fue Monge de San Benito del Monasterio de San Millán de la Cogulla y de Monge salió por Obispo, sin haber sido Abad a lo que yo imagino, porque en el Catálogo de los hijos ilustres de aquel Convento está: Martínus Monachus Episcopus."

1. Hinnebusch, *History of the Dominican Order*, 1:18; González, *Reino de Castilla*, 1:427–28; Vicaire, *Saint Dominic*, 40–42; Tugwell, "Notes," 34–47. The exceptions, of course, are those scholars working on the episcopate in Castile: Ayala Martínez, "Los obispos," 161; Ayala Martínez, "Alfonso VIII y la Iglesia," 270n97; Holndonner, *Kommunikation*, 434n100.
2. This example would not be lost on Martín's successor, Diego d'Acebo, but only Gallén has treated Diego in any detail: Gallén, "Les voyages de S. Dominique."
3. Jordan of Saxony, "Libellus," 28. Early Dominican histories and hagiographies frequently conflate Diego and Martín Bazán, and it was not until the twentieth-century scholarship of Mandonnet and Vicaire that Martín Bazán received any comment at all: Mandonnet, *St. Dominic*, 20–22; Vicaire, *Saint Dominic*, 33–45. Spanish antiquarians preserved the distinction between the two, although their work was hardly perfect: González Dávila, *Teatro eclesiástico*, 29; Loperráez Corvalán, *Descripción histórica*, 1:173–87; Argaíz, *La soledad laureada*, fol. 295r.
4. Reilly, "Alfonso VIII," 439, notes the importance of only one similar clan to the episcopal genetics of the kingdom of Castile. I would argue that the examples of the Blasquez at Ávila, Girón at Segovia, and Mathé at Burgos suggest that family networks of power in cathedral towns were deeply rooted.
5. Although the use of his surname, Bazán, is somewhat infrequently attested in diplomatics, the preservation of this name in Martín Bazán's epitaph is enough to render a positive family identification. The name "Baztán" shows up in a list of *linajes de ricos hombres* for the kingdom of Navarra. Loperráez Corvalán, *Descripcion histórica*, 1:187; Fortun Perez de Ciriza, *Sancho VII el Fuerte*, 110; Ramírez Vaquero, "La nobleza," 303–4. I have surveyed Martín Bazán's position within the larger makeup of the Castilian court: Lincoln, "Prosopography," 205, 207.
6. Argaíz, *La soledad laureada*, fol. 295. San Millán de la Cogulla was in Argaíz's mind enough for him to later note that Diego d'Acebo's alleged foundation of the Cistercian house of San Bernardo de Gumiel was in contrast to Martín Bazán's previous "black monk" persuasion (fol. 295–96). Reilly calls San Millán de la Cogulla one of the "seven great monasteries" of León-Castile: Reilly, *León-Castilla Under Alfonso VII*, 270. González notes that the monastery had important connections to Cluny with regard to its "vida espiritual": González, *Alfonso VIII*, 1:504. It also seems likely that Peter the Venerable may have visited San Millán during his visit to Iberia: Bishko, "Peter the Venerable's Journey"; Reglero de la Fuente, *Cluny en España*, 320–21.
7. The wealth of the Rioja was likely one of the prime factors that attracted Alfonso VIII's attention: Álvarez Borge, "La Rioja," 201–36.
8. On the library of San Millán de la Cogolla, see Reglero de la Fuente, *Cluny en España*, 140; Peña de San José, "La biblioteca del convento"; Camara Angulo, *Libros de matematicas*, passim.
9. González notes many of the locations held by Sancho VI and his son Sancho

VII, as late as 1196, in the larger region of the Rioja: González, *Alfonso VIII*, 1:91; Álvarez Borge, *Cambios y alianzas*, 389–401.

10. Peter the Venerable had visited Spain only forty-seven years before Martín's election (Bishko, "Peter the Venerable's Journey"), so it seems likely that the Cluniac reform ethos was still strong during Martín's time at the Suso community. The visit was at the behest of Alfonso VII and shored up Cluniac interests there, furthering this suggestion. Reilly, *León-Castilla Under Alfonso VII*, 73–74. Sweeney, "Innocent III," 34–35, notes with considerable detail the intellectual expectations placed on the judges-delegate in Hungary during a similar period.

11. On the broad influence of Cluny in Iberia: Reglero de la Fuente, *Cluny en España*, 9–25, 476–594.

12. I have examined elsewhere the context of other reform efforts in Castilian cathedral chapters in the 1190s and early 1200s: Lincoln, "'It Pleased the Lord Bishop,'" 271–75.

13. The specific details of the case and Celebruno's involvement is examined above.

14. Loperráez Corvalán, *Descripción histórica*, 1:161–62. The reign of Miguel as abbot of Arlanza for forty-eight years seems unlikely. Far more likely is that there were two men with the very common name of Miguel, one of whom, after a long reign as abbot, was named bishop and served at Osma for two years: Zaragoza i Pascual, "Abadologio del monasterio de San Pedro," 90. Because his article predated my research, Ayala Martínez expressed no definite opinion on the possibility, but my research has uncovered this connection: Ayala Martínez, "Los obispos," 161–62; Lincoln, "Prosopography," 202n38.

15. By foot, Burgo de Osma is seventy-six kilometers to San Pedro de Arlanza, while Burgos is only forty-seven kilometers.

16. Garrido Garrido, *Documentación*, 2:11–12.

17. Loperráez Corvalán, *Descripción histórica*, 1:146–61; Ayala Martínez, "Los obispos," 161–62; Lincoln, "Prosopography," 202n38.

18. The documents are edited in various locations. The Alexander letters are found in Rivera Recio and Vicaire: River Recio, *La Iglesia de Toledo*, 1:265n45, 1:266n46; Vicaire, "Saint Dominique," 40. The Lucius letter remains in the cathedral archive of Toledo: ACT X.2.C.1.6 (= *Papsturkunden in Spanien. Kastilien*, no. 221). The Innocent letter is in Mansilla: Mansilla, *La documentación pontificia*, 205.

19. Constable, *Reformation*, 296–328.

20. Lincoln, "'Holding the Place,'" 486–91.

21. Palacios Martín, "Alfonso VIII y . . . Plasencia."

22. González, *Alfonso VIII*, 2:956–58.

23. No document-based history of the twelfth-century town is possible, but the art-historical and archaeological evidence suggests that there was a sizable settlement in the Celtiberian and Roman periods. This settlement pattern likely persisted after the eighth-century conquests, and some evidence suggests that by the time Dominican convents were established, the town was again an important stop on the road from Soria toward Valladolid: Zalama, *Por tierras de Soria*, 73–76.

24. González, *Alfonso VIII*, 2:956–58; Loperráez Corvalán, *Descripción histórica*, 2:347–48.

25. This fact is so uniform in early Dominican hagiography that only a citation of Jordan of Saxony is necessary: Jordan of Saxony, "Libellus," 28. Dominic's transition from schoolboy to reformer is handled well in Tugwell, "Notes," 34–50.

26. Minguella y Arnedo, *Historia de Sigüenza*, 1:471.

27. The importance of these kinds of agreements has been sketched by Conedera in *Ecclesiastical Knights*, 112–40.

28. In an appendix, Holndonner has catalogued, in the manner of the Jaffé registries, the back-and-forth between the two dioceses: Holndonner, *Kommunikation*, 599–625.
29. Linehan, "Synod of Segovia," 38n30.
30. The provisions of the *hermandad* gave the usual assurances of mutual hospitality and inclusion in the prayer life of the respective chapters: Minguella y Arnedo, *Historia de Sigüenza*, 1:471. Martín's counterpart was San Martín de Finojosa. On Martín de Finojosa and his reputation for sanctity and subsequent canonization *ex antiquo*, see Manrique, *Santoral Cisterciense*, 2:107v. A good summary of the memorializing efforts supporting Martín's cult activity is found in González Cabrerizo, *Biografía*, 35–38; Astorga Arroya, "San Martín de Finojosa"; Romero, "Hacia una biografia científica."
31. Jordan of Saxony, "Libellus," 29.
32. Tugwell, "Notes," 34–50. I confess that even I, in earlier projects, was swayed by this logic, but canon law evidence unties the knotted logic too neatly to be denied. Porres Martín-Cleto, *Los Anales Toledanos*, 221; Tanner, *Decrees*, 198–99.
33. On Dominic's "thirst for theology," see Jordan of Saxony, "Libellus," 31–33. The subscriptions of canons survive in two documents at Osma from the late 1190s: one from 1195, where Dominic holds no office in the chapter, and one from 1199, where he appears as a sacristan. See Loperráez Corvalán, *Descripción histórica*, 3:41–47; Riaño Rodríguez and Gutierrez Aja, "Documentos," 236–37.
34. Early Dominican hagiographies attest to Dominic's particular devotion to the text of John Cassian's *Collationes patrum*, popular among reformers in that period. Jordan of Saxony, "Libellus," 33; Peter of Ferrand, *Petri Ferrandi Legenda*, 216; Constable, *Reformation*, 160, 270, 26–27.
35. Garrido Garrido, *Documentación*, 2:82–83.
36. Ayala Martínez observed that "aunque nada sabemos de las circunstancias de su elección, su persona no debió ser neutra en la consideración del rey Alfonso VIII." Ayala Martínez, "Los obispos," 161.
37. "Habita consideratione meritorum vestrorum et devotionem quam erga non geritis." González, *Alfonso VIII*, 3:57–59.
38. Ibid., 2:347–48.
39. On the crusade against Alfonso IX of León, see O'Callaghan, *Reconquest and Crusade*, 62–63, 83–84; Smith, "Iberian Legations," 40; Lincoln, "'Holding the Place,'" 491–92. For the punitive raid by Alfonso VIII of Castile and Alfons II of Aragon against the town of Castro de los Judíos near León: Soifer Irish, *Jews and Christians*, 27–28.
40. On the border raiding by the Almohads, see García Fitz, *Castilla y León*, 201–3.
41. The truce with the Almohads is not firmly dated, but it must be from after 1197, when the Almohads raided southern Castile for a second time: García Fitz, *Relaciones políticas y guerra*, 139–41. The marriage between Berenguela and Alfonso IX has been well studied: Bianchini, *Queen's Hand*, 37–68; Shadis, *Berenguela*, 51–72. The conquests of a number of Navarrese territories in the late 1190s amounted to a major addition to the lands of the king of Castile: Álvarez Borge, "La Rioja."
42. The renewal of the alliance between Aragon and Castile was a product of Pere II's reign, which began in early 1196, although good relations had existed as early as the reign of Alfons II: Alvira Cabrer, "*Si Possides Amicum*."
43. For the deaths of the bishops of Segovia and Ávila at Alarcos, see chapter 6.
44. The debate between Ruiz and Nieto Soria has articulated almost every possible angle, but current scholarly consensus favors Ruiz, albeit without a definitive knockout. Ruiz, "Oligarchy and Royal Power"; Ruiz, "Unsacred Monarchy"; Ruiz, "La formazione della monarchia"; Nieto Soria, "La monarquía bajomedieval castellana"; Ruiz, "Une royauté sans sacre"; Nieto Soria,

"Imágenes religiosas"; Nieto Soria, "La transpersonalización del poder real."

45. "Et legit ea coram rege dominus Martinus, Oxomensis episcopus, et, secundum quod invenerunt in privilegiis, iudicavit dominus rex et alcaldi." González, *Alfonso VIII*, 3:158.

46. Mansilla, *La documentación pontificia*, 176–77.

47. Ibid., 176: "Verum quoniam ipse in falsitate bullae nostrae fuit publice deprehensus et suspectus habetur."

48. Ibid. Of course, forgeries were not so uncommon in the medieval period that this was an unimaginable phenomenon.

49. Fletcher was so animated by the case as to label it "the Zamora Imbroglio." Furthermore, that Linehan addressed six separate consecutive rhetorical questions regarding the case betrays the energies it could stir up. Even Mansilla made specific mention of the intensity of the case, saying, "Al Papa no se le ocultaba la gravedad que encerraba esta última cuestión para dar sobre ella un fallo definitivo y de ahí su esfuerzo por encontrar una fórmula de compromiso." Linehan, "Un quirógrafo impugnado," 138; Fletcher, *Episcopate*, 202; Mansilla, "Disputas diocesanas," 108.

50. Mansilla, "Disputas diocesanas," 91–113.

51. Innocent's letter recounted the entire history of the decisions made at the papal curia on the matter and noted that the affair had been handled by "felicis recordationis Eugenius papa III predecessor noster . . . postmodum vero . . . a bone memorie Alexandro papa III ac demum a Lucio III predecessoribus nostris . . . felicis recordationis Urbanus papa III predecessor noster." Mansilla, *La documentación pontificia*, 251–52.

52. On the conferral of the metropolitan rights of Mérida to Santiago de Compostela, see Fletcher, *Saint James's Catapult*, 198–200.

53. The larger question of Zamora's controversial identification is admirably summarized in Fletcher, *Episcopate*, 195–203.

54. The letter containing Innocent's decision in favor of Compostela was dated 5 July 1199, and the letter appointing the appellate panel, 21 July 1199. As yet, I have found no other instance of the papacy's delegating the rights to a retrial to a panel of judges-delegate. Mansilla, *La documentación pontificia*, 220–26, 251–52.

55. Fletcher, *Episcopate*, 202. See also Innocent's bull of 5 July 1199 in which the sentence is handed down, and the bull of 21 July 1199 giving Martín, Brecio, and Martín the authority to retry the case in its entirety. Mansilla, *La documentación pontificia*, 220–26, 251–52.

56. Nearly every early modern and modern commentator on Plasencia falls short of identifying Brecio's post before Plasencia, but there is significant and frequent speculation as to his origins. In the most recent (and most careful) examination of the episcopology of Plasencia to date, no identification was even supportable: González Cuesta, "Sobre el episcopologio," 358–59. I have generally accepted González Cuesta's hypothesis that Brecio had previously served in the abbey of Valladolid, but this is a reasonable conjecture at best: Lincoln, "Prosopography," 212.

57. Mansilla, *La documentación pontificia*, 463–68. The best available précis of Martinho Rodrigues is that sketched by Oliveira, "Os bispos senhores da cidade," 175–83.

58. ACT X.2.C.2.2A; ACT X.2.C.1.6. The first of these two letters was edited by Vicaire: Vicaire, "Saint Dominique," 40.

59. Mansilla, *La documentación pontificia*, 205:

> Ordinem religionis plantare ac fovere plantatum ex officii nostri debito prevocamur, et sic Religionis locis Apostolicum nos convenit praebere patroncinium et favorem,

quod sub regimine ac gubernatione nostra assiduis proficere valeant incrementis. Intelleximus siquidem per scriptum authenticum sigillo tuo et Venerabilis fratris nostri Toletani Archiepiscopi communitum, quod tu de communi consensu totius capituli Oxomensis, auctoritate prefati Archiepiscopi consensu etiam et consilio karissimi in Christo filii nostri A. regis illustris Castelle deliberatione provida statuisti ut, secundum preceptum felicis recordationis Alexandri et Lucii Romanorum Pontificum in Oxomensi Ecclesia sint de cetero Canonici Regulares, nec aliquis in portionarium, vel saecularem canonicum recipiatur deinceps in eadem. Quaedam etiam alia capitula statuisti quae in eodem scripto prespeximus contineri. Volentes igitur quod a te videtur pia deliberatione statutum debita firmitate gaudere; constitutiones ipsas (quas possemus restitutiones potius nominare, cum a longis retro temporibus hoc ipsum de Oxomense Ecclesia fuerit, sicut asseris a Romanis Pontificibus ordinatum) sicut ipse rationabiliter factae sunt, et a tuo receptae capitulo, auctoritate Apostolica confirmamus et praesentis scripti pagina communimus.

60. Tanner, *Decrees*, 242.
61. Little, *Religious Poverty*, 152–58. The chapter had been Augustinian since its founding, but observance of the rule waxed and waned substantially: Portillo Capilla, "La regla de San Agustín." I am grateful to Dr. Jerrilyn Dodds for this reference.
62. Mansilla notes that the letter's text was incorporated into the *Compilatio tertia* (3.2.1) and into the *Liber Extra* (X 3.2.8). Mansilla, *La documentación pontificia*, 206. Friedberg's error is a common enough one, given the similarities between the Latin names for Exeter (Exoniensis) and Osma (Oxomensis), as Charles Duggan has observed: C. Duggan, "Case of Bernardo of Osma."
63. Linehan, *Spanish Church*, 20–34.
64. Ibid., esp. 29–31.
65. I have treated the embassies of Diego of Osma to Denmark on behalf of Alfonso VIII in a conference paper that was to be published as part of the proceedings of the ill-fated 2012 SSCLE meeting. It remains open-access on my Academia .edu page until it should be published in the volume: Lincoln, "The (Attempted) Alliance of Alfonso VIII of Castile and Valdemar II of Denmark: The *Infante* Fernando's Marriage Reconsidered."
66. González, *Alfonso VIII*, 3:341–47, here 3:346.
67. Garrido Garrido, *Documentación*, 2:82–83, 142–43, 143–44.
68. Gregory's second legation was in the 1195–96: Lincoln, "'Holding the Place,'" 473.
69. Tugwell, "Notes," 38–40.
70. Loperráez Corvalán, *Descripción histórica*, 1:187:

En lo restante del año que tuvo de vida este Prelado se mantuvo con quietud en el gobierno de su Iglesia, y murió en su Palacio a veinte y siete de Julio, como se sabe por los anales de su Iglesia, y un código antiguo que se hallaba en el archivo del Monasterio de la Vid; cuyo cuerpo habiendo estado algunos años en el pavimento de la Iglesia, fue después trasladado a la parte y lado de la Epístola de la capilla que llaman hoy del Santo Christo, venerándose antes en ella a Santo Domingo de Guzmán, cubriendo sus huesos una lápida con este breve epitafio de letra llamada comúnmente abacial. "Hic Jacet D. Martinus Bazan Episcopus Oxomensis."

71. I have compared these cathedral reforms elsewhere: Lincoln, "'It Pleased the Lord Bishop.'"

72. Mandonnet states this Premonstratensian hypothesis so matter-of-factly that in his era, it appears to have gone uncontested that Dominic adopted it because of his early experience: Mandonnet, *St. Dominic*, 36. Vicaire disagreed, noting that it was relatively unlikely that any such influence was either conscious or intended: Vicaire, *Saint Dominic*, 36–37.

Chapter 6
This chapter's epigraph is drawn from Garci-Gómez, *Cantar de Mío Cid*, 89, ll. 1793–96: "El obispo don Jerónimo, caboso coronado, / quando es farto de lidiar con amas las sus manos, / no tiene en cuenta los moros que ha matados, / lo que caíe a él mucho era sobejano."

1. We have a precise date for Martín's consecration, thanks to a missive from Celestine III to suffragans of Toledo, marked ACT A.6.G.1.1. (= *Papsturkunden in Spanien. Kastilien*, no. 274), informing the canons of Martín's confirmation and his receipt of the pallium from the hands of the pope himself.
2. Abajo Martín, *Documentación de Palencia*, 148–223; Ayala Martínez, "Breve semblanza"; Rivera Recio, *La Iglesia de Toledo*, 1:202–3.
3. Palacios Martín, "Alfonso VIII y . . . Plasencia; Nieto Soria, "La fundación del obispado."
4. I have treated the legations of Gregory of Sant'Angelo at length elsewhere: Lincoln, "'Holding the Place.'"
5. ACT A.6.G.1.1; Smith, "Iberian Legations," 85–111.
6. González, *Alfonso VIII*, 3:105–8.
7. Powers, *Society Organized for War*, 158.
8. No exact length of time can be specified for these raids, but municipal militias, which constituted the bulk of Castilian military muscle, were expected to serve three months: ibid., 116–18.
9. "Duxit autem idem archiepiscopus secum viros generosos et strenuos et multitudinem militum et peditum, cum quibus vastavit magnam partem terre Maurorum cismarine, spolians eam multis diviciis et infinita multitudine vacarum, peccorum et iumentorum." *CLRC*, 12, P. 44.
10. "Comovit arma in regem Africe et provocavit cito gentem Arabie. Populus eius instauravit acies et arma potencie direxit in Mauros. Exercitus eius transivit Bethim et dux eius presul Toleti. Magnates regni in consiliis presulis et exercitus omnis sub presule dignitatis. Nomen eius Martinus Magnus et genus eius a Pisorica. Cingulum eius zelus fidei et arma eius ad persecucionem blasphemie. Agmen omne ad nutum illius et sanguis Arabum in conspectus illius. Regio Bethica flammis succenditur et factum presulis prosperatur. Processit enim per castra Bethicae terras et oppida succendendo. Feliciter autem ad propria est reversus." *DRH*, VII.xxviii.11–24.
11. "A tierra de Guadalquevir pusol fuego ell arçobispo con la hueste, et quemola; et aproueCho alii ell fecho dell arçobispo, ca assi como cuenta del la estoria, andido por los castiellos de la prouincia de Guadalquevir ençendiendo las tierras et las fuertes pueblas, quemandolo todo, et en cabo tornosse pora su tierra con mucha bienandança. Aun ua la estoria adelant en estas cuentas de los fechos deste rey don Alffonsso de Castiella." *Primera crónica general*, 1001.
12. García Fitz, *Castilla y León*, 307; García Fitz, *Relaciones políticas y guerra*, 138–40; Ayala Martínez, *Las Cruzadas*, 311–12.
13. ʿAbd al-Wāḥid al-Marrākušī, *Kitāb al-Muʿjib fī taljīṣ ajbār al-Magrib*, 235.
14. "Lo atacaron todo en el Andalus por Oriente y por Occidente al mismo tiempo. Se extendió el contingente llegado a Sevilla por todo su territorio, saqueó sus regiones y atacó una de los castillos de su Ajarafe y estuvo a punto de aprovechar la ocasión, si no es por la vigilancia de los almohades, que se adelantaron a él y lo rechazaron de allí. Se retiraron después de ser muerto en el caso cierto número de ellos y Dios

les hizo fracasar en su empeño." Al-Gharnaṭi, "Comentario," 202.
15. Al-Athir, *Chronicle*, 3:19–20.
16. Al-Maqqarī says of the raids: "But to return to al-Mansur. When the [five-year] truce made with the Christians [in 1190] was over, or nearly so, a large party of them invaded the Muslim territory, and began to plunder and lay waste the country, and to commit all manner of ravages and depredations, which being reported to al-Mansur, who was then absent in Africa, he resolved upon chastising their insolence." Al-Maqqarī, *History*, 321.
17. Barton, *Aristocracy*, 19–20; Serrano, *El obispado de Burgos*, 2:72–73.
18. On the efforts of Ramón and Celebruno, see chapters 2 and 3.
19. The two bulls for Alarcos have been published, respectively, in Zerbi, *Papato*, 179, appendix 1, and Gómez and Lincoln, "'Sins,'" 62–63.
20. B. Hamilton, *Latin Church*, 65–67, 130–31; L. Duggan, *Armsbearing and the Clergy*, 103–5, 114; Barber, *Crusader States*, 25–26.
21. García Fitz, *Castilla y León*, 105; Gorosterratzu, *Don Rodrigo Jiménez de Rada*, 276–93.
22. ACT X.11.C.1.7. I have edited this text in Lincoln, "Beating Swords into Croziers," 103.
23. Gratian made this plain, and Lateran III confirmed the responsibility of local metropolitans: Gratian of Chiusi, *Decretum*, C.9 q.3 c.2, D.51 c.5, D.64 c.1, D.64 c.5, D.64 c.6; Tanner, *Decrees*, 212.
24. Rodrigo Gutiérrez was the royal *mayordomo* for a considerable length of time: Barton, *Aristocracy*, 170.
25. Colmenares provides the specific identification of Gutierre's parents as "conde don Rodrigo González Girón y de doña Mayor Núñez de Lara, su mujer." Colmenares, *Historia*, 162; Barton, *Aristocracy*, 170; ACT X.2.B.1.1.
26. Tanner, *Decrees*, 212.
27. For Martín Bazán, see chapter 5. For Rodrigo, see chapter 7.
28. *Compilatio prima*, book 1, title 4.
29. E.g., Abajo Martín, *Documentación de Palencia*, 203–27; Villar García, *Documentación*, 132–43.
30. Lourie, *Curia and Cortes*, 11–13, 227–29; O'Callaghan, *Cortes of Castile-León*, 13, 153, 156.
31. Gutierre's father was a longtime *mayordomo* of the king: González, *Alfonso VIII*, 1:357–59. Rodrigo names the family members at Las Navas as "Gonzalvus Roderici et fratres eius," a group that Alvira Cabrer has confirmed to be the very same sons of Rodrigo Girón: *DRH*, VIII.iii; Alvira Cabrer, *Las Navas de Tolosa 1212*, 240.
32. Power, *Society Organized for War*, 1–3, 30, 37, 53, 58.
33. Colmenares, *Historia*, XVIII.xi.
34. On the rebellions against Celebruno of Poitiers, see chapter 2.
35. "Fere omnes parrochiales vestri clerici in tantam sunt perlapsi nequitiam ut vobis obedire contumiter contradicant novas et detestabiles conspirationes et coniurationes pretextu confratriarum adversum vos ineuntes." ACT A.6.G.1.10.
36. The aftermath of Alarcos included raids against the Toledan hinterland by both the Leonese king and the Almohad caliph in 1196 and 1197: García Fitz, *Castilla y León*, 307, 448; García Fitz, *Relaciones políticas y guerra*, 138–40; Ayala Martínez, *Las Cruzadas*, 311–12.
37. Hitchcock, *Mozarabs*, 75–98; Molénat, "La fin des chrétiens arabisés."
38. The earliest letter to this effect is ACT A.6.H.1.4, but the tenor of the text suggests that it was not the first.
39. "La de absolver e imponer la correspondiente penitencia a quienes hubieran incurrido en excomunión por haber maltratado físicamente a clérigo u hombre de religión, siempre que de resultas de ello no hubiera perecido o quedado mutilado." Ayala Martínez, "Breve semblanza," 361.
40. ACT A.6.G.1.3 (= *Papsturkunden in Spanien. Kastilien*, no. 284).

41. Ibid.
42. The background of Julián ben Tauro is detailed at length in chapter 9.
43. Martín and Julián collaborated in assisting the reforms of Sigüenza five years later, but there are no lawsuits by Toledo against Cuenca or vice versa preserved from the period when both Martín and Julián were the heads of their dioceses: Hernández Sánchez, *Los cartularios*, 241–69; Chacón Gómez-Monedero, Canorea Huete, and Salamanca López, *Catálogo*, 80–98.
44. Pluralism was flatly forbidden by the Council of Tours and Third Lateran: Somerville, *Pope Alexander III*, 49; Tanner, *Decrees*, 1:218–19. However, pluralism was practiced regularly among the clerical elite in Iberia, as extant wills by cathedral canons show: Barrios García, *Documentos*, 84.
45. Jiménez Monteserín, *Vere pater pauperum*, 405–6.
46. Hernández Sánchez, *Los cartularios*, 256.
47. The early history of the diocese of Cuenca has already received significant attention: Nieto Soria, "La fundación del obispado," 111–13; Nieto Soria, "El equipamiento económico"; Powers, "Early Reconquest Episcopate."
48. Both Martín Bazán and Alderico di Palacio served on numerous delegations, examined in detail above.
49. Villar García, *Documentación*, 145–47; Mansilla, *La documentación pontificia*, 332, 336–39, 353–54.
50. The marriage between Berenguela and Alfonso IX has been the subject of significant and thoughtful commentary: Bianchini, *Queen's Hand*, 37–103; Shadis, *Berenguela*, 73–97.
51. Alfonso IX raided the region around Toledo almost immediately after Alarcos: Martín, "Alfonso IX y sus relaciones con Castilla," 16. Alfonso IX's raids coincided with those of the Almohad caliph in 1196/97 and led Celestine to call on the Portuguese to crusade against Alfonso IX: García Fitz, *Castilla y León*, 448–49; Smith, "Iberian Legations," 110–11.
52. Only Oviedo appears to have spoken out against the match, and Alfonso IX punished him for breaking rank: Fletcher, *Episcopate*, 76. Innocent sent his confessor, Rainier da Ponza, to resolve the marriage's dissolution, which was the only papally sanctioned option: Mansilla, *La documentación pontificia*, 168–70; Powell, *Deeds*, 73–75.
53. The first letter, edited by Mansilla (Mansilla, *La documentación pontificia*, 168–70), dated to 1198, but Berenguela and Alfonso did not separate until 1204, as the letter from that year attests (ibid., 332–33).
54. Only one of the children, Infanta Leonor, died young. The children would all play peculiar roles in the unification of Castile and León. Alfonso de Molina would serve an important role under Fernando, who took control of Castile in 1217 and León in 1230. Infanta Constanza was one of the Ladies of Las Huelgas in Burgos, and Infanta Berenguela married John of Brienne. On this branch of the Leonese royal family, see Bianchini, "Foreigners and Foes."
55. On the resolution of this *arras* property's holdings, see Bianchini, *Queen's Hand*, 80–86.
56. Mansilla, *La documentación pontificia*, 332.
57. Ibid., 336–39.
58. Gratian included many canons relating to incest in the first recension of the *Decretum*: D.27 c 9, D83 c.1, C.3 q.4 c.4, C.6 q.1 c.17, C.23 q.5 c.45, C27 q.1 c.14&17, C.35 q.2&3 c.7&10.
59. The very first passage of the *Gesta Innocentii* makes his mercy a key part of his character: Powell, *Deeds*, 3. For the privilege granting Martín the right to absolve Berenguela: Mansilla, *La documentación pontificia*, 332–33. It is worth noting that Martín and Alderico di Palacio were part of the delegation that begged for papal leniency toward the incestuous marriage in the first place: Bianchini, *Queen's Hand*, 72.

60. The towns listed in the dissolution of the marriage: Mansilla, *La documentación pontificia*, 336–39. This clearly echoes the Treaty of Cabreros's contents: Bianchini, *Queen's Hand*, 80–86.
61. T. Martin, "Hacia una clarificación"; Bianchini, "*Infantazgo*"; Henriet, "Deo votas"; Rodríguez López, "Dotes y arras."
62. On the bishop of Oviedo and his criticism of Alfonso IX, see Fletcher, *Episcopate*, 76.
63. On Palencia's holdings in the Tierra de Campos, see the chapters on Ramón de Minerva and Alderico di Palacio.
64. Tanner, *Decrees*, 216–17.
65. González, *Alfonso VIII*, 2:779–80.
66. Ibid. On the appellation of Martín as King Alfonso's friend, see Rivera Recio, *La Iglesia de Toledo*, 2:84.
67. There are no surviving purchases from Gonzalo Pérez during his archiepiscopate recorded in González Palencia, *Los mozárabes*, nos. 170–220.
68. Ibid., nos. 322a, 322b, 329, 334, 335, 349.
69. Abajo Martín, *Documentación de Palencia*, 256–63; Barrios García, *Documentos*, 146–57.
70. González Palencia, *Los mozárabes*, nos. 322b, 335. On the status of clerics under the *fuero* of Toledo: Muñoz y Romero, *Colección de fueros*, 1:363–69; González, *Alfonso VIII*, 2:326–27.
71. This was not a smooth process everywhere: Foote, *Lordship*, 93–103; Miller, *Formation*, 122–41; B. Hamilton, *Latin Church*, 137–58; Burger, *Bishops, Clerks*, 110–16; Madden, *Enrico Dandolo*, 27–32.
72. Bisson, *Crisis*, 312–14.
73. Burger, *Bishops, Clerks*, 110.
74. Linehan, *History and the Historians*, 313.
75. "Honor gentis vita eius et stola eius diadema Ecclesie. Sapiencia eius pax multorum et lingua eius informatio discipline. Manus eius ad subsidium pauperum et cor eius ad compassionem humilum." *DRH*, VII.xxviii.11–24.
76. Rodrigo's "thesis" is well studied: Linehan, *History and the Historians*, 350–84; Reilly, "*De rebus Hispanie*"; Pick, *Conflict and Coexistence*, 14–20; Linehan, "On Further Thought."
77. Rivera Recio, *La Iglesia de Toledo*, 2:84.

Chapter 7

This chapter's epigraph is drawn from Alcázar, *Vida, virtudes, y milagros*, fol. 1r: "San Julián, segundo Obispo de Cuenca, honra de nuestra España, ornamento de la Iglesia Universal, idea de Santos Prelados, maravilla grande de la gracia, y una de las más brillantes lumbreras, que lucen en la Gloria; admirable en la vida, excelso en las virtudes, y prodigioso en los milagros, es el assumpto de esta Historia."

1. González, *Alfonso VIII*, 1:929.
2. Estepa Díez, "El Reino," 49; García Fitz, *Castilla y León*, 103–4; Krasner Balbale, "Between Kings and Caliphs," 204–9; Bennison, *Almoravid and Almohad Empires*, 89–98.
3. Holt, "*In eo tempore*," 7; González, *Alfonso VIII*, 2:462–568; Martínez Díez, *Alfonso VIII*, 104–6; Estepa Díez, "Memoria y poder real," 191–92; García Fitz, *Relaciones políticas y guerra*, 127–31.
4. This is Linehan's speculation, but it has a strong rationale: Linehan, *History and the Historians*, 290.
5. Nieto Soria, "La fundación del obispado"; Nieto Soria, "Los obispos fundadores," 37–39; Díaz Ibáñez, "La iglesia de Cuenca," 31–56; Powers, "Early Reconquest Episcopate," 5–8.
6. Nieto Soria, "El equipamiento económico," 316, 320.
7. Julián first appears in 1197 as a bishop of Cuenca in the royal charters: Díaz Ibáñez, "La iglesia de Cuenca," 119–20, esp. 119n149; Powers, "Early Reconquest Episcopate,"16.
8. Díaz Ibáñez, "La iglesia de Cuenca," 119–20; Nieto Soria, "Los obispos fundadores," 37.
9. González Palencia, *Los mozárabes*, 2:214–15.
10. Díaz Ibáñez, "La iglesia de Cuenca," 119–20.
11. Olstein, *La era mozárabe*, 51–81.

12. González Palencia, *Los mozárabes*, 1:214–15; Hernández Sánchez, *Los cartularios*, 254–55.
13. Oliva Manso, "Enigmas monetarias," 334; Hernández Sánchez, "Las postras publicadas," 257, 259.
14. While Julián was not well attested in Olstein's sample, Martín was: Olstein, *La era mozárabe*, 127. Later evidence about the cult of San Julián de Cuenca using onomastic analysis has given greater weight to Julián's short-term staying power as a name in the first decade after his remains were translated in the cathedral, despite its nonexistence in Mozarabic sources: Nalle, "Saint for All Seasons," 30.
15. González Palencia, *Los mozárabes . . . : Volumen preliminar*, 183; Olstein, *La era mozárabe*, 112.
16. Hernández Sánchez, *Los cartularios*, 213–14.
17. Ibid., 236–37. For this charter from Martín, see chapter 6. The rule that Martín was modifying was the reform of Celebruno.
18. Nieto Soria, "El equipamiento económico," 312–13.
19. Carl makes a strong case for the innovative qualities of both internal and external frontiers on the administration of the diocese of Calahorra: Carl, *Bishopric*, 155–263.
20. Trenchs Oden, "El necrologio-obituario," 371; Díaz Ibáñez, "La iglesia de Cuenca," 119; Hernández Sánchez, *Los cartularios*, 242–44. Hernández Sánchez mistakenly transcribes a charter, preserved in several copies, from 25 May 1198 as containing the subscription of "J(ohannes) Conchensis episcopus," but since Juan was already dead, the abbreviation may suggest Julián was the witness in the charter.
21. ACC, III, Inventarios, leg. 74, no. 13, fol. 16r–v.
22. Hernández Sánchez, *Los cartularios*, 254–55.
23. González, *Alfonso VIII*, 3:158–60; Trenchs Olden, "El necrologio-obituario," 352; Díaz Ibáñez, "La iglesia de Cuenca," 119n149.
24. Harris has suggested that, while records of the ceremonies are scarce, they were important for reclaiming the space of the newly conquered towns and provided the best use of conquered resources: Harris, "Mosque to Church Conversion." To that effect, Díaz Ibáñez helpfully details the evidence for both the cathedral and (from the smaller, neighborhood mosques) parish churches: Díaz Ibáñez, "La iglesia de Cuenca," 37–38, 51.
25. Powers describes the case of Gíl of Cuenca but mistakenly suggests that Gíl was buying out the "Magellario" family. "Macellarius" is one word for "butcher" in Latin, and the transposition of a "c" to a "g" is orthographically common. Powers, "Early Reconquest Episcopate," 11–12. I have treated Gíl's career extensively in Lincoln, "About Three Clerics."
26. Whitcombe has shown that Mauricio of Burgos was both financially and intellectually active in the region and that his project at Burgos drew talent from across the European continent: Whitcombe, "Building Heaven on Earth," 46–59.
27. ACC, III, Inventarios, leg. 74, no. 13, fols. 13r–v.
28. Nickson, *Toledo Cathedral*, 48–55, 69–75.
29. E.g., Barrow, *Clergy*, 279–81; Loud, *Latin Church*, 422–23.
30. I have examined this reform in context with the reforms at Osma and Sigüenza in Lincoln, "'It Pleased the Lord Bishop.'"
31. Cuenca, like all the frontier provinces, had been hit by Almohad raiding in 1196 and 1197, while famines in Palencia in 1192 and flooding on the Tajo River in 1200 and 1203 point to a decade of poorer-than-usual agricultural yields: Porres Martín-Cleto, *Los Anales Toledanos*, 160–65, 220–21. On the price edicts of 1207: Hernández Sánchez, "Las posturas publicadas," 257–65.

32. Jiménez Monteserín, *Vere pater pauperum*, 405–6.
33. Ibid., 405: "Canonicus vero hereditatem annivesarii quam conduxerit sub constituta locatione, omnibus diebus vite sue possideat et eius usum fructum habeat."
34. "Anniversarii quod fuerit LX mencales et amplius, due partes sint vestiarii, tertia sit comestiarii, et ista tertia pars distribuatur in die anniversarii tam canonicis quam porcionariis sicut beneficium refectorii. Alie due partes rediguntur in vestiario. Has ergo dividant canonici mansionarii equaliter inter se. Pene nummi sint comestiarii. Et horum anniversariorum quorum reditus ad presentes redacti sunt in vestiarium, due scilicet partes, quia, ut diximus, tertia pars est comestiarii." Ibid.
35. "Ita tamen quod dum canonicus vel portionarius in infirmitate positus, testamentum condiderit, eligat quem voluerit de canonicis, in cuius dispositione remaneat portio illa ad opus missarum celebrandum et exeat qui pro canonico vel portionario defuncto celebraverit super tumulum defuncti usque ad annum sicut conseuetudine." Ibid.
36. ACC, I, caja 2, no. 7.
37. González, *Alfonso VIII*, 3:280–82, 3:311–12.
38. ACC, III, Libros, no. 717, fol. 2r. The letter is curiously given as originating from Lyon rather than Ferentini, where the pope was residing at the time, as the Potthast registrum notes: Potthast, *Regesta pontificium Romanorum*, nos. 1977–88.
39. ACC, III, Inventarios, leg. 74, no. 13, fols. 26v–27r.
40. Miller, *Clothing the Clergy*, 21–23, 197–98; Loud, *Latin Church*, 424–27. Constable's commentary on the symbolic impact of clothing in monastic reform controversies should also indicate that debates about symbolism were not alien to clerical discourses about clothing: Constable, *Reformation*, 188–92.
41. Ladero Quesada, "La renta de sal," 823.
42. Powers, *Code of Cuenca*, 18–23.
43. Chamocho Cantudo, *Los fueros del reino*, 144–46.
44. Valmaña Vicente, *El fuero de Cuenca*. Powers translated the text of the *fuero* of Cuenca with annotations: Powers, *Code of Cuenca*.
45. The bibliography on the legal implications of the *fuero* of Cuenca is immense, but Chamocho Cantudo's summary bibliography is quite useful for a first reference: Chamocho Cantudo, *Los fueros del reino*, 149–50.
46. Powers, *Code of Cuenca*, 3.
47. Ibid., 31, 126.
48. ACC, I, caja 2, no. 8; González, *Alfonso VIII*, 3:396–97.
49. ACC, I, caja 2, no. 8; González, *Alfonso VIII*, 3:396–97.
50. For the Henry II vs. Becket controversy's "criminous clerks" angle, see Thomas's comments in *Secular Clergy*, which summarizes the quarrel thoughtfully and places it in a larger context (209–26). On the concept of "libertas ecclesiae," see the summative comments of Bisson in *Crisis*, 9, 212, 488.
51. There are no modifications to the rights of the clerics under the *fuero* for nearly fifty years, when the terms were confirmed by Alfonso X in 1255: ACC, III, Libros, no. 717, fol. 17v.
52. The records of his translation are preserved in the *Libro de Actas* of the cathedral chapter: ACC, Actas 1516, fol. 33r. The Gothic cathedral in Cuenca was completed in a number of phases, but a substantive treatment of it like that of Nickson's work on Toledo has yet to be completed. The best work remains that of Albares, but it is in need of considerable expansion: Albares Albares, "La Catedral."
53. Trenchs Oden, "El necrologio-obituario," 364; Jiménez Monteserín, *Vere pater pauperum*, 283–84.

54. Nalle, "Saint for All Seasons," 42–44.
55. Jiménez Monteserín, *Vere pater pauperum*, 279.
56. Nalle, "Saint for All Seasons," 30.
57. Jiménez Monteserín, *Vere pater pauperum*, 418–531.
58. Ibid., 419, 425, 429, 474, 484.
59. For Alderico's reliquary sandals, see chapter 4.
60. Nalle ("Saint for All Seasons," 26–30) was working, in part, from the hagiographical account of Escudero: Escudero, *Vida y milagros*, fols. 1r–23r.
61. Abajo Martín, *Documentación de Palencia*.
62. Jiménez Monteserín, *Vere pater pauperum*, 544–45.
63. Ibid.
64. Jiménez Monteserín, *Vere pater pauperum*, 546–61.
65. Ariazaleta and Jean-Marie, "En el umbral de santidad," 1–14.
66. Escudero, *Vida y milagros*, fols. 1r–23r.
67. Valenzuela y Velazquez, *Discurso*, 3–57.
68. Martir Riço, *Historia*, 144–46.
69. On Joscelmo's arm-crypt in the Capilla del Doncel in the cathedral of Sigüenza: Peces Rata, *Paleografía y epigrafía*, 51.
70. Linehan, *History and the Historians*, 313.
71. B. Hamilton, *Latin Church*, 116–17, 122–23; Loud, *Latin Church*, 170–71, 173–74, 259–78. On this trend generally, see Barrow, *Clergy*, 49–51.
72. Anonymous, *Novena al glorioso S. Julian*.
73. Nalle, "Saint for All Seasons," 28–30.

Chapter 8

This chapter's epigraph is drawn from Sánchez Portocarrero, *Nuevo catálogo*, 24–25: "Mostró su valor don Rodrigo asistiendo mucho al valoroso Rey don Alonso VIII. Con quien se halló en la milagrosa batalla de las Navas año 1212 assi lo afirman nustras historias, y en la muerte, y entierro del mismo Rey."

1. The use of the "Verdejo" name, often used in connection to this bishop of Sigüenza, cannot be substantiated for Rodrigo. Although Minguella y Arnedo attributed his name to "el primitivo catologo de los once Obispos primeros," no such catalog exists in any of the inventories from before Minguella y Arnedo's time, and his lack of citations for the attribution of "de Verdejo" is troublesome. Even Joseph Duggan's cautious research was unable to uncover proof of Rodrigo's supposed origins in Verdejo, despite Reilly's use of Duggan's work to support such a claim. Moreover, there is no mention of Rodrigo's ancestry in any of the early modern histories whose titles bear resemblance to a work of this kind, and the most likely candidate for the attribution begins his narration of Rodrigo's episcopate with the following: "Don Rodrigo, de cuya patria no se sabe nada." Minguella y Arnedo, *Historia de Sigüenza*, 1:175–76; J. Duggan, *"Cantar de Mio Cid,"* 87–88; Reilly, "Alfonso VIII," 438–39; Sánchez Portocarrero, *Nuevo catálogo*, 24.
2. Of course, Rodrigo was not alone in spanning this gap of clerics. See the appendix for their biographical details.
3. Minguella y Arnedo, *Historia de Sigüenza*, 1:465.
4. Archivo Capitular de Sigüenza, Particulares 18.
5. Minguella y Arnedo, *Historia de Sigüenza*, 1:175. The exact relationship between the two men is untraceable, but most assume that he was Martín's nephew, based on Minguella y Arnedo's citation of an ineluctable "primitivo catologo." As was outlined in the first note to this chapter, the evidence is not traceable.
6. Ibid., 1:453, 1:465.
7. On the family of Esteban of Zamora, see Fletcher, *Episcopate*, 42–46. For the other three families, see the appendix at the end of this volume.
8. Reilly, "Alfonso VIII," 448–51.
9. See the examples of Martín López de Pisuerga and Ramón de Minerva in chapters 2 and 3.
10. One suspects that, if the conspiracy mentioned by Reilly were in place, then

a short tenure for Archbishop Martín López would have been assumed. That seems unlikely, given that Martín appears as a member of the cathedral chapter of Palencia for a decade or two, and, if he was appointed to the position at the earliest canonical age because of his family's position, then he would have been in his late forties at the time he was elevated to the Toledan dignity. The archbishop's imminent demise, in 1192, would have been unlikely grounds to support a conspiracy. Even if he had reached the ripe old age of eighty at his death, he would not have been more than sixty-five at his election, which was far from being "too old" to be elected to the episcopate.

11. We know the exact day of Rodrigo's consecration thanks to a charter that preserves his own memorialization, albeit three years later: Minguella y Arnedo, *Historia de Sigüenza*, 1:479–50.

12. Ibid., 1:477.

13. E.g., ibid., *Historia de Sigüenza*, 1:475–76; Constable, *Reformation*, 54–58.

14. Minguella y Arnedo, *Historia de Sigüenza*, 1:481–82.

15. Ibid., 1:478–79.

16. Ibid., 1:479.

17. On Martín López's raid, see above, chapter 6.

18. Minguella y Arnedo, *Historia de Sigüenza*, 1:480. It is likely that these were for the residences of the bishop and his *familiares*, since Martín López was required to approve the purchase and archbishops rarely tolerated other clerical bodies encroaching on their territory.

19. Muñoz y Romero, *Colección de fueros*, 1:529–31.

20. Olea Álvarez, *Sigüenza*, 1:207–8.

21. "Ad presentium posteorumque noticiam perveniat quod cum clerici de medina propter quosdam excessus suos essent excomunicati quidam eorum suum errorem cognoscentes et de eo resipiscere volentes iuraverunt mandatum domini R. segointini episcopi promitentes se in omnibus ejus preceptis satisfacturos et parituros." Minguella y Arnedo, *Historia de Sigüenza*, 1:482.

22. Ibid., 1:482–83: "Alii vero in suo errore et nequicia perdurantes ad nequicie sue solacium laicos omnes de medina ita comoverunt et adversus clericos qui mandatum iuraverunt armaverunt quod domos eorum violenter fregerunt et rebus suis eos spoliaverunt."

23. Although I have investigated the legations of Gregory, my study found no direct evidence of a stop in Medinaceli or Sigüenza: Lincoln, "'Holding the Place,'" 473. I suspect that the claim was heard at one of the legate's stops during the second legation, from which far fewer sources survive.

24. "Quapropter cum prefatus episcopus domino gregorio diachono cardinali tunc temporis apostolice sedis legato, super tam atroci facto de laicis conquereretur ipse cardinlis predictis laicis ut coram eo super hoc responsuri venirent mandavit. Verum cum ejus mandato parere negligerent ipso eos sententia excommunicationis innodavit et omnes ecclesias medine tam ville quam aldearum interdicto supposuit." Minguella y Arnedo, *Historia de Sigüenza*, 1:483.

25. "Cautum etiam insuper fecerunt ut qui mortuum suum non sepeliret eis centum aureos pectaret et quod nullus decimas daset." Ibid.

26. "Contra ius et consuetudinem contra etiam mandatum domini Aldefonsi illustrissimi regis castelle conpulere aldeanos ut singuli vicini bina kaficia medii tres fanegas quartarii singular kaficia ad villam defferrent." Ibid.

27. I base my calculations on Ruiz's figures, but, given the variety of crops, it seems most likely that the land measurement (in terms of a *fañega*'s worth of seed) rather than the raw produce in terms of bushels is intended. Forty-five bushels of grain, 1,585 liters of produce, is enormous. While Rodrigo may be

exaggerating for rhetorical effect, a land-based tax seems more likely than precise measurement. Ruiz, *Crisis and Continuity*, 328.

28. "Fecerunt etiam edictum ut quicumque in domibus episcopi habitaret vel eas conduceret vel vineas aut agros ipsius excoleret aut in illius molendinis moleret eis LX mencallos solveret et qui mandatum episcopi de cetero iuraret centum aureos eis pectaret et domos ejus funditus everterentur." Minguella y Arnedo, *Historia de Sigüenza*, 1:483. On the conversion of these sums, see Todesca, "Money of Account."

29. Ortego Rico, "Las salinas," 208–18.

30. For the fortress of Medinaceli, see Zalama, *Por tierras de Soria*, 100–101.

31. Minguella y Arnedo, *Historia de Sigüenza*, 1:487–89.

32. Ibid., 1:494–95.

33. Ibid., 1:502–3.

34. Muñoz y Romero, *Colección de fueros*, 1:529–31.

35. "Trató de restablecer la disciplina claustral en todo su esplendor primitivo." Minguella y Arnedo, *Historia de Sigüenza*, 1:184.

36. Ibid., 1:500–502.

37. The parties attested to in the charter included both the Toledan archbishop and the bishop of Sigüenza, along with the archdeacon of Molina, the sacristan, and several other untitled members of the cathedral. Ibid.

38. Ibid., 1:501: "Super questione de mille mencallis de pozancos et patrimonio episcopi et questione de centum viginti aureis et questione de la madera et questione de domibus dompni vincentii canonicis silentium imponimus et episcopum ab hujusmodi impetitione absolvimus." For the conversion of *menkales* to maravedíes or *morabetinos*: Todesca, "Money of Account."

39. "Super questione de fossada et mobilium archipresbiteri de Molina condempnamus episcopum ut solvat canonicis medietatem." Minguella y Arnedo, *Historia de Sigüenza*, 1:501–2.

The bishop of Sigüenza was given the *fuero* of Medinaceli as the basis for his dominion in his diocese by Alfonso VII (r. 1126–57). That *fuero* gave the clerics of the city exemption from the *fonsado* tax, ostensibly because theirs was a position nominally exempt from military service: Julia Sevilla Muñoz, "Una consecuencia"; Muñoz y Romero, *Colección de fueros*, 1:529–31.

40. "Super questione quod prohibit dominus episcopus canonicos votivas donations ab extraneis recipere mandamus quod de extraneis qui in vita sua vel morte pro remedio anime sue aliquid canonicis nominatim conferre voluerit canonici licite sine contradictione aliqua recipiant." Minguella y Arnedo, *Historia de Sigüenza*, 1:502.

41. "Super questione qua dicunt canonici episcopum dare beneficia ecclesiastica extraneis et non filiis ecclesie dicimus quod episcopus canonicos sive extraneos sibi fideliter servientes digna faciat remuneratione gaudere." Ibid. One presumes that they meant "sons of the Church" in a figurative rather than literal sense.

42. "A quatuor vero questionibus que restant videlicet de personis et rebus earum et redecimatione laboriès cum aldeis et salinis et Cabrera et de usu pallium cuniculorum et vineis a claustralibus emendis non omnino desistimus sed causa maioris consilii iudicare deferimus. Nos igitur utramque sententiam predictorum arbitrorum in presentia nostra latam approbamus et confirmamus et ad majoris roboris plenitudinem obtinendam tam nostri quam venerabilium fratrum nostrorum R[oderici] segontini et J[uliani] conchensi episcoporum nec non et segontini conventus." Ibid. By 1206, these disputes between the bishop and his chapter must have been sufficiently resolved, since the churches of Sigüenza and Segovia signed a *hermandad*: Archivo Capitular de Sigüenza, Pergaminos Particulares 18.

43. The conflict between Sigüenza and Osma was a long-running dispute: Holndonner, *Kommunikation*, 599–625. Holndonner missed one papal bull at Sigüenza, which Celestine III sent to confirm the decision of Cardinal Guido when he was on legation in 1136 at the Council of Burgos, regarding the case between Sigüenza and Osma: Archivo Capitular de Sigüenza, Pontificia 11; Weiss, *Die Urkunden*, 118.
44. Minguella y Arnedo, *Historia de Sigüenza*, 1:507–8.
45. Ibid., 1:508.
46. On Martín López de Pisuerga's settlement of his own dispute, see above, chapter 6. The text of canon 9 of Lateran III was clear on this issue: Tanner, *Decrees*, 1:215–17.
47. The two examples that seem most pertinent here are Thomas Becket, whose cult spread quickly to Castile under the patronage of Queen Leonor Plantagenet, and that of Berenguer de Vilademuls, the archbishop of Tarragona, who was less famously but just as brutally killed by a young Catalan noble called Guilhelm Ramón de Moncada. See Barlow, *Thomas Becket*, 225–50; Smith, "Reconciliation."
48. The contemporary examples of the *fuero* of Cuenca and the *fuero* of Palencia, both from towns with strong episcopal influences, demonstrate that clerics were either exempt from secular courts or given substantial recourse to ecclesiastical courts: Abajo Martín, *Documentación de Palencia*, 178; Powers, *Code of Cuenca*, 3. On Julián's negotiating of these tricky legal corridors, see chapter 7.
49. The fuero of Palencia, issued in 1180, makes *calumpnia* equate to physical violence: "De calumpniis. Pro livoribus in corpore hominis factis, eligat maiorinus episcopi unam tantum calumpniam, quam voluerit, de duobus livorbus vel multis. Si quis percusserit aliquem in dentibus, ita ut perdat aliquos dentes, pro octo anterioribus, scilicet, quatuor superioribus et quatuor inferioribus, pro quolibet dente istorum pectet LX solidos usque ad CCC solidos et non amplius; aliis dentibus, pro quolibet dente, V solidos." Abajo Martín, *Documentación de Palencia*, 176. Later titles in the *fuero* of Palencia detailed more egregious injuries and employed similar formulations.
50. "The fueros of Coria, Cáceres, and Usagre assigned the same fine for calling somebody a 'Jew,' a 'cuckold,' a 'traitor,' or a 'leper.'" Soifer Irish, *Jews and Christians*, 177n31. Also: "He who calls someone a leper, hornbearer [cuckold], fornicator, or son of a fornicator should pay two *aurei* if he [the victim] can prove it." Powers, *Code of Cuenca*, 86.
51. ACT X.1.F.1.3.
52. Mansilla, *La documentación pontificia*, 431–33.
53. Ibid., 433–34.
54. Ibid., 432.
55. Lincoln, "Note on the Authorship."
56. Minguella y Arnedo, *Historia de Sigüenza*, 1:517.
57. Ibid., 1:517–18.
58. Hernández Sánchez, *Los cartularios*, 282–83.
59. *DRH*, VIII.x.
60. E.g., Sánchez Portocarrero, *Nuevo catálogo*, 25; Renales Carrascal, *Catalatto seguntino*, 38; González Dávila, *Teatro eclesiástico*, 1:150.
61. Minguella y Arnedo, *Historia de Sigüenza*, 1:524–25.
62. Ibid., 1:526–27.
63. The death of Alfonso VIII is recorded in many (near) contemporary Christian chronicles, usually with lamentations and praises: Porres Martín-Cleto, *Los Anales Toledanos*, 183–84; *CLRC*, 68–69; *DRH*, VIII.xv; "La Cronica de la población de Ávila," 43–44.
64. The best narratives are Shadis's and Bianchini's: Shadis, *Berenguela*, 97–121; Bianchini, *Queen's Hand*, 104–39.
65. García y García, *Historia del Concilio IV Lateranense*, 30–31.

66. ACT X.2.B.2.6; ACT I.4.A.1.7A. Rivera Recio edited these documents in his article "Personajes hispanos asistentes," 340–41.
67. García y García, *Historia del Concilio IV Lateranense*, 87–106.
68. Bianchini, *Queen's Hand*, 140–79.
69. Minguella y Arnedo, *Historia de Sigüenza*, 1:531.
70. Ibid.
71. Ibid., 1:533–34.
72. Ibid., 1:198.
73. Desprèe, *La batalla de Sigüenza*, 177–227; Manrique García, *Sangre en La Alcarria*, 77–87.
74. Minguella y Arnedo, *Historia de Sigüenza*, 1:198.
75. Ibid., 1:539–40: "Postea vero morte venerabilis predecessoris nostri Domini R. Segoniti episcopi interveniente presens carta sigillo suo sigillari non potuit."
76. González, *Reinado y diplomas*, 2:161–62, 2:178–79.
77. Ibid., 1:166–68.
78. Ibid., 1:665–66.
79. Ángel Martínez, "Inscripciones medievales."
80. Molina de la Torre, "Epigrafía medieval y moderna."
81. Castresana López, *Corpus Inscriptionum*.
82. García Lujan, *Cartulario*, 113–14; Gorosterratzu, *Don Rodrigo Jiménez de Rada*, 375–88; Mantilla de los Ríos Rojas et al., *Vestiduras pontificiales*.
83. On Alderico's cult, see chapter 5. For the inscriptions on the tomb of Bernardo de Agen and Joscelmo, see Peces Rata, *Paleografía y epigrafía*, 51, 64–66.

Chapter 9
This chapter's epigraph is drawn from Linehan, *Spanish Church*, 1–2.
1. For the recoverable biographical information, see the appendix.
2. There were six bishops in a fifteen-year span, from 1198 to 1213, at Burgos, which indicates the instability of the diocese in the period: Lincoln, "Prosopography," 211.
3. González Cuesta, "Sobre el episcopologio," 358–59.
4. The importance of *palea* in the second recension of Gratian and afterward is, in part, my reasoning for deploying their legacy as "husks" to indicate the future avenues of study: Brundage, *Medieval Canon Law*, 190–91.
5. Riley-Smith, *Crusades*, 112–37, 169–71; Ayala Martínez, *Las Cruzadas*, 295–320; García Fitz and Novoa Portela, *Cruzadas en la Reconquista*, 69–100; Phillips, *Second Crusade*, 136–67, 244–68; Purkis, *Crusading Spirituality*, 120–78.
6. On the nature of these earlier *parias* conflicts, see García Fitz, *Relaciones políticas y guerra*, 29–76; O'Callaghan, *Reconquest and Crusade*, 1–49; Ayala Martínez, "On the Origins of Crusading," 229–35.
7. The expansion of the crusading movement into the Iberian Peninsula has considerable scholarly support: Phillips, *Second Crusade*, 136–67, 244–68; Purkis, *Crusading Spirituality*, 139–78; O'Callaghan, *Reconquest and Crusade*, 23–50; Riley-Smith, *Crusades*, 169–71; Ayala Martínez, *Las Cruzadas*, 295–320; García Fitz and Novoa Portela, *Cruzadas en la Reconquista*, 69–100; Ayala Martínez, "On the Origins of Crusading," 229–39.
8. Linehan, "Synod of Segovia," 42.
9. Alvira Cabrer, *Las Navas de Tolosa 1212*, 92–103; Gómez, "Las Navas de Tolosa," 70–86.
10. Lincoln, "'Beating Swords into Croziers'"; L. Duggan, *Armsbearing and the Clergy*, 102–44; Nakashian, *Warrior Clergy*, 64–124, 184–228.
11. Colmenares, *Historia*, XVIII.11. On Martín López's investigation of Gutierre Rodríguez Girón, see chapter 7. Given Gutierre's family's involvement in campaigns in the kingdom and his previous position as chancellor, it seems likely that he himself was closely connected to the crusade. Family memory, even in Spain, could be a powerful motivator for crusading and its

associated activities: Paul, *To Follow in Their Footsteps*, 200–203, 251–94.
12. Barrios García, *Documentos*, 88. On the men of Ávila: Gomez-Moreno, "La Crónica"; Powers, *Society Organized for War*, 1–3, 29–30, 46–47, 57–58.
13. See also Alvira Cabrer, *Las Navas de Tolosa 1212*, 337.
14. These similarities are described in greater detail in the next section of this chapter.
15. Sobrino González, "Palacios catedralicios," 565, fig. 7.
16. See the description of Celebruno's *fuero* concession in chapter 2.
17. Powers, *Code of Cuenca*, 174.
18. Nieto Soria, "El equipamiento económico"; Díaz Ibañez, "Las fortalezas medievales"; Powers, "Early Reconquest Episcopate," 1–16.
19. Díaz Ibáñez, "La iglesia de Cuenca," 119–26.
20. González, *Alfonso VIII*, 3:856–59.
21. On the organization of the towns, see Powers, *Society Organized for War*, 11–39.
22. Bolton, *Medieval Reformation*, 104.
23. Constable, *Reformation*, 325–28.
24. Linehan has rightly noted that Cardinal d'Abbeville was shocked at certain habits of the Castilian clerics, but a Parisian intellectual's horror at frontier life may be less instructive of practiced reality than the idealized *forma vivendi* of the schoolrooms: Linehan, *Spanish Church*, 20–34.
25. Chenu, *Nature, Man, and Society*, 202–39.
26. On Martín's reform, see chapter 5.
27. On the reforms of the Sigüenza chapter, see chapter 8.
28. On these reforms in the context of the episcopate of Julián, see chapter 7.
29. The charter detailing the chapter's reform was edited by Jiménez Monteserín in *Vere pater pauperum*, 405–6. I have treated this reform in Lincoln, "'It Pleased the Lord Bishop,'" 275–78.
30. Abajo Martín, *Documentación de Palencia*, 197–200.
31. Nickson, *Toledo Cathedral*, 7–11, 197–220.
32. For these cases, see the discussion of Ramón de Minerva in chapter 3 and the reform of Osma during Celebruno's reign in chapter 2.
33. ACT A.6.F.1.10.
34. ACT XI.F.1.3A.
35. On this example: Barrios Garcia, *Documentos*, 75; Engel and Martín Martín, *Provincia Compostellana*, 4:42–43.
36. On Sigüenza vs. Osma: Holndonner, *Kommunikation*, 599–605. On Palencia vs. Segovia: Villar García, "Un conflicto interdiocesano."
37. Kosto, "Reconquest," 101–4.
38. García y García, *Derecho común*, 51; Linehan, *History and the Historians*, 299, 346.
39. Lincoln, "Note on the Authorship."
40. García y García, "La canonística Ibérica."
41. D'Alverny and Vajda, "Marc de Tolède," in *Al-Andalus* 16, no. 2 (1951): 267–68, 268–69.
42. I have examined this trend in Lincoln, "Prosopography," 207–8.
43. Antecedents: Garrido Garrido, *Documentación*, 1:286–87. Helias: ibid., 1:324, 2:284–85. Odo: ibid., 2:6–9, 24–25, 74–75, 138. Melendo: ibid., 2:18–20, 22–23, 39–40, 64–65, 90–91, 109–11, 206–7, 215–16, 219, 234–35, 269–70, 284–85, and Abajo Martín, *Documentación de Palencia*, 252–54. Martín: Garrido Garrido, *Documentación*, 2:190–91, 206–7, 208, 220, 234–35. Rodrigo: ibid., 2:200–201, 208–9, 213–16, 234–35, 262–63, 284–85. Gíl: ibid., 2:206–8, 234–35.
44. Juan: Garrido Garrido, *Documentación*, 2:174–75. Martín: ibid., 2:237–38.
45. Garsias: Abajo Martín, *Documentación de Palencia*, 122–24. Martin: ibid., 141–43, 163–65. Guillermo de Peñafiel: ibid., 194–97, 212–18. Parens: ibid., 212–15. Ponç: ibid., 215–18, and Garrido Garrido, *Documentación*, 2:266–69. Sares: Abajo Martín, *Documentación de Palencia*, 215–18. Lanfranc: ibid., 230–34,

238–41, 263–64. Giraldo di Lombardo: ibid., 231–34, 234–35, 237–38. Guillermo de Maranac: ibid., 251–52. Lope: ibid., 252–54, 254–55. Aprile: ibid., 252–54, and Hernández Sánchez, *Los cartularios*, 300–301. Michael: Abajo Martín, 252–54. Enrico: ibid.

46. Pedro: Barrios García, *Documentos de Ávila*, 91–92. Juan: ibid., 85–88.
47. Giraldo: Minguella y Arnedo, *Historia de Sigüenza*, 1:456–57, 465–66, 491, 492, 493. Fortún: ibid., 1:482–84, 494–96. Benedictus: ibid., 1:504.
48. A[rnaldus?]: Abajo Martín, *Documentación de Palencia*, 227–28. Guillermo de Soria: Minguella y Arnedo, *Historia de Sigüenza*, 1:457.
49. Domingo: Hernández Sánchez, *Los cartularios*, 136, 37. Ricardus: ibid., 93–94, 94–95, 97–98, 116–17, 129–30. Giraldo: ibid., 116–17, 160–61,1 67–68. Robert: ibid., 152–55, 155–56, 160–61, 161–62, 167–68, 175. Michael: ibid., 163. Mauricio (later bishop of Burgos): Garrido Garrido, *Documentación*, 2:268–69; Hernández Sánchez, *Los cartularios*, 275–76, 289–90, 290–91, 293–94, 294–95, 300–301, 301–2, 302, 307–8. Gonzalo: ibid., 297–98. Domingo: ibid., 312–13, 315–16.
50. Nieto Soria, "La fundación del obispado," 22. Judging from the records of Cuenca, it seems quite likely that several other clerics may have employed the title, but because the witness lists were poorly preserved in the copying of earlier privileges, they have since been lost. The usual practice in authentic texts from the period suggests that only the officers of the chapter subscribed charters, while simple canons witnessed texts for their friends or business partners: Chacón Gomez-Monedero, *Documentos medievales*, files 001–01F.
51. Maffei, "Fra Cremona," 35–51; Rucquoi, "La double vie," 725–26.
52. Fidora, "La recepción de San Isidoro"; Fidora, "Dominicus Gundissalinus"; Rucquoi, "Gundisalvus." On the methodological problems of describing the work carried out at Toledo as a "school" in any formal sense, see Gonzálvez Ruiz, "La escuela de Toledo"; Jacquart, "La Escuela de Traductores"; Benito Ruano, "Ámbito y ambiente"; Burnett, "Coherence"; Gargatagli, "La historia de la escuela."
53. D'Alverny and Vajda, "Marc de Tolède," in *Al-Andalus* 16, no. 1 (1951): 99–132; Ayala Martínez, *Ibn Tumart*, 13–60; Burman, *Reading the Qur'ān*; Burman, "Tafsīr and Translation."
54. Barrios García, *Documentos*, 81–84.
55. Michael Scot and Gerard of Cremona have left strong biographical imprints: see *Oxford Dictionary of National Biography*, s.v. "Michael Scot," https://doi.org/10.1093/ref:odnb/24902; *Dizionario Biografico degli Italiani*, s.v. "Gherardo da Cremona," http://www.treccani.it/enciclopedia/gherardo-da-cremona_ (Dizionario-Biografico).
56. Haskins, *Renaissance of the Twelfth Century*, 41–44, 52–53, 284–90.
57. Lincoln, "Prosopography," 207–8.
58. Barrow, *Clergy*, 49–51.
59. Loud, *Latin Church*, 170–71, 173–74, 259–78.
60. B. Hamilton, *Latin Church*, 116–17, 122–23.
61. Foote, *Lordship*, 38–40, 84, 130–34.
62. Miller, *Formation*, 61, 74–75, 167–68.
63. Eldevik, *Episcopal Power*, 9–10.
64. Barrow, *Clergy*, 271–74, 301–7.
65. Fletcher, *Episcopate*, 31–86.
66. Branco, "Reis, bispos e cabidos."
67. Haskins, *Renaissance of the Twelfth Century*, 41–44, 52–53, 285–90. For a criticism of this quality of Haskins's work, see Kosto, "Reconquest," 101–4.
68. Haskins, *Renaissance of the Twelfth Century*, passim.
69. Southern, "Schools of Paris," 133–37.
70. Gomes, "Escolares e Universidade," 1:511–13.
71. Yolles has shown that the intellectual and literary production of the Latin East was not mediocre, as had been wrongly presumed, but instead poorly preserved: Yolles, "Latin Literature," 9–170.

72. The series of studies in the final part of the volume edited by Parisse demonstrates that this was a widespread phenomenon in the Latin Church: Parisse, *Les chanoines réguliers*, 361–524. Researchers working in other regions have shown that these trends fit long-twelfth-century Christendom broadly: Hamilton, *Latin Church*, 101–2; Barrow, *Clergy*, 100–114; Calvo Gómez, "Los canónigos regulares," 55–78; Burton, "Regular Canons"; Thompson, *Cities of God*, 153. The bibliography of scholarship on the secular clergy compiled by Carcel Ortí is instructive, even if cathedral chapters were not the focus of all of these projects: Cárcel Ortí, "El clero secular," 971–1047.

73. Chenu, *Nature, Man, and Society*, 202–38; Little, *Religious Poverty*, 99–112.

74. Fletcher, *Episcopate*, 221.

75. On the obedience oaths, see, as examples, ACT X.1.E.1.6; ACT X.2.B.1.1; ACT X.2.B.1.1B.

Appendix

1. Hernández Sánchez, *Los cartularios*, 54–64, 88–138; Villar García, *Documentación*, 93–97.
2. Rivera Recio, *La Iglesia de Toledo*, 1:198–99.
3. Linehan, "Synod of Segovia," 42; Fita, "Concilios nacionales," 470–75; Häring, "Die spanischen Teilnehmer"; Somerville, *Pope Alexander III*, 28.
4. Hernández Sánchez, *Los cartularios*, 63–106; Minguella y Arnedo, *Historia de Sigüenza*, 1:119–21.
5. Rivera Recio, *La Iglesia de Toledo*, 1:202–3.
6. Fita, "Concilios nacionales," 470–75; Häring, "Die spanischen Teilnehmer"; Somerville, *Pope Alexander III*, 28; Linehan, "Synod of Segovia," 34n15; Mansi, *Sacrorum Conciliorum*, 22:216.
7. González, *Alfonso VIII*, 2:96–678; Marcos Díez, *La Abadía de Santa María de Husillos*, 35–38, 310–17.
8. Rivera Recio, *La Iglesia de Toledo*, 1:200–202; García y García, *Derecho común*, 67; García y García, *Iglesia, sociedad y derecho*, 1:70; González, *Alfonso VIII*, 1:416–17; Riu y Cabanas, "Primeros cardenales," 137–41.
9. Mansi, *Sacrorum Conciliorum*, 22:216, lists the attendants, but Pedro is not among them. It stands to reason that, while at the Third Lateran Council, the pope was impressed enough with Pedro that he later named him cardinal.
10. Hernández Sánchez, *Los cartularios*, 117–92. The data on Gonzalo Pérez is remarkably slim, and even Linehan was unwilling to say more than that he existed: Rivera Recia, *La Iglesia de Toledo*, 1:202; Linehan, *History and the Historians*, 313.
11. Abajo Martín, *Documentación de Palencia*, 148–223.
12. Ayala Martínez, "Breve semblanza"; Rivera Recio, *La Iglesia de Toledo*, 1:202–4.
13. González, *Alfonso VIII*, 3:446–507.
14. Linehan, *History and the Historians*, 313–18; Pick, *Conflict and Coexistence*, 30–34; Reilly, "Alfonso VIII."
15. Rivera Recio, "Personajes hispanos asistentes," 347; Gorosterratzu, *Don Rodrigo Jiménez de Rada*, 380–83, 466–67.
16. Garrido Garrido, *Documentación*, 1:237–39.
17. Somerville, *Pope Alexander III*, 29. Pedro Pérez was the one cleric from Castile who was absent from the Third Lateran Council: Mansi, *Sacrorum Conciliorum*, 22:216.
18. The surname of Mathé is attested to by Serrano and confirmed by Ayala Martínez, and a substantive link between Marino and the Mathé family is supported by the cathedral obituary (and a precedent property exchange between his sister Estefania and brother Juan): Serrano, *El obispado de Burgos*, 2:116; Ayala Martínez, "Los obispos," 158–59; Serna Serna,

Los obituarios, 458; Garrido Garrido, Documentación, 2:131–32.
19. Garrido Garrido, Documentación, 1:271–90.
20. Ibid., 2:64–66.
21. Ibid., 2:139–40.
22. Ayala Martínez, "Los obispos," 159n26; González, Alfonso VIII, 1:432–33; Serrano, El obispado de Burgos, 2:171–72.
23. Ayala Martínez, "Los obispos," 159; Serrano, El obispado de Burgos, 2:176–79, 2:188–89.
24. Garrido Garrido, Documentación, 2:20–22, 54–55, 139–40.
25. Hernández Sánchez, Los cartularios, 281–96.
26. Rivera Recio, "Personajes hispanos asistentes," 348.
27. Reglero de la Fuente, Cluny en España, 340–42, 732–34.
28. Holndonner, Kommunikation, 343; Lomax, "Don Raimundo," 279.
29. Mansi, Sacrorum Conciliorum, 22:216.
30. Minguella y Arnedo, Historia de Sigüenza, 1:135–36, 440–52.
31. Mansi, Sacrorum Conciliorum, 22:216.
32. Villar García, Documentación, 156–57.
33. Rodriguez Salcedo, "Memorias de don Tello Téllez de Meneses," 13–36; Salcedo Tapia, "Vida de Don Tello Téllez de Meneses," 87–246.
34. Villar García, Documentación, 91–93; Loperráez Corvalán, Descripción histórica, 1:123–46.
35. Linehan, "Royal Influence"; C. Duggan, "Case of Bernardo of Osma"; Loperráez Corvalán, Descripción histórica, 1:146–61; Riaño Rodríguez and Gutiérrez Aja, "Documentos," 228–32.
36. On Miguel's pre-episcopal qualifications and the problems of the abbatology of San Pedro de Arlanza, see my extended comment in Lincoln, "Prosopography," 217n42.
37. Mansi, Sacrorum Conciliorum, 22:216.
38. Loperráez Corvalán, Descripción histórica, 1:170, makes his observations based on a now lost set of annals from Osma.
39. Argaiz, La soledad laureada, 295; Loperráez Corvalán, Descripción histórica, 1:173–87; Riaño Rodríguez and Gutiérrez Aja, "Documentos," 236–37.
40. Loperráez Corvalán, Descripción histórica, 1:187–95; Riaño Rodríguez and Gutiérrez Aja, "Documentos," 236–37.
41. Jordan of Saxony is the first to report the affiliation of Diego d'Acebo with Cîteaux: Jordan of Saxony, "Libellus," 35.
42. Loperráez Corvalán, Descripción histórica, 1:187; González, Alfonso VIII, 1:428.
43. González, Alfonso VIII, 3:446–507; Gorosterratzu, Don Rodrigo Jiménez de Rada, 33–43.
44. Pick, Conflict and Coexistence, vii–viii; Reilly, "Alfonso VIII"; Gorosterratzu, Don Rodrigo Jiménez de Rada, 7–32.
45. Rivera Recio, "Personajes hispanos asistentes," 348.
46. Garrido Garrido, Documentación, 2:18–85.
47. On the identification of Melendo as a monk of Santa Cruz de Coimbra, see Branco or Linehan: Branco, "Portuguese Ecclesiastics," 91–93; Linehan, "Columpna firmissima," 247–49.
48. Rivera Recio, "Personajes hispanos asistentes," 348.
49. Hernández Sánchez, Los cartularios, 54–119.
50. Somerville, Pope Alexander III, 28.
51. Colmenares, Historia, 161–62.
52. Ayala Martínez, "Los obispos," 162; Barón Faraldo, Grupos y dominios aristocráticos, 171.
53. Mansi, Sacrorum Conciliorum, 22:216.
54. ACT X.2.B.1.1; Colmenares, Historia, 162–63; O'Callaghan, "Ideas of Kingship," 12.
55. Ayala Martínez, "Los obispos," 162; González, Alfonso VIII, 1:239–43.
56. González Palencia, Los mozárabes, 1:247.
57. Colmenares, Historia, 163.
58. Ibid., 1.XIX.xii, 1.XX.xiv–xv.
59. Rivera Recio, "Personajes hispanos asistentes," 347. Gerardo famously went

mad after returning from Lateran IV: García García, *Historia del Concilio*, 113–22.
60. Hernández Sánchez, *Los cartularios*, 63–106.
61. Fita, "Concilios nacionales," 470–75; Häring, "Die spanischen Teilnehmer"; Somerville, *Pope Alexander III*, 28; Linehan, "Synod of Segovia," 34n15; Mansi, *Sacrorum Conciliorum*, 22:216.
62. Lincoln, "Prosopography," 219n65; Villar García, *Documentación*, 108–9; Minguella y Arnedo, *Historia de Sigüenza*, 1:117–18, 424.
63. In a wall-side crypt, only Joscelmo's arm is buried in the Capilla del Doncel in Sigüenza: Peces Rata, *Paleografía y epigrafía*, 51.
64. Garrido Garrido, *Documentación*, 1:247–99.
65. Mansi, *Sacrorum Conciliorum*, 22:216.
66. This is Minguella y Arnedo's speculation in *Historia de Sigüenza*, 1:140–41.
67. García Lujan, *Cartulario*, 60–72, 75–79.
68. *Diccionario biográfico español*, s.v. "Martín de Finojosa," http://dbe.rah.es/biografias/24457/san-martin-de-finojosa.
69. Romero, "Hacia una biografia científica"; Astorga Arroya, "San Martín de Finojosa."
70. Minguella y Arnedo, *Historia de Sigüenza*, 1:473–74.
71. Ibid., 1:175–77.
72. Rivera Recio, "Personajes hispanos asistentes," 349.
73. Barrios García, *Documentos*, 35–36.
74. Somerville, *Pope Alexander III*, 28; Mansi, *Sacrorum Conciliorum*, 22:216.
75. Barrios García, *Documentos*, 51–52.
76. Ibid.
77. Ibid., 88; Tello Martínez, *Cathalago sagrado*, 149.
78. Barrios García, *Documentos*, 78–80.
79. Ibid., 88; Villar García, *Documentación*, 156–57; González, *Alfonso VIII*, 3:317–18, 48.
80. Barrios García, *Documentos*, 94–96.
81. Rivera Recio, "Personajes hispanos asistentes," 348.
82. Hernández Sánchez, *Los cartularios*, 167–68, 188–89, 202.
83. González Palencia, *Los mozárabes*, 1:214–15; Hernández Sánchez, *Los cartularios*, 254–55.
84. Hernández Sánchez, *Los cartularios*, 231–32, 263–64, 272–73.
85. González offered the conjecture that Brecio was the sacristan of Valladolid (González, *Alfonso VIII*, 1:471–2), and his speculation may be correct: Mañueco Villalobos and Zurita Nieto, *Documentos*, 1:256–57.
86. González suspected that Domingo was the abbot of Valladolid (González, *Alfonso VIII*, 1:471–2), and his suspicion may have merit: Mañueco Villalobos and Zurita Nieto, *Documentos*, 2:36–40.

Bibliography

Archival Sources
Archivo Capitular de Sigüenza
Archivo Capitular de Sigüenza, Pontificia 11
Archivo Capitular de Sigüenza, Particulares 18

Archivo Catedralicio de Cuenca
ACC, I, caja 2, no. 1
ACC, I, caja 2, no. 7
ACC, I, caja 2, no. 8
ACC, III, Inventarios, leg. 74, no. 13
ACC, III, Libros, no. 717
ACC, Actas 1516

Archivo Catedralicio de Palencia
Acta Capitulares, 39, fol. 250r
Armario I, Legajo 1, no. 15, modern no. 15 (1501), fol. 9r
Armario I, Legajo 3, no. 48, modern no. 48 (1637)
Armario IV, Legajo 8, no. 1, modern no. 884 (1481/82)

Archivo Catedralicio de Toledo
ACT A-6.D.1.12
ACT A.6.E.1.18
ACT A.6.F.1.10
ACT A.6.G.1.1
ACT A.6.G.1.3
ACT. A.6.G.1.10
ACT A.6.H.1.4
ACT E.7.C.2.7
ACT I.4.A.1.7A
ACT I.9.G.1.1A
ACT X.1.E.1.6
ACT X.1.F.1.3
ACT X.1.F.1.3A
ACT X.2.A.2.2
ACT X.2.A.2.3A
ACT X.2.A.2.3B
ACT X.2.A.2.3D
ACT X.2.A.2.7
ACT X.2.A.2.11
ACT X.2.B.1.1
ACT X.2.B.1.1b
ACT X.2.B.2.6
ACT X.2.C.1.6
ACT X.2.C.1.8
ACT X.11.C.1.7
ACT Z.1.G.1.9A

Biblioteca Nacional de España
BNE MS 10839, fols 81r–83r
BNE MS 13035

Edited Primary Sources

Abajo Martín, Theresa, ed. *Documentación de la catedral de Palencia*. Fuentes Medievales Castellano-Leonesas 103. Burgos: Gráficas Cervantes, 1986.

'Abd al-Wāḥid al-Marrākušī, Abū Muḥammad. *Kitāb al-Muʿyib fī taljīs ajbār al-Magrib*. Edited and translated by Ambrosio Huici Miranda. Tetuán: Editora Marroquí, 1955.

Alfonso X, Fernán Sánchez de Valladolid, Sancho IV, and Ramón Menéndez Pidal. *Primera crónica general de España que mandó componer Alfonso el Sabio y se continuaba bajo Sancho IV en 1289*. Madrid: Editorial Gredos, 1955.

Ángel Martínez, Lorenzo Miguel. "Inscripciones medievales de la provincia de Segovia." PhD thesis, Universidad de León, 1999.

Anonymous [Juan de Osma]. "Chronica Latina Regum Castellae." In *Chronica Hispana Saeculi XIII*, edited by Luis Charlo Brea, 7–118. Corpus Christianorum: Continuatio Medievalis. Turnhout: Brepols, 1997.

Anonymous. *Historia Compostellana*. Edited by Emma Falque. Corpus Christianorum: Continuatio Medievalis. Turnhout: Brepols, 1988.

Argaíz, Gregorio de, Gabriel de León, and Bernardo de Hervada. *La soledad laureada por San Benito y sus hijos en las Iglesias de España y Teatro monastico de la provincia Cartaginense*. Madrid: por Bernardo de Herbada, 1675.

Athir, Ibn al-. *The Chronicle of Ibn al-Athir for the Crusading Period from al-Kamil fi'l-Ta'rikh*. Translated by D. S. Richards. 3 vols. Crusade Texts in Translation. Burlington, VT: Ashgate, 2010.

Barrios García, Ángel. *Documentos de la Catedral de Ávila (Siglos XII–XIII)*. Fuentes históricas abulenses. Ávila: Ediciones de la Institución "Gran Duque de Alba," 2004.

Barton, Simon, and Richard Fletcher. *The World of El Cid: Chronicles of the Spanish Reconquest*. New York: Manchester University Press, 2000.

Berger, Daniel. *Dioeceses exemptae: Dioecesis Burgensis*. Vol. 1 of *Iberia pontificia: sive, Repertorium privilegiorum et litterarum a Romanis pontificibus ante annum MCLXXXXVIII Hispaniae et Portugaliae, ecclesiis monasteriis civitatibus singulisque personis concessorum*. Gottingen: Vandenhoeck & Ruprecht, 2012.

———. *Provincia Toletana. Dioecesis Palentina*. Vol. 3 of *Iberia pontificia: sive, Repertorium privilegiorum et litterarum a Romanis pontificibus ante annum MCLXXXXVIII Hispaniae et Portugaliae, ecclesiis monasteriis civitatibus singulisque personis concessorum*. Gottingen: Vandenhoeck & Ruprecht, 2015.

Berger, Daniel, Klaus Herbers, and Thorsten Schlauwitz. *Papsturkunden in Spanien III. Kastilien. Vorabeiten zur Hispania (Iberia) Pontificia*. Berlin: De Gruyter, 2021.

Castejón y Fonseca, Diego de. *Primacia de la Santa Iglesia de Toledo, su origen, sus medras, sus progresos, en la continua serie de prelados que la governaron, a vista de las mayores persecuciones de la católica religión defendida contra las impugnaciones de Braga*. Madrid: por Diego Diaz de la Carrera, 1645.

Castresana López, Álvaro. *Corpus Inscriptionum Christianarum et Mediaevalium Provinciae Burgensis (ss. IV–XIII)*. Oxford: Archaeopress, 2015.

Chacón Gómez-Monedero, Francisco A., ed. *Documentos medievales de la catedral de Cuenca, 1182–1399*. Madrid: Digibis, 2009. DVD-ROM.

Chacón Gómez-Monedero, Francisco A, Julián Canorea Huete, and Manuel J. Salamanca López. *Catálogo de la Sección Institucional del Archivo de la Catedral de Cuenca*. Madrid: Ediciones de la Universidad de Castilla-La Mancha, 2008.

Chamocho Cantudo, Miguel Ángel. *Los fueros del reino de Toledo y Castilla la Nueva*. Madrid: Agencia estatal Boletín Oficial el Estado, 2017.

Colmenares, Diego de. *Historia de la insigne ciudad de Segovia y compendio de las historias de Castilla*. Segovia: Imprenta Real, 1637.

Correa y Roldán, Juan. "Anales de la Santa Iglesia Catedral de Plasencia desde su fundación." In *Historias Placentinas Inéditas*, edited by Domingo Sánchez Loro, 29–78. Cáceres: Institución Cultural "El Brocense" de la Excma. Diputación Provincial de Cáceres, 1983.

Engel, Franco, and Juan Luis Martín Martín, eds. *Provincia Compostellana. Dioeceses Abulensis, Salmanticensis, Cauriensis, Civitatensis, Placentina*. Vol. 4 of *Iberia pontificia: sive, Repertorium privilegiorum et litterarum a Romanis pontificibus ante annum MCLXXXXVIII Hispaniae et Portugaliae, ecclesiis monasteriis civitatibus singulisque personis concessorum*. Gottingen: Vandenhoeck & Ruprecht, 2016.

Estepa Díez, Carlos. "El Reino de Castilla de Alfonso VIII." In *Poder real y sociedad: Estudios sobre el reinado de Alfonso VIII (1158–1214)*, edited by Carlos Estepa Díez, Ignacio Álvarez Borge, and José María Santamarta Luengos, 11–63. León: Universidad de León, 2011.

Fernández de Madrid, Alonso. *Silva Palentina*. 3 vols. Edited by Matías Vielva Ramos. Palencia: Diputación Provincial de Palencia, 1932.

García Lujan, José Antonio. *Cartulario del Monasterio de Santa María de Huerta*. Almazán: Monasterio de Santa Maria de Huerta, 1981.

Garci-Gómez, Miguel, ed. *Cantar de Mío Cid*. Madrid: CUPSA Editorial, 1977.

Garrido Garrido, José Manuel, ed. *Documentación de la catedral de Burgos*. Vol. 1, *804–1183*. Vol. 2, *1184–1222*. Fuentes Medievales Castellano-Leonesas 13 and 14. Burgos: Gráficas Cervantes, 1983.

Gharnaṭi, Sharīf al-. "Comentario a la Qasīda maqṣūra de Ḥazim al-Qarṭājanī." In *Las grandes batallas de la reconquista durante las invasiones africanas*, edited by Ambrosio Huici Miranda, 197–206. Granada: Editorial Universidad de Granada, 2000.

Gómez-Moreno, Manuel. "La Crónica de la población de Ávila." *Boletín de la Real Academia de la Historia* 113, no. 1 (1943): 11–56.

González, Julio. *Regesta de Fernando II*. Madrid: CSIC, 1943.

———. *Reinado y diplomas de Fernando III*. 2 vols. Cordóba: Publicaciones del Monte de Piedad y Caja de Ahorros de Córdoba, 1983.

———. *El reino de Castilla en la epoca de Alfonso VIII*. 3 vols. Madrid: Escuela de Estudios Medievales, 1960.

González Chantos y Ullauri, Diego Eugenio. *Santa Librada, Vírgen y Mártir, Patrona de la Santa Iglesia, Ciudad y Obispado de Sigüenza*. Madrid: Imprenta de la Administración del Real Arbitrio, 1806.

González Dávila, Gíl. *Teatro eclesiástico de las iglesias metropolitanas y catedrales de los Reynos de las dos Castillas: Vidas de sus Arzobispos y Obispos; y cosas memorables de sus sedes*. Madrid: En la Imprenta de Francisco Martínez, 1645.

González Palencia, Ángel. *Los mozárabes de Toledo en los siglos XII y XIII*. 4 vols. Madrid: Instituto de Valencia de Don Juan, 1926–30.

Gratian of Chiusi. *Decretum Gratiani sive Concordia Discordantium Canonum. First Recension*. Edited by Anders Winroth et al. New Haven: Yale University and Stephan Kuttner Institute of Medieval Canon Law, 2015. https://sites.google.com/a/yale.edu/decretumgratiani/.

———. *Decretum Gratiani*. [Second Recension.] In *Corpus Iuris Canonici*, edited by Emil Friedberg. Graz: Akademische Drucku. Verlagsanstalt, 1955.

Hernández Sánchez, Francisco J., ed. *Los cartularios de Toledo: Catálogo documental*. Monumenta Ecclesiae Toletanae Historica 1. Madrid: Fundación Ramon Areces, 1985.

Ḥimyarī, Muḥammad ibn Abd Allāh al-. *Kitab ar-Rawd al Mi'tar*. Translated by

Maria Pilar Maestro Gonzalez. Valencia: Gráficas Bautista, 1963.

Honorius of Autun. "Gemma Animae." In *Patrologia Latina*, edited by Jean-Paul Migne, 172, cols. 0541–0738B.

Hugh of St. Victor. "Speculum de Mysterriis Ecclesiae." In *Patrologia Latina*, edited by Jean-Paul Migne, 177, cols. 0335–380D.

Ibn Ṣāḥib al-Ṣalāh, 'Abd al-Malik ibn Muḥammad. *Al-Mann bil-Imāma: Estudio preliminar, traducción e indices*. Translated by Ambrosio Huici Miranda. Valencia: Editorial Anubar, 1969.

Jordan of Saxony. "Libellus de Principiis Ordinis Praedicatorum." Edited by D. H-C. Scheeben. In *Monumenta historica sancti patris nostri Dominici*, 25–88. Monumenta Ordinis Praedicatorum Historica. Rome: Institutum Historicum Fratrum Praedicatorum, 1935.

Lipskey, Glenn. "The Chronicle of Alfonso the Emperor: A Translation of the *Chronica Adefonsi imperatoris*, with Study and Notes." PhD diss., Northwestern University, 1972.

Loperráez Corvalán, Juan. *Descripción histórica del obispado de Osma*. 3 vols. Madrid: Imprenta Real, 1778. Reprint, Turner Reprints, 1978.

Lotario di Segni. "Legis et Sacramentis Eucharistiae Libri Sex." In *Patrologia Latina*, edited by Jean-Paul Migne, 217, cols. 0763–0915.

Lucas Tudensis. *Chronicon Mundi*. Corpus Christianorum: Continuatio Medievalis. Turnhout: Brepols, 2003.

Mansi, Giovanni Domenico, ed. *Sacrorum Conciliorum Nova Amplissima Collectio*. 31 vols. Florence: Antonio Zatta, 1758–98.

Mansilla, Demetrio Reoyo. *La documentación pontificia hasta Inocencio III (965–1216)*. Rome: Instituto Español de Estudios Eclesiasticos, 1955.

Mañueco Villalobos, Manuel, and José Zurita Nieto. *Documentos de la Iglesia Colegial de Santa María la Mayor*. 3 vols. Valladolid: Sociedad de Estudios Históricos Castellanos, 1917–1920.

Maqqarī, Aḥmed b. al-. *The History of the Mohammedan Dynasties in Spain*. Translated by Pascual de Guyangos. London: Oriental Translation Fund of Great Britain and Ireland, 1840–43.

Marcos Díez, David. *La Abadía de Santa María de Husillos: Estudio y colección documental*. Palencia: Diputación de Palencia, 2011.

Marrākušī, Ibn 'Iḏārī al-. *Al-Bayān al-Mugrb fi Ijtiṣār ajbār muluk al-Andalus wa al-Magrib*. Translated by Ambrosio Huici Miranda. Colección de Crónicas Árabes de la Reconquista 2. Tetuán: Editora Marroquí, 1953.

Minguella y Arnedo, Toribio. *Historia de la diócesis de Sigüenza y de sus obispos*. Madrid: Imprenta de la "Revista de Archivos, Bibliotecas y Museos," 1910–13.

Molina de la Torre, Francisco Javier. "Epigrafía medieval y moderna en la Provincia de Valladolid." PhD. Diss. Universidad de Valladolid, 2013.

Morales y Tercero, Ascensio de. "Inventario General de los privilegios, bulas e instrumentos separados en los Archivos de la Ciudad de Plasencia." In *Historias Placentinas Inéditas*, edited by Domingo Sánchez Loro, 250–93. Cáceres: Institución Cultural "El Brocense" de la Excma. Diputación Provincial de Cáceres, 1983.

Muñoz y Romero, Tomás. *Colección de fueros municipales y cartas pueblas de los reinos de Castilla, León, Corona de Aragón y Navarra*. Madrid: J. M. Alonso, 1847.

Peces Rata, Felipe-Gíl. *Paleografía y epigrafía en la Catedral de Sigüenza*. Sigüenza: Gráficas Carpintero, 1988.

Peter of Ferrand. *Petri Ferrandi Legenda sancti Dominici*. Edited by Simon Tugwell. Rome: Angelicum University Press, 2015.

Porres Martín-Cleto, Julio, ed. *Los Anales Toledanos I y II*. Toledo: Instituto Provincial de Investigaciones y Estudios Toledanos, 1993.

Potthast, August. *Regesta pontificium Romanorum, inde ab a. post Christum Natum MCXCVIII ad a. MCCCIV*. Berlin: Rudolph Decker, 1874.

Powell, James M., trans. *The Deeds of Pope Innocent III by an Anonymous Author*. Washington, DC: Catholic University of America Press, 2004.

Powers, James F. *The Code of Cuenca: Municipal Law on the Twelfth-Century Castilian Frontier*. Philadelphia: University of Pennsylvania Press, 2000.

Renales Carrascal, José. *Catalatto seguntino, serie pontificia y annales diocesanos*. Madrid: por los Herederos de la Viuda de Juan García Infanzón, 1742.

Riaño Rodríguez, Timoteo, and María del Carmen Gutiérrez Aja. "Documentos de los siglos XII y XIII del archivo de la Catedral de Burgo de Osma." *Archivo de Filología Aragonesa* 18/19 (1976): 217–84.

Sánchez Portocarrero, Diego. *Nuevo catálogo de los obispos de la santa iglesia di Siguenza: Epilogo de sus memorables acciones*. Madrid: Diaz de la Carrera, 1646.

Sandoval, Francisco de. *San Antonino Español: Discurso apologético*. Valladolid: por la viuda de Cordova, 1633.

San Martín Payo, Jesus. "Inscripciones en la Catedral de Palencia." *Publicaciones de la Institución de la Tello Téllez de Meneses* 39 (1977): 41–86.

Serna Serna, Sonia. *Los obituarios de la Catedral de Burgos*. Fuentes y Estudios de Historia Leonesa. Léon: Caja España de Inversiones y Archivo Histórico Diocesano de León, 2008.

Tanner, Norman P., S.J., ed. *Decrees of the Ecumenical Councils*. Washington, DC: Georgetown University Press, 1990.

Tello Martínez, José, ed. *Cathalago sagrado de los obispos que han regido a la santa Yglesia de Ábila, desde el primero que fue san Segundo, mártyr clarísimo con notas varias*. Ávila: Ediciones de Institución "Gran Duque de Alba" de la Excma. Diputación Provincial de Ávila, 2001.

Trenchs Oden, José. "El necrologio-obituario de la catedral de Cuenca." *Anuario de Estudios Medievales* 12 (1982): 341–80.

Valmaña Vicente, Alfredo, ed. *El fuero de Cuenca*. 2nd ed. Cuenca: Editorial Tormo, 1978.

Villar Garcia, Luis Miguel, ed. *Documentación medieval de la Catedral de Segovia (1115–1300)*. Salamanca: Ediciones Universidad de Salamanca y Ediciones Universidad de Deusto, 1990.

Walz, Angelus, ed. "Acta Canonizationis Sancti Dominici." In *Monumenta historica sancti patris nostri Dominici*. Monumenta Ordinis Praedicatorum Historica 16. Rome: Institutum Historicum Fratrum Praedicatorum, 1935.

Ximénez de Rada, Rodrigo. *De Rebus Hispaniae sive Historia Gothicorum*. Corpus Christianorum: Continuatio Medievalis. Turnhout: Brepols, 1987.

Secondary Sources

Albares Albares, Miguel Ángel. "La Catedral, espacio sagrado y laboratorio de cultura." *Revista de Museología: Publicación Científica al Servicio de la Comunidad Museológica* 73 (2018): 155–68.

Alcázar, Bartholomé, S.J. *Vida, virtudes, y milagros, de San Julian, segundo obispo de Cuenca*. Madrid: Juan García Infanzon, 1692.

Alfani, Guido. *Fathers and Godfathers: Spiritual Kinship in Early-Modern Italy*. Aldershot: Ashgate, 2009.

Alfani, Guido, Vincent Gourdon, and Agnese Vitali. "Social Customs and Demographic Change: The Case of Godparenthood in Catholic Europe." *Journal for the Scientific Study of Religion* 51, no. 3 (2012): 482–504.

Álvarez Borge, Ignacio. *Cambios y alianzas: La politica regia en la frontera del Ebro en el reinado de Alfonso VIII de Castille (1158–1214)*. Madrid: CSIC, 2008.

———. "La Rioja en el reino y reinado de Alfonso VIII." In *1212, un año, un* reinado, un tiempo de despegue: XXIII Semana de Estudios Medievales, Nájera, del 30 de julio al 3 de agosto de 2012, edited by Esther López Ojeda, 201–36. Logroño: Instituto Estudios Riojanos, 2013.

Alvira Cabrer, Martín. *Las Navas de Tolosa 1212: Idea, liturgia y memoria de la batalla*. Madrid: Silex, 2012.

———. "Prendiendo el fuego de la guerra: Operaciones militares en las fronteras cristiano-almohades entre 1209 y 1211." In *Iglesia, guerra y monarquía en la Edad Media: Miscelánea de estudios medievales*, edited by José Peña González and Manuel Alejandro Rodríguez de la Peña, 139–92. Madrid: CEU Ediciones, 2014.

———. "'Si Possides Amicum, in Temptatione Posside Illum': Alfonso VIII and Peter the Catholic." In Gómez, Lincoln, and Smith, *King Alfonso VIII of Castile*, 185–203.

Alvira Cabrer, Martín, and Pascal Buresi. "'Alphonse, par la grâce de Dieu, Roi de Castille et de Tolède, Seigneur de Gascogne': Quelque remarques à propos des relations entre Castillans et Aquitains au début du XIIIe siècle." In *Aquitaine-Espagne (VIIIe–XIII siècle)*, edited by Philippe Sénac, 219–32. Poitiers: Université de Poitiers, 2001.

Anonymous. *Novena al glorioso S. Julian, obispo, y patrón, de la ciudad de Cuenca y su obispado: Compuesta a un devoto suyo*. Madrid: Gabriel Ramirez, n.d. [likely mid-eighteenth century]. Preserved at http://liburutegibiltegi.bizkaia.eus /bitstream/handle/20.500.11938/73473 /b11063543.pdf.

Ariazaleta, Amaia, and Stéphanie Jean-Marie. "En el umbral de santidad: Alfonso VIII de Castilla." In *Pratiques hagiographiques dans l'Espagne du Moyen Âge et du Siècle d'Or*, edited by Amaia Arizaleta, Françoise Cazal, and Claude Chauchadis, 2:573–83. Toulouse: Presses Universitaires du Midi, 2005.

Astorga Arroya, Maria Ignacio. "San Martín de Finojosa, la gran figure histórica del Real Monasterio de Santa María de Huerta." *Cistercium* 14, no. 82 (1962): 229–36.

Ayala Martínez, Carlos de. "Alfonso VII y la cruzada: Participación de los obispos en la ofensiva reconquistadora." In *Castilla y el mundo feudal: Homenaje al profesor Julio Valdeón*, edited by María Isabel del Val Valdivieso and Pascual Martínez Sopena, 2:513–30. Valladolid: Junta de Castilla y León, 2009.

———. "Alfonso VIII: Cruzada y cristiandad." *Espacio, Tiempo y Forma* 29 (2016): 75–113.

———. "Alfonso VIII y la Iglesia de su reino." In *1212, un año, un reinado, un tiempo de despegue: XXIII Semana de Estudios Medievales, Nájera, del 30 de julio al 3 de agosto de 2012*, edited by Esther López Ojeda, 237–96. Logroño: Instituto de Estudios Riojanos, 2013.

———. "Breve semblanza de un arzobispo de Toledo en tiempos de cruzada: Martín López de Pisuerga." In *Mundos medievales: Espacios, sociedades y poder: Homenaje al Profesor José Ángel García de Cortázar y Ruiz de Aguirre*, edited by Beatriz Arízaga Bolumburu et al., 1:355–62. Santander: Universidad de Cantabria, 2012.

———. *Las Cruzadas*. Madrid: Sílex, 2004.

———. "Holy War and Crusade During the Reign of Alfonso VIII." In Gómez, Lincoln, and Smith, *King Alfonso VIII of Castile*, 118–42.

———. *Ibn Tumart, el arzobispo Jiménez de Rada y la "cuestión sobre Dios."* Madrid: Ediciones La Ergastula, 2017.

———. "Iglesia y violencia en torno a la idea de cruzada siglo XII." *Hispania Sacra* 49 (1997): 349–61.

———. "Los obispos de Alfonso VIII." In *Carreiras eclesiásticas no Ocidente Cristão*, edited by Ana María Jorge, Hermínia Vilar, and Martia João Branco, 153–86. Lisbon: Universidade Católica Portugesa, 2007.

———. "Los obispos leoneses y las guerras santas de Fernando II." In *Homenaje a profesor Eloy Benito Ruano*, 1:91–105. Madrid: Sociedad Española de Estudios Medievales, 2010.

———. "On the Origins of Crusading in the Peninsula: The Reign of Alfonso VI

(1065–1109)." *Imago Temporis: Medium Aevum* 7 (2013): 225–69.

Barber, Malcolm. *The Crusader States*. New Haven: Yale University Press, 2014.

———. *The Two Cities: 1050–1320*. New York: Routledge, 1992.

Barlow, Frank. *Thomas Becket*. Berkeley: University of California Press, 1986.

Barón Faraldo, Andres. *Grupos y dominios aristocráticos en la Tierra de Campos oriental, siglos X–XIII*. Palencia: Diputación Provincial de Palencia, 2006.

Barrigón, María. "A Not So Royal Shoe: Revisiting the So-Called 'Ankle Boot of Eleanor Plantagenet.'" *Dress: The Journal of the Costume Society of America* 42, no. 1 (2016): 1–14.

Barrow, Julia S. *The Clergy in the Medieval World: Secular Clerics, Their Families and Careers in North-Western Europe, c. 800–c. 1200*. New York: Cambridge University Press, 2015.

Bartolomé Herrero, Bonifacio. "Obispos extranjeros al frente de la Diócesis de Segovia (1120–1742)." *Estudios Segovianos* 105 (2005): 19–54.

Barton, Simon. *The Aristocracy in Twelfth-Century León and Castile*. New York: Cambridge University Press, 2002.

———. *Conquerors, Brides, and Concubines: Interfaith Relations and Social Power in Medieval Iberia*. Philadelphia: University of Pennsylvania Press, 2015.

———. "The Count, the Bishop and the Abbot: Armengol VI of Urgel and the Abbey of Valladolid." *English Historical Review* 111, no. 440 (1996): 85–103.

———. "El Cid, Cluny and the Medieval Spanish *Reconquista*." *English Historical Review* 126, no. 520 (2011): 517–43.

———. "Two Catalan Magnates in the Courts of the Kings of León-Castile: The Careers of Ponce de Cabrera and Ponce de Minerva Re-Examined." *Journal of Medieval History* 18, no. 3 (1992): 233–66.

Baucells i Reig, Josep. *Vivir en la Edad Media: Barcelona y su entorno en los siglos XIII y XIV (1200–1344)*. Barcelona: CSIC, 2004.

Baury, Ghislain. "Los ricoshombres y el rey en Castilla: El linaje Haro (1076–1322)." *Territorio, Sociedad y Poder* 6 (2011): 53–72.

Bell, Rudolph M., and David Weinstein. *Saints and Society: The Two Worlds of Western Christendom, 1000–1700*. Chicago: University of Chicago Press, 1982.

Benito Ruano, Eloy. "Ámbito y ambiente de la 'Escuela de Traductores de Toledo.'" *Espacio, Tiempo y Forma, Serie III, Historia Medieval* 13 (2000): 13–28.

Bennison, Amira K. *The Almoravid and Almohad Empires*. New York: Edinburgh University Press, 2016.

Bianchini, Janna. "Daughters, Wives, Widows, Lords: Dynastic Identity and Affective Bonds Among Infantas in Twelfth-Century León-Castile." In *Reginae Iberiae: El poder regio femenino en los reinos medievales peninsulares*, edited by Miguel García-Fernández and Silvia Cernadas Martínez, 11–30. Santiago de Compostela: Universidade de Santiago de Compostela, 2014.

———. "Foreigners and Foes in the Leonese Succession Crisis." In *The Emergence of León-Castile c. 1065–1500: Essays Presented to Joseph F. O'Callaghan*, edited by James Todesca, 47–68. Burlington, VT: Ashgate, 2015.

———. "The *Infantazgo* in the Reign of Alfonso VIII." In Gómez, Lincoln, and Smith, *King Alfonso VIII of Castile*, 59–79.

———. *The Queen's Hand: Power and Authority in the Reign of Queen Berenguela of Castile*. Philadelphia: University of Pennsylvania Press, 2010.

Bishko, Charles Julian. "Peter the Venerable's Journey to Spain." *Studia Anselmiana* 40 (1956): 152–75.

Bisson, Thomas N. *The Crisis of the Twelfth Century: Power, Lordship, and the Origins of European Government*. Princeton: Princeton University Press, 2009.

Bolton, Brenda. *The Medieval Reformation*. London: Edward Arnold, 1983.

Boyle, Leonard, O.P. "The Constitution 'Cum ex eo' of Boniface VIII: Education of

Parochial Clergy." *Mediaeval Studies* 24 (1962): 263–302.

Branco, Maria Joâo Violante. "Portuguese Ecclesiastics and Portuguese Affairs Near the Spanish Cardinals in the Roman Curia (1213–1254)." In *Carreiras Eclesiásticas no Ocidente Cristão (séc. XII–XIV): Ecclesiastical Careers in Western Christianity (12th–14th c.)*, 79–100. Lisbon: Centro de Estudos de História Religiosa Universidade Católica Portuguesa, 2007.

———. "Reis, bispos e cabidos: A diocese de Lisboa durante o primeiro século da sua restauraçâo." *Lusitania Sacra*, 2nd ser., 10 (1998): 55–94.

Brooke, C. N. L. *Churches and Churchmen in Medieval Europe*. New York: Bloomsbury, 2003.

Brown, Peter. *Augustine of Hippo: A Biography*. Berkeley: University of California Press, 1967.

———. *The Body and Society: Men, Women, and Sexual Renunciation in Early Christianity*. New York: Columbia University Press, 1988.

Brundage, James. *Medieval Canon Law*. New York: Routledge, 2014.

Burger, Michael. *Bishops, Clerks, and Diocesan Governance in Thirteenth-Century England: Reward and Punishment*. New York: Cambridge University Press, 2012.

Burman, Thomas E. *Reading the Qurʾān in Latin Christendom, 1140–1560*. Philadelphia: University of Pennsylvania Press, 2007.

———. "Tafsīr and Translation: Traditional Arabic Qurʾān Exegesis and the Latin Qurʾāns of Robert of Ketton and Mark of Toledo." *Speculum* 73, no. 3 (1998): 703–32.

Burnett, Charles. "The Coherence of the Arabic-Latin Translation Program in Toledo in the Twelfth Century." *Science in Context* 14, no. 1/2 (2001): 249–88.

———. "John of Seville and John of Spain: A *Mise au Point*." *Bulletin de Philosophie Médiévale* 44 (2002): 59–78.

Burton, Janet. "The Regular Canons and Diocesan Reform in Northern England." In *The Regular Canons in the Medieval British Isles*, edited by Janet E. Burton and Karen Ströber, 41–59. Turnhout: Brepols, 2012.

Calvo Gómez, Juan Antonio. "Los canónigos regulares del Santo Sepulcro de Jerusalén en la Península Ibérica." *Medievalismo* 25 (2015): 55–84.

Camara Angulo, R. *Libros de matematicas y astronomia en la biblioteca del monasterio de Yuso de San Millán de la Cogolla*. Logroño: Instituto de Estudios Riojanos, 1992.

Cárcel Ortí, Maria Milagros. "El clero secular en Europa en la baja edad media. Bibliografía." *Anuario de Estudios Medievales* 35, no. 2 (2005): 971–1050.

Carl, Carolina. *A Bishopric Between Three Kingdoms: Calahorra, 1045–1190*. Leiden: Brill, 2011.

Catlos, Brian. *Kingdoms of Faith: A New History of Islamic Spain*. New York: Basic Books, 2018.

Celada, Gregorio. "La enseñanza de la Teologia en los estudios medievales y Santo Domingo." In *Santo Domingo de Caleruega: Contexto Cultural, III Jornadas de Estudios Medievales*, edited by Cándido Aniz Iriarte and Luís Vicente Día Martín, 113–42. Salamanca: Editorial San Esteban, 1994.

Cerda Costabal, José Manuel. "The Assemblies of Alfonso VIII of Castile: Burgos (1169) to Carrión (1188)." *Journal of Medieval Iberian Studies* 3 (2011): 61–77.

———. "La dot gasconne d'Aliénor d'Angleterre: Entre royaume de Castille, royaume de France et royaume d'Angleterre." *Cahiers de Civilisation Médiévale* 54 (2011): 225–41.

———. "Leonor Plantagenet y la consolidación castellana en el reinado de Alfonso VIII." *Anuario de Estudios Medievales* 42, no. 2 (2012): 629–52.

———. "The Parliamentary Calendar of Spanish and English Assemblies in the Twelfth Century." *Parliaments, Estates and Representation* 26 (2006): 1–18.

Cerda Costabal, José Manuel, and Félix Martínez Llorente. "Un documento inédito y desconocido de la cancillería de la reina Leonor Plantagenet." *En la España Medieval* 42 (2019): 59–90.

Chenu, Marie-Dominique. *Nature, Man, and Society in the Twelfth Century.* Translated by Jerome Taylor and Lester K. Little. Medieval Academy Reprints for Teaching. Toronto: University of Toronto Press, 1997.

Clemente Ramos, Julián. "Buenos y malos fueros: Aportación al estudio de la renta feudal en Castilla-León (ss. XI al XIII)." *Norba: Revista de Historia* 5 (1984): 116–26.

Cole, Joshua, and Carol Symes. *Western Civilizations: Brief Fifth Edition.* New York: W. W. Norton, 2020.

Conedera, Sam. *Ecclesiastical Knights: The Military Orders in Castile, 1150–1350.* New York: Fordham University Press, 2015.

Constable, Giles. *The Reformation of the Twelfth Century.* New York: Cambridge University Press, 1996.

Corral, Fernando Luis. "Alfonso VIII of Castile's Territorial Litigation at Henry II of England's Court: An Effective and Valid Arbitration?" *Nottingham Medieval Studies* 50 (2006): 22–42.

Dalché, Jean Gautier. *Historia urbana de León y Castilla en la Edad Media (siglos IX–XIII).* 2nd ed. Madrid: Siglo Veintiuno, 1989.

D'Alverny, Marie-Thérèse, and Georges Vajda. "Marc de Tolède, traducteur d'Ibn Tumart." *Al-Andalus: Revista de las Escuelas de Estudios Árabes de Madrid y Granada* 16, no. 1 (1951): 99–140; 16, no. 2 (1951): 259–307; 17, no. 1 (1952): 1–56.

Desprèe, Jaime. *La batalla de Sigüenza: Diario de guerra, 14 de julio, 16 de octubre de 1936.* Sigüenza: El Europeo Comunicación y Multimedia, 2004.

Díaz Ibáñez, Jorge. "Los fortalezas medievales de la Iglesia de Cuenca." In *La fortaleza medieval: Realidad y simbolo*, edited by Juan Antonio Barrio Barrio and José Vicente Cabezuelo Pliego, 305–12. Murcia: Compobell, 1997.

———. "La iglesia de Cuenca en la Edad Media (siglos XII–XV): Estructura y relaciones de poder." Universidad Complutense de Madrid, 2002.

Díez Herrera, Carmen. "El obispado de Burgos en la baja edad media: Formas de fortalecer su jurisdicción frente al monasterio de San Salvador de Oña." *Anuario de Estudios Medievales* 45, no. 2 (2015): 753–82.

Doubleday, Simon. *The Lara Family: Crown and Nobility in Medieval Spain.* Cambridge, MA: Harvard University Press, 2001.

Duggan, Anne J. "Conciliar Law 1123–1215: The Legislation of the Four Lateran Councils." In *The History of Canon Law in the Classical Period, 1140–1234: From Gratian to the Decretals of Pope Gregory IX*, edited by Wilfried Hartmann and Kenneth Pennington, 318–66. Washington, DC: Catholic University of America Press, 2008.

Duggan, Charles. "The Case of Bernado of Osma: Royal Influence and Papal Authority in the Diocese of Osma." In *The Church and Sovereignty, c. 590–1918: Essays in Honor of Michael Wilks*, edited by Diana Wood, 77–96. London: Basil Blackwell, 1991.

Duggan, Joseph. *The "Cantar de Mio Cid": Poetic Creation in Its Economic and Social Contexts.* New York: Cambridge University Press, 2008.

Duggan, Lawrence G. *Armsbearing and the Clergy in the History and Canon Law of Western Christianity.* New York: Boydell Press, 2013.

Eldevik, John. *Episcopal Power and Ecclesiastical Reform in the German Empire: Tithes, Lordship, and Community, 950–1150.* New York: Cambridge University Press, 2012.

Erdmann, Carl. "Das Papsttum und Portugal im ersten Jahrhundert der portugiesischen Geschichte." *Abhandlungen der preussischen Akademie der Wissenschaften* (1928): 51–63.

Escudero, Francisco, S.J. *Vida y milagros del glorioso confesor Sant Iulian, segundo obispo de Cuenca.* Toledo: Pedro Rodríguez, 1589.

Estepa Díez, Carlos. "Memoria y poder real bajo Alfonso VIII (1158–1214)." In *La construcción medieval de la memoria regia*, edited by Pascual Martínez Sopena and Ana Rodríguez, 189–208. Valencia: Universitat de Valencia, 2011.

Estepa Díez, Carlos, Ignacio Álvarez Borge, and José María Santamarta Luengos. *Poder real y sociedad: Estudios sobre el reinado de Alfonso VIII (1158–1214)*. León: Universidad de León, 2011.

Fancy, Hussein. *The Mercenary Mediterranean: Sovereignty, Religion, and Violence in the Medieval Crown of Aragon*. Chicago: University of Chicago Press, 2016.

Fidora, Alexander. "Dominicus Gundissalinus and the Introduction of Metaphysics into the Latin West." *Review of Metaphysics* 66 (2013): 691–712.

———. "La recepción de San Isidoro de Sevilla por Domingo Gundisalvo (ca. 1110–1181): Astronomía, astrología y medicina en la Edad Media." *Mirabilia: Revista Electrónica de História Antiga e Medieval* 1 (2001): 137–49.

Fita, Fidel. "Concilios nacionales de Salamanca en 1154 y de Valladolid en 1155." *Boletín de la Real Academia de la Historia* 24 (1894): 449–75.

———. "Obispos mozárabes, refugiados en Toledo a mediados del siglo XII." *Boletín de la Real Academia de la Historia* 30 (1897): 529–32.

Fletcher, R. A. *The Episcopate in the Kingdom of León in the Twelfth Century*. Oxford: Oxford University Press, 1978.

———. *Saint James's Catapult: The Life and Times of Diego Gelmírez of Santiago de Compostela*. New York: Oxford University Press, 1984.

Foote, David. *Lordship, Reform, and the Development of Civil Society in Medieval Italy: The Bishopric of Orvieto, 1100–1250*. Notre Dame: Notre Dame University Press, 2004.

Fortún Peréz de Ciriza, Luis Javier. "La quiebra de la soberan.a navarra en.lava, Guip.zcoa y el Duranguesado (1199–1200)." *Revista del Instituto de Estudios Vascos* 45, no. 2 (2000): 439–94.

———. *Sancho VII el Fuerte*. Iruña: Mintzoa, 2003.

Freedman, Paul. *The Diocese of Vic: Tradition and Regeneration in Medieval Catalonia*. New Brunswick: Rutgers University Press, 1983.

Fromherz, Alan. "Making 'Great Battles' Great: Christian and Muslim Views of Las Navas de Tolosa." *Journal of Medieval Iberian Studies* 4, no. 1 (2012): 33–38.

Fuente Pérez, María Jesús. *El estudio general de Palencia: La primera universidad hispana*. Palencia: Ediciones Calamo, 2012.

Fumagalli Beono Brocchieri, Mariateresa. "The Intellectual." In *The Medieval World*, edited by Jacques Le Goff and translated by Lydia Cochrane, 181–210. London: Collins and Brown, 1990.

Gallén, Jarl. "Les voyages de S. Dominique au Danemark: Essai de datation." In *Xenia medii aevi historiam illustrantia oblata Thomae Kaeppeli O.P.*, edited by Raymond Creytens and Pius Künzle, 1:73–84. Rome: Edizione di Storia e Letteratura, 1978.

García Fitz, Francisco. *Castilla y León frente al Islam: Estrategias de expansión y tácticas militares (siglos XI–XIII)*. Seville: Universidad de Sevilla, 1998.

———. *Relaciones políticas y guerra: La experiencia castellano-leonesa frente al Islam: Siglos XI–XIII*. Seville: Universidad de Sevilla, 2002.

———. "Was Las Navas a Decisive Battle?" *Journal of Medieval Iberian Studies* 4, no. 1 (2012): 5–9.

García Fitz, Francisco, and Feliciano Novoa Portela. *Cruzados en la Reconquista*. Madrid: Marcial Pons, 2014.

García-Gallo de Diego, Alfonso. "Aportación al estudio de los fueros." *Anuario de Historia del Derecho Español* 26 (1956): 387–446.

———. "Los fueros de Toledo." *Anuario de Historia de Derecho Español* 45 (1975): 341–488.

García-Serrano, Francisco. *Preachers in the City: The Expansion of the Dominican Order in Castile (1217–1348)*. New Orleans: University Press of the South, 1997.

García y García, Antonio. "La canonística Ibérica (1150–1250) en la investigación reciente." *Bulletin of Medieval Canon Law*, n.s., 41 (1981): 41–75.

———. *Derecho común en España: Los juristas y sus obras*. Murcia: Universidad de Murcia, 1991.

———. *Historia del Concilio IV Lateranense de 1215*. Salamanca: Centro de Estudios Orientales y Ecuménicos "Juan XXIII," 2005.

———. *Iglesia, sociedad y derecho*. Salamanca: Universidad Pontificia de Salamanca, 1985.

Gargatagli, Marietta. "La historia de la escuela de traductores de Toledo." *Quaderns: Revista de Traducció* 4 (1999): 9–13.

Gerrard, Daniel M. G. *The Church at War: The Military Activities of Bishops, Abbots and Other Clergy in England, c. 900–1200*. New York: Routledge, 2016.

Giebfried, John J. "Crusader Constantinople's 1205 'Magna Carta.'" Conference paper, Saint Louis University Third Symposium on Medieval and Renaissance Studies, 15 June 2015.

Gomes, Saul Antonio. "Escolares e Universidade na Coumbra Medieval: Breves Notas Documentais." In *Estudos em Homenagem a João Francisco Marques*, 1:509–31. Porto: Faculdade de Letras da Universidade do Porto, 2001.

Gómez, Miguel D. "Alfonso VIII and the Battle of Las Navas de Tolosa." In Gómez, Lincoln, and Smith, *King Alfonso VIII of Castile*, 141–73.

———. "Las Navas de Tolosa: The Practice and Culture of Crusade in Medieval Iberia." PhD diss., University of Tennessee, Knoxville, 2011.

Gómez, Miguel D., and Kyle C. Lincoln. "'The Sins of the Sons of Men': A New Letter of Pope Celestine III Concerning the Crusade of Alarcos." *Crusades* 16 (2017): 55–63.

Gómez, Miguel, Kyle C. Lincoln, and Damian Smith, eds. *King Alfonso VIII of Castile: Government, Family, and War*. New York: Fordham University Press, 2019.

González, Julio, ed. *Historia de Palencia*. 2 vols. Palencia: Diputación Provincial de Palencia, 1990.

González Cabrerizo, Eliseo. *Biografía del insigne soriano San Martín de Finojosa: Abad de Huerta y Obispo de Sigüenza*. Soria: Imprenta de E. las Heras, 1929.

González Cuesta, F. "Sobre el episcopologia de Plasencia." *Hispania Sacra* 95 (1995): 347–76.

González Minguez, César. "Fueros palentinos en la época de Alfonso VIII." *Publicaciones de la Institución "Tello Téllez de Meneses"* 67 (1996): 57–76.

———. "Notas sobre la economía palentina en la Edad Media." *Publicaciones de la Institución "Tello Téllez de Meneses"* 72 (2001): 99–126.

González Palencia, Ángel. *El Arzobispo Don Raimundo de Toledo*. Barcelona: Labor, 1942.

Gonzálvez Ruiz, Ramón. "La escuela de Toledo durante el reinado de Alfonso VIII." In *Alarcos 1195 = Arak 592: Actas del Internacional Conmemorativo del VIII Centenario de la Batalla de Alarcos (1995, Ciudad Real)*, edited by Ricardo Izquierdo Benito and Francisco Ruiz Gómez, 169–210. Cuenca: Ediciones de la Universidad de Castilla-La Mancha, 1996.

———. *Hombres y libros de Toledo*. Monumenta Ecclesiae Toletanae Historica. Madrid: Fundación Ramón Areces, 1997.

Goodich, Michael. *Vita Perfecta: The Ideal of Sainthood in the 13th Century*. Monographien zur Geschichte des Mittelalters 25. Stuttgart: Anton Hiersemann, 1982.

Gorosterratzu, Javier. *Don Rodrigo Jimenez de Rada, gran estadista, escritor y prelado: Estudio documentado de su vida, de los cuarenta años de su Primacia en la Iglesia de España y de su Cancillerato en Castilla, y en particular la prueba de su asistencia al Concilio IV de Litran tan debatida en la controversia de la venida de Santiago a España*. Pamplona: Vdª de T. Bescansa, 1925.

Guijarro González, Susana. "Las escuelas catedralicias castellanas y su aportación a la historia del pensamiento medieval

(1200–1500)." In *Pensamiento medieval hispano: Homenaje a Horacio Santiago-Otero*, edited by José María Soto Rábanos, 1:703–36. Madrid: CSIC, 1998.

———. "Las escuelas y la formación del clero de las catedrales en las diócesis castellano-leonesas (siglos XI al XV)." In *La enseñanza en la edad media: X Semana de Estudios Medievales, Nájera 1999*, edited by José Angel García de Cortázar y Ruiz de Aguirre, Francisco Javier García Turza, and José Ignacio de la Iglesia Duarte, 61–95. Logroño: Instituto de Estudios Riojanos, 2000.

———. "Estudiantes, universidades y cabildos catedralicios en las diócesis castellanas durante la baja edad media." *Edades: Revista de Historia* 4 (1998): 39–55.

———. "La formación cultural del clero catedralicio palentino en la edad media (siglos XIV–XV)." In *Actas del II Congreso de Historia de Palencia, 27, 28 y 29 de abril de 1989*, edited by María Valentina Calleja González, 4:651–66. Palencia: Diputación de Palencia, 1990.

———. "Masters and Schools in the Castilian Cathedrals During the Spanish Middle Ages, 1000–1300." *Medieval History* 4 (1994): 218–47.

Hamilton, Bernard. *The Latin Church in the Crusader States*. London: Variorum Publications, 1980.

Hamilton, Sarah. *Church and People in the Medieval West, 900–1200*. New York: Routledge, 2013.

Häring, Nicholas M. "Die spanischen Teilnehmer am Konzil von Rheims im März 1148." *Medieval Studies* 32 (1970): 159–71.

Harris, Julie A. "Mosque to Church Conversion in the Spanish Reconquest." *Medieval Encounters* 3, no. 2 (1997): 158–72.

Haskins, Charles Homer. *The Renaissance of the Twelfth Century*. Cambridge, MA: Harvard University Press, 1927.

Henriet, Patrick. "Deo votas: L'Infantado et la fonction des infantes dans la Castille et le León des Xe–XIIe siècles." In *Au cloître et dans le monde: Femmes, hommes, et sociétés (IXe–XVe siècle): Mélanges en l'honneur de Paulette L'Hermite-Leclercq*, edited by Patrick Henriet and Anne-Marie Legras, 89–203. Cultures et Civilizations Médiévales. Paris: Presses de l'Université de Paris-Sorbonne, 2000.

Hernández Sánchez, Francisco J. "Los mozárabes del siglo XII en la ciudad y la iglesia de Toledo." *Toletum: Boletín de la Real Academia de Bellas Artes y Ciencias Históricas de Toledo* 16 (1985): 57–124.

———. "Las posturas publicadas por las Cortes de Toledo de 1207 (nueva edición)." *Historia. Instituciones. Documentos* 38 (2011): 255–66.

Hernández Sánchez, Francisco J., and Peter Linehan. *The Mozarabic Cardinal: The Life and Times of Gonzalo Pérez Gudiel*. Florence: SISMEL Galuzzo, 2004.

Heras Hernandez, Felix de las. *Los obispos de Ávila: Su acción pastoral en el ambiente histórico de su tiempo a partir de la predicación apostólica*. Ávila: Diputación de Ávila, 2004.

Herrero de la Fuente, Marta. "Los documentos sobre la concordia compromiso entre las diócesis de Palencia y Segovia del año 1190." In *Actas del II Congreso de Historia de Palencia: 27, 28, y 29 de abril de 1989*, edited by María Valentina Calleja González, 2:261–87. Palencia: Diputación Provincial, Departamento de Cultura, 1990.

Hinnebusch, William A. *The History of the Dominican Order*. Staten Island, NY: Alba House, 1966.

Hitchcock, Richard. *Mozarabs in Medieval and Early Modern Spain: Identities and Influences*. Burlington, VT: Ashgate, 2008.

Holt, Edward L. "*In eo tempore*: The Circulation of News and Reputation in the Charters of Fernando III." *Bulletin of Spanish and Portuguese Historical Studies* 42, no. 1 (2017): 4–22.

Holndonner, Andreas. *Kommunikation—Jurisdiktion—Integration: Das Papsttum und das Erzbistum Toledo im 12. Jahrhundert (ca. 1085–ca. 1185)*. Abhandlungen der Akademie der

Wissenschaften zu Göttingen. Berlin: Walter de Gruyter, 2014.

Honeycutt, Lois. "Queenship Studies Comes of Age." *Medieval Feminist Forum* 51, no. 2 (2015): 9–16.

Hoose, Adam. "The *Sabatati*: The Significance of Early Waldensian Shoes, c. 1184–c. 1300." *Speculum* 91, no. 2 (2016): 257–73.

Izquierdo Benito, Ricardo, and Francisco Ruiz Gómez, eds. *Alarcos 1195 = Arak 592: Actas del Congreso Internacional Conmemorativo del VIII Centenario de la Batalla de Alarcos (1995, Ciudad Real)*. Cuenca: Ediciones de la Universidad de Castilla-La Mancha, 1996.

Jacquart, Danielle. "La Escuela de Traductores." In *Toledo, siglos XII–XIII: Musulmanes, cristianos y judíos: La sabiduría y la tolerancia*, edited by Louis Cardaillac and translated by José Luis Arántegui, 183–98. Madrid: Alianza, 1992. [Originally published Paris: Éditions Autrement, 1991.]

Jervis, Anna Valeria, Maria Rita Giuliani, Marcella Ioele, Michael Jung, Marica Mercalli, and Federica Moretti. "Stepping Across the Mediterranean: Conservation of a Pair of Pontifical Sandals of the Thirteenth Century AD." *Studies in Conservation* 55, numbered supplement 2 (2010): 113–19.

Jiménez Monteserín, Miguel. *Vere pater pauperum: El culto de San Julián en Cuenca*. Cuenca: Diputación de Cuenca, Departamento de Cultura, 1999.

Julian-Jones, Melissa. Review of *Bishops in the Political Community of England, 1213–1272*, by S. T. Ambler. *Speculum* 94, no. 2 (2019): 497.

Jussen, Bernhard. *Spiritual Kinship as Social Practice: Godparenthood and Adoption in the Early Middle Ages*. Newark: University of Delaware Press, 2000.

Kantorowicz, Ernst. *The King's Two Bodies: A Study in Medieval Political Theology*. Princeton: Princeton University Press, 1957.

Kennedy, Hugh. *Muslim Spain and Portugal: A Political History of al-Andalus*. New York: Routledge, 1996.

Kosto, Adam. "Reconquest, Renaissance, and the Histories of Iberia, ca. 1000–1200." In *European Transformations: The Long Twelfth Century*, edited by John Van Engen and Thomas F. X. Noble, 93–117. Notre Dame: University of Notre Dame Press, 2012.

Krasner Balbale, Abigail. "Between Kings and Caliphs: Religion and Authority in Sharq al-Andalus (1145–1244 CE)." PhD diss., Harvard University, 2012.

Ladero Quesada, Miguel Angel. *Ciudades de la España medieval*. Madrid: Dykinson, 2010.

———. *Las ferias de Castilla: Siglos XII a XV*. Madrid: Comité Español de Ciencias Históricas, 1994.

———. "La renta de sal en la Corona de Castilla: Siglos XIII–XVI." In *Homenaje al profesor Juan Torres Fontes*, edited by Universidad de Murcia, 1:821–38. Murcia: Universidad de Murcia, 1987.

Lay, Stephen. *The Reconquest Kings of Portugal: Political and Cultural Reorientation on the Medieval Frontier*. New York: Palgrave Macmillan, 2009.

Lincoln, Kyle C. "About Three Clerics and Towards a 'History from the Middle': Miguel de San Nicolas, Gíl of Cuenca, and Lanfranc di Palacio of Palencia." *Journal of Religious History* (2022): 1–20. doi: 10.1111/1467-9809.12831.

———. "Beating Swords into Croziers: A Case Study of Warrior Bishops in the Kingdom of Castile, c. 1158–1214." *Journal of Medieval History* (2018): 83–103.

———. "The Episcopate in the Kingdom of Castile During the Reign of Alfonso VIII (1158–1214)." PhD diss., Saint Louis University, 2016.

———. "'Holding the Place of the Lord Pope Celestine': The Legations of Gregory, Cardinal-Deacon of Sant'Angelo (1192–4 & 1196–7)." *Anuario de la Historia de la Iglesia* 24 (2014): 471–500.

———. "'It Pleased the Lord Bishop': Episcopal Agency and Cathedral Chapter Reform in the Kingdom of Castile at the End of the Long Twelfth Century

(c. 1195–1205)." In *Episcopal Power and Personality in Medieval Europe, 900–1480*, edited by Peter Coss, Chris Dennis, Melissa Julian-Jones, and Angelo Silvestri, 265–84. Church History 42. Turnhout: Brepols, 2020.

———. "*Mihi pro fidelitate militabat*: Cruzada, guerra santa y guerra justa contra cristianos durante el reino de Alfonso VIII de Castilla según las fuentes episcopales." In *Actas del Congreso de Hombres de Guerra y Religion*, edited by Carlos de Ayala Martínez and J. Santiago Palacios Ontalva, 13–33. Madrid: Silex, 2018.

———. "A Note on the Authorship of the *Collectio Seguntina*." *Bulletin of Medieval Canon Law*, n.s., 33 (2016): 137–144.

———. "A Prosopography of the Castilian Episcopate in the Reign of Alfonso VIII." In Gómez, Lincoln, and Smith, *King Alfonso VIII of Castile*, 204–20.

———. "(Re)Writing a History of Castilian Dominance in the Age of the Separation of the Crowns of Leon-Castile (1031–1252)." In *Rewriting History in the Central Middle Ages*, edited by Emily Winkler and C. P. Lewis, 295–314. Turnhout: Brepols, 2022.

———. "*Una cum Uxore Mea*: Alfonso VIII, Leonor Plantagenet, and Marriage Alliances at the Court of Castile." *Revista Chilena de los Estudios Medievales* 4 (2013): 11–32.

Linehan, Peter. "*Columpna firmissima*: D. Gil Torres, the Cardinal of Zamora." In *Cross, Crescent and Conversion: Studies on Medieval Spain and Christendom in Memory of Richard Fletcher*, edited by Simon Barton and Peter Linehan, 241–62. Leiden: Brill, 2008.

———. *History and the Historians of Medieval Spain*. New York: Clarendon Press, 1993.

———. "On Further Thought: Lucas of Túy, Rodrigo of Toledo and the Alfonsine Histories." *Anuario de Estudios Medievales* 27, no. 1 (1997): 415–36.

———. "Un quirógrafo impugnado: Zamora y la cultura jurídica zamorana a comienzo del siglo XIII." *Anuario de Estudios Medievales* 39, no. 1 (2009): 127–76.

———. "Royal Influence and Papal Authority in the Diocese of Osma: A Note on 'Quia requisitis' (JL 13728)." *Bulletin of Medieval Canon Law*, n.s., 31 (1990): 31–42.

———. *Spain, 1157–1300: A Partible Inheritance*. Malden, MA: Blackwell, 2008.

———. *The Spanish Church and the Papacy in the Thirteenth Century*. New York: Cambridge University Press, 1971.

———. "The Synod of Segovia." *Bulletin of Medieval Canon Law*, n.s., 10 (1980): 31–44.

Little, Lester K. *Religious Poverty and the Profit Economy in Medieval Europe*. Ithaca: Cornell University Press, 1978.

Lomax, Derek W. "Don Ramón, Bishop of Palencia (1148–1184)." In *Homenaje a Jaime Vicente Vivens*, edited by Juan Maluquer de Motes y Nicolau, 1:279–91. Barcelona: Facultad de Filosofía y Letras, 1965.

López Pita, Paulina. "Contribución al estudio de la familia mozarabe de los Polinchení." *Al-Qantara* 1, no. 1 (1980): 429–34.

Lorenzo, Santiago Francia. "Palencia en la época de Santo Domingo de Guzmán: Instituciones Eclesiásticas." In *Santo Domingo de Caleruega: Contexto Cultural, III Jornadas de Estudios Medievales*, edited by Cándido Aniz Iriarte and Luís Viliente Día Martín, 161–96. Salamanca: Editorial San Esteban, 1994.

Loud, Graham. *The Latin Church in Norman Italy*. New York: Cambridge University Press, 2007.

Madden, Thomas F. *Enrico Dandolo and the Rise of Venice*. Baltimore: Johns Hopkins University Press, 2003.

Maffei, Domenico. "Fra Cremona, Montpellier e Palencia nel secolo XII ricerche su Ugolina da Sesso." *Revista Española de Derecho Canonico* 47, no. 128 (1990): 35–51.

Mandonnet, Pierre. *St. Dominic and His Work*. Translated by Mary Benedicta Larkin. New York: B. Herder, 1944.

Manrique, Angel. *Santoral Cisterciense hecho de varios discursos, predicables en todas las fiestas de nuestra Señora, y otros Sanctos.* Barcelona: Hieronymo Margarit, en la calle de Pedritxol, delante N.S. del Pino, 1613.

Manrique García, José María. *Sangre en La Alcarria: Sigüenza en la guerra (1936–39).* Valladolid: Galland Books, 2009.

Mansilla, Demetrio Reoyo. "Disputas diocesanas entre Toledo, Braga y Compostela en los siglos XII al XV." *Anthologica Annua* 3 (1955): 89–143.

———. "Inocencio III y los reinos hispanos." *Anthologica Annua* 2 (1954): 9–49.

Mantilla de los Ríos Rojas, M. Socorro, et al. *Vestiduras pontificiales del arzobispo Rodrigo Ximénez de Rada, S. XIII: Su estudio y restauración.* Madrid: Ministerio de Cultura, Direccion General de Bellas Artes y de Conservación y Restauración de Bienes Culturales, Instituto de Conservación y Restauración de Bienes Culturales, 1995.

Martin, Georges. "Hilando un reinado: Alfonso VI y las mujeres." *e-Spania: Revue Interdisciplinaire d'Études Hispaniques Médiévales et Modernes.* http://e-spania.revues.org/20134.

Martín, José-Luis. "Alfonso IX y sus relacions con Castilla." *Espacio, Tiempo y Forma, Serie III, Historia Medieval* 7 (1994): 11–31.

Martin, Therese. "Fuentes de potestad para reinas e infantas: El in-fantazgo en los siglos centrales de la Edad Media." *Anuario de Estudios Medievales* 46, no. 1 (2016): 97–136.

———. "Hacia una clarificación del infantazgo en tiempos de la reina Urraca y su hija la infanta Sancha (ca. 1107–1159)." *e-Spania: Revue Interdisciplinaire d'Études Hispaniques Médiévales et Modernes.* https://e-spania.revues.org/12163.

Martínez Díez, Gonzalo. *Alfonso VIII rey de Castilla y Toledo (1158–1214).* Gijón: Ediciones Trea, 2007.

———. "La Universidad de Palencia: Revision critica." In *Actas del II Congreso de Historia de Palencia,* edited by Maria Valentine Calleja Gonzalez, 4:155–170. Palencia: Diputación Provincial de Palencia, 1990.

Martir Riço, Juan Pablo. *Historia de la muy noble y leal ciudad de Cuenca.* Madrid: Viuda de P.o de Madrigal, 1629.

McKiernan Gonzalez, Eileen Patricia. "Monastery and Monarchy: The Foundation and Patronage of Santa María la Real de Las Huelgas and Santa María la Real de Sigena." PhD diss., University of Texas, 2005.

Miller, Maureen C. *Clothing the Clergy: Virtue and Power in Medieval Europe, c. 800–1200.* Ithaca: Cornell University Press, 2014.

———. *The Formation of a Medieval Church: Ecclesiastical Change in Verona, 950–1150.* Ithaca: Cornell University Press, 1993.

Molénat, Jean-Pierre. "La fin des chrétiens arabisés d'al-Andalus: Mozarabes de Tolède et du Gharb au XIIe siècle." In *¿Existe una identidad mozárabe? Historia, lengua y cultura de los cristianos de al-Andalus (siglos IX–XII),* edited by Cyrille Aillet, Mayte Penelas, and Philippe Roisse, 287–98. Madrid: Casa de Velazquez, 2008.

Nakashian, Craig. *Warrior Churchmen of Medieval England, 1000–1250.* New York: Boydell & Brewer, 2016.

Nalle, Sara. "A Saint for All Seasons: The Cult of San Julián." In *Culture and Control in Counter-Reformation Spain,* edited by Anne J. Cruz and Mary Elizabeth Perry, 25–50. Hispanic Issues 7. Minneapolis: University of Minnesota Press, 1992.

Nickson, Tom. *Toledo Cathedral: Building Histories in Medieval Castile.* University Park: Penn State University Press, 2015.

Nieto Soria, José Manuel. "El equipamiento económico de una sede episcopal castellana de nueva creación: Cuenca, 1180–1280." *Anuario de Estudios Medievales* 12 (1982): 311–40.

———. "La fundación del obispado de Cuenca (1177–1183): Consideraciones político-eclesiásticas." *Hispania Sacra* 34, no. 69 (1982): 111–32.

———. "Imágenes religiosas del rey y del poder real en la Castilla del siglo XIII." *En la España Medieval* 7 (1986): 709–29.

———. "La monarquía bajomedieval castellana ¿Una realeza sagrada?" In *Homenaje al profesor Juan Torres Fontes*, edited by Universidad de Murcia, 2:1225–37. Murcia: Universidad de Murcia, 1987.

———. "Los obispos fundadores: Biografía, poder y memoria en la diócesis de Cuenca." *Erebea: Revista de Humanidades y Ciencias Sociales* 3 (2013): 25–47.

———. "La transpersonalización del poder real en la Castilla bajomedieval." *Anuario de Estudios Medievales* 17 (1987): 559–70.

O'Callaghan, Joseph. *The Cortes of Castile-León, 1188–1350*. Philadelphia: University of Pennsylvania Press, 1989.

———. *A History of Medieval Spain*. Ithaca: Cornell University Press, 1975.

———. "Ideas of Kingship in the Preambles of Alfonso VIII's Charters." In Gómez, Lincoln, and Smith, *King Alfonso VIII of Castile*, 11–29.

———. *Reconquest and Crusade in Medieval Spain*. Philadelphia: University of Pennsylvania Press, 2003.

Olea Álvarez, Pedro. *Sigüenza entre las dos Castillas y Aragón*. 3 vols. Sigüenza: P. A. Olea, 2009.

Oliveira, Miguel de. "Os bispos senhores da cidade." In *Historia da Cidade do Porto*, edited by Artur de Magalhâes Basto, 175–83. Porto: Exma. Diputacao do Porto, 1962.

Olstein, Diego. *La era mozárabe: Los mozárabes de Toledo (siglos XII y XIII) en la historiografía, las fuentes y la historia*. Salamanca: Ediciones Universidad de Salamanca, 2006.

Ortego Rico, Pablo. "Las salinas de Atienza, Medinaceli y Molina de Aragón en la baja edad media: Propiedad, comercio y fiscalidad." *Historia. Instituciones. Documentos* 40 (2013): 207–49.

Palacios Martín, Bonifacio. "Alfonso VIII y su política de frontera en Extremadura." *Anuario de Estudios Medievales* 19 (1989): 155–65.

———. "Alfonso VIII y su política de frontera en Extremadura: La creación de diócesis de Plasencia." *En la España Medieval* 15 (1992): 77–96.

Parisse, Michel, ed. *Les chanoines réguliers: Émergence et expansion (XIe–XIIIe siècles); Actes du sixième colloque international du CERCOR, Le Puy en Velay, 29 juin–1er juillet 2006*. Saint-Etienne: Publications de l'Université de Saint-Etienne, 2009.

Paul, Nicholas L. *To Follow in Their Footsteps: The Crusades and Family Memory in the High Middle Ages*. Ithaca: Cornell University Press, 2017.

Peces Rata, Felipe-Gíl. *Los obispos en la Ciudad del Doncel (589–2012)*. Sigüenza: Gráficas Carpintero, 2012.

Peña de San José, Joaquín. "La biblioteca del convento de San Millán de la Cogolla." *Berceo* 39 (1956): 183–94.

Perry, David. *Sacred Plunder: Venice and the Aftermath of the Fourth Crusade*. University Park: Penn State University Press, 2015.

Phillips, Jonathan. *The Second Crusade: Extending the Frontiers of Christendom*. New Haven: Yale University Press, 2007.

Pick, Lucy K. *Conflict and Coexistence: Archbishop Rodrigo and the Muslims and Jews of Medieval Spain*. Ann Arbor: University of Michigan Press, 2004.

Pixton, Paul. *The German Episcopacy and the Implementation of the Decrees of the Fourth Lateran Council, 1216–1245: Watchmen on the Tower*. Leuven: Brill, 1995.

Portillo Capilla, Teófilo. "La regla de San Agustín en la catedral de Santa María de Osma." In *Santo Domingo de Caleruega: Contexto eclesial religioso. IV Jornadas de Estudios Medievales*, edited by Luis Vicente Díaz Martín and Cándido Ániz Iriarte, 225–44. Salamanca: Editorial San Esteban, 1996.

Powers, James. "The Early Reconquest Episcopate at Cuenca, 1177–1284." *Catholic Historical Review* 87 (2001): 1–16.

———. *A Society Organized for War: The Iberian Municipal Militias in the Central*

Middle Ages, 1000–1284. Berkeley: University of California Press, 1987.

Procter, Evelyn. *Curia and Cortes in León and Castile, 1072–1295.* New York: Cambridge Univesity Press, 1980.

Purkis, William. *Crusading Spirituality in the Holy Land and Iberia, c. 1095–1187.* Rochester, NY: Boydell Press, 2008.

Ramírez Vaquero, Eloisa. "La nobleza bajomedieval Navarra: Pautas de comportamiento y actitudes políticas." In *La nobleza peninsular en la Edad Media*, edited by Juan Ignacio Ruiz de la Peña Solar and Cesar Álvarez Álvarez, 299–323. Ávila: Fundación Sánchez Albornoz, 1999.

Reeves, Andrew. "Education and Religious Instruction." In *The Routledge History of Medieval Christianity*, edited by Robert Swanson, 103–16. New York: Routledge, 2015.

Reglero de la Fuente, Carlos Manuel. *Cluny en España: Los prioratos de la provincia y sus redes sociales (1073–ca. 1270).* León: Centro de Estudios e Investigación "San Isidoro," 2008.

Reilly, Bernard F. "Alfonso VIII, the Castilian Episcopate, and the Accession of Rodrigo Jiménez de Rada as the Archbishop of Toledo in 1210." *Catholic Historical Review* 99, no. 3 (2013): 437–54.

———. "The Court Bishops of Alfonso VII of Leon-Castile, 1147–1157." *Mediaeval Studies* 36 (1974): 67–78.

———. "The *De rebus Hispanie* and the Mature Latin Chronicle in the Iberian Middle Ages." *Viator* 43, no. 2 (2012): 131–45.

———. *The Kingdom of León-Castilla Under King Alfonso VI, 1065–1109.* Princeton: Princeton University Press, 1988.

———. *The Kingdom of León-Castilla Under King Alfonso VII, 1126–1157.* Philadelphia: University of Pennsylvania Press, 1998.

———. *The Kingdom of León-Castilla Under Queen Urraca, 1109–1126.* Princeton: Princeton University Press, 1982.

———. "On Getting to Be a Bishop in Leon-Castile: The 'Emperor' Alfonso VII and the Post-Gregorian Church." *Studies in Mediaeval and Renaissance History* 1 (1978): 35–68.

Reynolds, Susan. *Fiefs and Vassals: The Medieval Evidence Reinterpreted.* Oxford: Clarendon Press, 1994.

Riley-Smith, Jonathan. *The Crusades: A History.* 3rd ed. New Haven: Yale University Press, 2014.

Riu y Cabanas, Ramón. "Primeros cardenales de la Silla Primada." *Boletín de la Real Academia de la Historia* 27 (1895): 137–47.

Rivera Recio, Juan Francisco. *La Iglesia de Toledo en el siglo XII (1086–1208).* Vol. 1. Rome: Iglesia nacional española, 1966.

———. *La Iglesia de Toledo en el siglo XII (1086–1208).* Vol. 2. Toledo: Diputación Provincial de Toledo, 1976.

———. "Personajes hispanos asistentes en 1215 al IV concilio de Letran." *Hispania Sacra* 4, no. 8 (1951): 335–55.

Robinson, I. S. *The Papacy, 1073–1193: Continuity and Innovation.* New York: Cambridge University Press, 1990.

Rodríguez López, Ana. "Dotes y arras en la política territorial de la monarquía feudal castellana: Siglos XII–XIII." *Arenal* 2, no. 2 (1995): 271–93.

Rodríguez Salcedo, Severino. "Memorias de don Tello Téllez de Meneses." *Publicaciones de la Institución Tello Téllez de Meneses* 1 (1949): 13–38.

Romero, Maria Agustín. "Hacia una biografia cientifica de San Martin de Finojosa." *Celtiberia* 23, no. 1 (1962): 93–115.

Rosenwein, Barbara, et al. *A Short History of the Middle Ages.* 5th ed. Toronto: University of Toronto Press, 2018.

Rubenstein, Jay. *Guibert of Nogent: Portrait of a Medieval Mind.* New York: Taylor and Francis, 2013.

Rucquoi, Adeline. "Ciudad e Iglesia: La colegiata de Valladolid en la Edad Media." *En la España Medieval* 5 (1986): 961–84.

———. *Dominicus Hispanus: Ochocientos años de la Orden de Predicadores.* Madrid: Junta de Castilla y León, 2016.

———. "Las dos vidas de la Universidad de Palencia (c.1180–1250)." In *Rex, sapientia, nobilitas: Estudios sobre la Península Ibérica medieval*, 87–124. Granada: Universidad de Granada, 2006.

———. "Éducation et société dans la Péninsule Ibérique médiévale." *Histoire de l'Éducation* 69 (1996): 3–36.

———. "La double vie de l'université de Palencia (c. 1180–c. 1250)." *Studia Gratiana* 29 (1998): 723–48.

———. "Gundisalvus ou Dominicus Gundisalvi?" *Bulletin de Philosophie Médiévale* 41 (1999): 85–106.

———. *Rex, sapientia, nobilitas: Estudios sobre la Península Ibérica medieval*. Granada: Universidad de Granada, 2006.

———. "Las rutas del saber: España en el siglo XII." *Cuadernos de Historia de España* 95 (1998): 41–58.

Ruiz, Teofilo F. *Crisis and Continuity: Land and Town in Late Medeval Castile*. Philadelphia: University of Pennsylvania Press, 1994.

———. "La formazione della monarchia non consacrata: Simboli e realtà di potere nell Castiglia medioevale." In *Federico II e il mondo mediterraneo*, edited by Pierre Toubert and Agostino Paravicini Bagliani, 230–47. Palermo: Salerio, 1994.

———. *From Heaven to Earth: The Reordering of Castilian Society, 1150–1350*. Princeton: Princeton University Press, 2004.

———. "Oligarchy and Royal Power: The Castilian Cortes and the Castilian Crises 1248–1350." *Parliaments, Estates and Representation* 2 (1982): 95–101.

———. "Prosopografía burgalesa, Serracín y Bonifaz." *Boletín de la Institución Fernán González* 54 (1975): 467–99.

———. "Une royauté sans sacre: La monarchie castillane du Bas Moyen Âge." *Annales* 39 (1984): 429–53.

———. "Unsacred Monarchy: The Kings of Castile in the Late Middle Ages." In *Rites of Power: Symbolism, Ritual, and Politics Since the Middle Ages*, edited by Sean Wilentz, 109–44. Philadelphia: University of Pennsylvania Press, 1985.

———. *Sociedad y poder real en Castilla. Burgos en la Edad Media*. Barcelona: Ariel, 1981.

Salcedo Tapia, Modesto. "Vida de don Tello Téllez de Meneses, obispo de Palencia." *Publicaciones de la Institución Tello Téllez de Meneses* 53 (1985): 79–266.

San Martín Payo, Jesús. "Catalogo del Archivo de la Catedral de Palencia." *Publicaciones de la Institución Tello Téllez de Meneses* 50 (1983): 1–149.

Sayers, Jane. *Papal Judges Delegate in the Province of Canterbury, 1198–1254: A Study in Ecclesiastical Jurisdiction and Administration*. New York: Oxford University Press, 1971.

Serrano, Luciano. *D. Mauricio, obispo de Burgos y fundador de su catedral*. Madrid: Instituto de Valencia de Don Juan, 1922.

———. *El obispado de Burgos y Castilla primitiva desde el siglo V al XIII*. 3 vols. Madrid: Instituto de Valencia de Don Juan, 1935.

Sevilla Muñoz, Julia. "Una consecuencia de la reconquista de Guadalajara: La repoblación de Sigüenza por un obispo aquitano." *Wad-al-Hayara: Revista de Estudios de Guadalajara* 12 (1985): 43–56.

Shadis, Miriam. *Berenguela of Castile and Political Women in the High Middle Ages*. New York: Palgrave Macmillan, 2009.

———. "Happier in Daughters than in Sons: The Children of Alfonso VIII of Castile and Leonor Plantagenet." In Gómez, Lincoln, and Smith, *King Alfonso VIII of Castile*, 80–101.

Sirantoine, Hélène. *Imperator Hispaniae: Les idéologies impériales dans le royaume de León (IXe–XIIe siècles)*. Madrid: Casa de Velazquez, 2013.

Smith, Damian. *Crusade, Heresy, and Inquisition in the Lands of the Crown of Aragon, c. 1167–1276*. Leiden: Brill, 2010.

———. "The Iberian Legations of Cardinal Hyacinth Bobone." In *Pope Celestine III: Diplomat and Pastor*, edited by John Doran and Damian Smith, 84–115. Aldershot: Ashgate, 2008.

———. "The Reconciliation of Guilhelm Ramón de Moncada." In *The Fourth*

Lateran Council and the Crusade Movement: The Impact of the Council of 1215 on Latin Christendom and the East, edited by Jessalynn Bird and Damian J. Smith, 131–50. Turnhout: Brepols, 2018.

Sobrino González, Miguel. "Palacios catedralicios, catedrales palatinas." Anales de Historia del Arte, extra, 2 (2013): 551–67.

Soifer Irish, Maya. Jews and Christians in Medieval Castile: Tradition, Coexistence and Change. Washington, DC: Catholic University of America Press, 2016.

———. "Tamquam domino proprio: Contesting Ecclesiastical Lordship over Jews in Thirteenth-Century Castile." Medieval Encounters: Jewish, Christian and Muslim Culture in Confluence and Dialogue 19 (2013): 534–66.

Somerville, Robert. Pope Alexander III and the Council of Tours (1163): A Study of Ecclesiastical Politics and Institutions in the Twelfth Century. Berkeley: University of California Press, 1977.

Southern, R. W. "The Schools of Paris and the School of Chartres." In Renaissance and Renewal in the Twelfth Century, edited by Robert Louis Benson, Giles Constable, and Carol Dana Lanham, 113–37. Toronto: Medieval Academy Reprints for Teaching, 1991.

Spinks, Bryan D. Early and Medieval Rituals and Theologies of Baptism: From the New Testament to the Council of Trent. Burlington, VT: Ashgate, 2006.

Suárez Fernández, Luis, ed. León en torno a las Cortes de 1188. León: La Robla, 1987.

Sweeney, James Ross. "Innocent III, Canon Law, and Papal Judges Delegate in Hungary." In Popes, Teachers, and Canon Law in the Middle Ages, edited by James Ross Sweeney and Stanley Chodorow, 26–52. Ithaca: Cornell University Press, 1986.

Thomas, Hugh. The Secular Clergy in England, 1066–1216. New York: Oxford University Press, 2016.

Thompson, Augustine. Cities of God: The Religion of the Italian Communes, 1125–1325. University Park: Penn State University Press, 2005.

Todesca, James J. "Money of Account and Circulating Coins in Castile-León c. 1085–1300." In Problems of Medieval Coinage in the Iberian Area: A Symposium Held by the Sociedade Numismática Scalabitana and the Instituto de Sintra on 4–8 October 1988, edited by Mário Gomes Marques and D. M. Metcalf, 271–86. Santarém: Instituto de Sintra, 1988.

———. "Selling Castile: Coinage, Propaganda, and Trade in the Reign of Alfonso VIII of Castile." In Gómez, Lincoln, and Smith, King Alfonso VIII of Castile, 30–58.

Tugwell, Simon. "Notes on the Life of St. Dominic IV: Dominic's Date of Birth." Archivum Fratrum Praedicatorum 67 (1997): 27–59.

Vaca Lorenzo, Angel. "El obispado de Palencia desde sus orígenes hasta su definitive restaución en el siglo XI." Hispania Sacra 52, no. 105 (2000): 21–72.

Vajay, Szabolcs de. "L'aspect politique des trois mariages de Raymond Bérenger le Grand." Assembles d'estudis. Besalu 1 (1968): 35–73.

Valenzuela y Velazquez, Juan Bautista. Discurso en comprobación de la santidad de vida, y milagros del glorioso San Julian, segundo obispo de Cuenca. Cuenca: Bartolome de Selme, 1611.

Vann, Teresa. "The Town Council of Toledo During the Minority of Alfonso VIII (1158–1169)." In Medieval Iberia: Essays on the History and Literature of Medieval Spain, edited by Donald Kagay and Joseph Snow, 43–60. New York: Peter Lang, 1997.

Vauchez, André. Sainthood in the Later Middle Ages. Translated by Jean Birrell. New York: Cambridge University Press, 1997.

Vicaire, M. H. Saint Dominic and His Times. Translated by Kathleen Pond. New York: McGraw-Hill, 1964.

———. "Saint Dominique chanoine d'Osma." Archivum Fratrum Praedicatorum 63 (1993): 5–41.

Vila da Vila, María Margarita. "Repoblación y estructura urbana de Ávila en la Edad Media." In *La ciudad y el mundo urbano en la historia de Galicia*, edited by Ramón Villares Paz, 137–54. A Coruña: Universidad de Santiago de Compostela, 1988.

Villar García, Luis Miguel. "Un conflicto interdiocesano en la Edad Media: Palencia y Segovia y la División de Wamba." In *Actas del I Congreso de Palencia*, edited by María Valentina Calleja González, 2:385–400. Valladolid: Diputación de Palencia, 1987.

Walker, Rose. "Leonor of England, Plantagenet Queen of King Alfonso VIII of Castile, and Her Foundation of the Cistercian Abbey of Las Huelgas: In Imitation of Fontevraud?" *Journal of Medieval History* 31 (2005) 346–68.

Ward, Benedicta. *Miracles and the Medieval Mind: Theory, Record, and Event, 1000–1215*. Philadelphia: University of Pennsylvania Press, 1982.

Weiss, Stefan. *Die Urkunden der päpstlichen Legaten von Leo IX. bis Coelestin III. (1049–1198)*. Cologne: Böhlau Verlag, 1995.

Witcombe, Teresa. "Building Heaven on Earth: Bishop Maurice and the *novam fabricam* of Burgos Cathedral." *Bulletin for Spanish and Portuguese Historical Studies* 42, no. 1 (2017): 46–60.

Winroth, Anders. "The Legal Revolution of the Twelfth Century." In *European Transformations: The Long Twelfth Century*, edited by Thomas F. X. Noble and John Van Engen, 338–53. Notre Dame: Notre Dame University Press, 2012.

Yolles, Julian. "Latin Literature and Frankish Culture in the Crusader States (1098–1187)." PhD diss., Harvard University, 2015.

Zalama, Miguel Ángel. *Por tierras de Soria*. León: Ediciones Lancia, 1995.

Zaragoza i Pascual, Ernesto. "Abadología del monasterio de San Pedro de Arlanza (siglos X–XIX)." *Boletín de la Institución Fernán González* 210 (1995): 85–110.

———. "Abadología del monasterio de San Salvador de Oña (siglos XI–XIX)." *Burgense: Collectanea Scientifica* 35, no. 2 (1994): 557–94.

Zerbi, Piero. *Papato, impero e "respublica christiana" dal 1187 al 1198*. 2nd ed. Milan: Vita e Pensiero, 1980.

Index

Abbat, Per, 85
de Abbeville, Cardinal Jean, 80
'Abd al-Wāḥid al-Marrākušī, Abū Muḥammad, 88
ben Abdullah al-Polincheni, Domingo, Archp. of Toledo, 31
d'Acebo, Diego, bp. of Osma, 69, 73, 74, 80, 83
Adrian IV (pope), 17
de Agen, Bernardo, Bp. of Sigüenza, 126
Alarcos, Crusade of (1195), 89, 92, 127
   aftermath, 8, 95
   call and recruitment, 7, 89, 116
   defeat and casualties, 8, 75, 123, 131
Alcázar, Bartholomé, 101
al-Mansur, Yaqub
   Almohad Caliph, 7, 88
   campaigns in Iberia, 75, 132
al- Maqqarī, Aḥmed, 88, 89
Álava, 80
Albarracín-Segorbe, diocese of, 3, 9, 103
de Alcázar, Bartholome, 101
Alexander III (pope), 17, 20, 28, 29, 32, 44, 45, 47, 56, 78, 79, 101, 134
Alfonso, Bp. of Ourense, 61, 62
Alfonso VI, K. of Léon, 57

Alfonso VII, K. of León and Castile, 4, 19, 20, 33, 36, 37, 49, 95
   death, 4
   coronation, 18
   imported clerics, 20, 52, 57
Alfonso VIII, K. of Castile, 1, 6, 7, 9, 16, 19, 22, 24, 25, 79, 86, 99, 113, 115, 123, 125
   attempted canonization, 109
   control of Gascony, 8
   knighthood at San Zoilo, 38, 39, 42
   minority, 5, 6, 17, 20, 23, 34, 35, 36, 37, 38, 41, 46, 70 ,101
   reign as a chronological unit, 4, 5, 12, 13, 66, 129, 131, 137
   relationship with clerics and the Church, 18, 22, 23, 25, 33, 41, 42, 44, 48, 50, 55, 62, 75, 80, 83, 96, 99, 105
   wars against León, 6, 8, 43, 44, 45
   wars against Navarra, 6, 8, 45, 46, 75, 83
   Will and Testament in 1204, 8, 28, 80, 81, 106, 117
Alfonso IX, K. of León, 3
   Cortes of Valladolid, 3
   knighting by Alfonso VIII at Carrión, 7
   marriage to Berenguela of Castile, 61, 66, 75, 94, 95, 96, 98
   Putative 1196 Crusade against, 8, 75

Alfonso Alfonsez de Molina, 95
Almazán, 120
Alvárez Borge, Ignacio, 70
Amiens, Hugh of, 138
Anales Toledanos, 73
Anthony, St., 49
de Argaíz, Gregorio, 35, 69, 70, 84
Astorga, diocese of, 9
Ibn al-Athir, 88
Atienza, 120
Augustinian Rule, 79, 80
Ávila, 134, 135, 136
  archives, 11
  cathedral chapter, 60
  diocese of, 3, 9, 54, 97, 129
  dispute with Segovia, 54
  frontier position, 11
  militia, 131, 132
  separation of Plasencia from, 7, 10
  walls, 132
de Ayala Martínez, Carlos, 12, 13, 75
Azaña, 102

de Bazán, Martín, Bp. of Osma, 16, 28, 69, 75, 76, 84, 90, 137, 140
  early life and family, 70
  cultivation of patronage, 72, 75, 81, 82
  papal judicial delegations, 60, 74, 76, 77, 81
  reform of the chapter, 29, 69, 71, 74, 73, 74, 78, 79, 80, 81, 82, 133
Belinchón, 25, 26, 27, 32, 33, 53, 132
Becket, Thomas, 107
Berengaria, wife of Alfonso VII, 36, 37
Berenguela, Q. of León and Castile, 7, 10, 61, 67, 94, 95, 96, 98, 123, 124, 125
Berenguela Alfonsez, daughter of Berenguela and Alfonso IX, 95
Bernardo of Osma, Bp. of Osma, 28, 29, 30, 32, 54, 71, 78, 134
Bianchini, Janna, 1, 16, 39, 96
Bisson, Thomas, 97
Blanca, Q. of France, 7
Bobone, Hyacinth (cardinal). *See* Celestine III (pope)
Bolton, Brenda, 133
Braga, archdiocese of, 21, 77, 78
Brecio, Bp. of Plasencia, 78, 129
Burger, Michael, 97
Burgos, 55, 58, 61, 71, 74, 81, 126, 135

archives, 11
bishops, 54
diocese of, 3, 9, 61, 76
1169 *Cortes* of, 6, 24, 38

Cáceres, 10
Calahorra, diocese, 75
Calatrava, 93, 101, 103, 132
Calatrava, Military Order of, 54
Caleruega, 74
Canterbury, 14
Cañete, 106
de Cardona, Pedro, 135, 137, 138
Carl, Carloina, 13
Carlos I (Charles V), 66
Carrión, 1188 *Cortes* of, 7
Cassian, John, 58
de Castéjon y Fonseca, Diego, 17, 34
de Castellmorum/de Segovia, Juan, Abp. of Toledo, 19, 23
Castro family, 17
  Gutierre Fernández de, 38
Celebruno, bp. of Sigüenza and Archbp. of Toledo, 15, 17, 29, 30, 49, 85, 89, 134, 140
  Canon of Toledo, 19, 20
  comital godfather, 20
  cultivating patronage, 18, 22, 30, 31, 34
  election to Sigüenza, 19, 32
  elevation to Toledo, 23, 32
  Episcopate in Sigüenza, 20, 21, 23, 53
  Fuero of Belinchón, 25, 26, 27, 32, 132
  jurisdictional disputes, 21,
  reform efforts, 45, 71
  reform of the chapter, 28, 30, 31, 32
  royal godfather, 5, 18, 19, 20, 22, 23, 32, 38
Celestine III (pope), 75, 92, 93, 95, 116, 118
  election as Pope, 7
  legations in Iberia, 6, 21, 86
Centellas, 77
Chamocho Cantudo, Miguel, 106
Chartres, Fulcher of, 138
Chenu, Marie-Dominique, 63
Ciudad Rodrigo, diocese of, 9
Clairvaux, Bernard of, 127
Clement III (pope), 60
Clermont, 1095 Council of, 131
Collationes Patrum, 58
Collectio Seguntina, 122, 135
de Colmenares, Diego, 91

Compilatio prima, 32, 90
Compilatio tertia, 80
Conrad, D. of Swabia, 7
Constable, Giles, 115, 133, 134
  Constanza, daughter of Berenguela and Alfonso IX, 95
Córdoba, 9
Coria, diocese of, 9
Corral, Fernando Luis, 46, 47
Cremona, Gerald of, 136
Cuenca, 16, 101, 133, 135
  1177 conquest, 6, 8, 91, 101
  cathedral/mosque, 104, 107, 109
  cathedral chapter, 93, 94, 138
  diocese of, 3, 9
  foundation of fiocese, 6, 86, 101
  Fuero, 106, 107, 132

Damian, Peter, 135
Deva, River, 61
Díaz Ibáñez, Jorge, 102
Dominic of Osma/Domingo de Caleruega, St., 11, 14, 57, 74, 135, 140
  Order of Preachers, 70, 79, 80
  role in reform of Osma, 16, 69, 73, 74, 80, 82, 83
  student at Palencia, 56, 58, 59, 60, 63, 73, 74, 109
Duggan, Lawrence, 131
Duero, River, 72

Ebro, River, 70
Eleanor of Aquitaine, 6
Enrique, K. of Castile, 123, 124, 125
Escudero, Francisco, 109
Esteban, bp. of Zamora, 114

Fernández de Madrid, Alonso, 51, 62, 63, 65
Fernando, *Infante* of Castile (d. 1211)
  as heir to Casitle, 7
  1210 Raiding of Murcia, 9
  leadership of 1212 Crusade of Las Navas de Tolosa, 9
Fernando II, K. of Leon, 19, 22, 36, 37
  control in Castilian territory, 4, 17, 23, 38, 42, 43, 44
  as heir to Castile presumptive, 5
Fernando III, K. of Castile and León, 10, 12, 57, 89, 95, 124, 125, 126
Finojosa, (St.) Martín de

Bishop of Sigüenza, 73, 114
  Abbot of Huerta, 124, 137
Finojosa, Rodrigo de, 7, 90, 113, 121, 123, 124, 125, 126, 141
  Bishop of Sigüenza, 16, 66, 116
  early life and election to episcopate, 114, 115
  compilation of *Collectio Seguntina*, 122, 135
  conflict over homicide accusations, 121, 122
  conflict with Medinaceli, 116, 117, 118, 119, 120, 125, 127
  cultivation of patronage, 115, 118, 119, 124
  reform of cathedral chapter, 83, 93, 106, 115, 119, 120, 127, 133
Fletcher, Richard, 1, 11, 13, 48, 78, 130, 139
Foote, David, 14
Freedman, Paul, 14
Friedberg, Emil, 80
Friesing, Otto von, 138
Frodericus, Archd. of Calatrava, 103

G., archdeacon of Segovia, 90
Garcés de Lerma, Gonzalo Pérez, 102
García, Bp. of Osma, 71
García Fitz, Francisco, 6
García y García, Antonio, 124
Garrard, Daniel, 49
Gascony, Bishops from, 8
Gelmírez, Diego, Abp. of Santiago de Compostela, 13, 48, 55, 58
Gerardo, Bp. of Segovia, 122, 126
Gíl, canon of Cuenca, 104
González, Julio, 12, 39, 46, 125
González, Domingo, Archd. of Cuéllar, 59, 135
González Dávila, Gíl, 65
González Palencia, Ángel, 102, 103
González Telmo, (St.) Pedro, 64
Gonzalo Miguel, Bp. of Segovia, 62
Gratian, 136, 138
  Decretum, 29, 60
Gregory, Cardinal-Deacon of Sant'Angelo, 72
  legations in Iberia, 7, 72, 81, 86, 117
Gregory IX (pope), 57, 80
Granada, 9
Guillermo, bp of Zamora, 114
Guipuzcoa, 80
Gutiérrez Girón, Gonzalo, bp. of Segovia, 1, 2, 16, 54, 74, 90
Gutiérrez Girón, Count Rodrigo, 89, 91

Hamilton, Bernard, 14, 49, 110
Haskins, Charles Homer, 135, 136, 138
Henry II of England, 6, 107
   negotiations between Castile and Navarra at court, 6, 45, 46, 47
Historia Compostellana, 18
Holndonner, Andreas, 14
Honorius III (pope), 89
Hospital, Military Order of the, 120
Huecar, River, 101
Huesca, 77
Huete, 105
Huici Miranda, Ambrosio, 88
Husillos, 134

I[oannes?]., Master of the School at Palencia, 62
Ibáñez, Pedro, Abt. of San Salvaror de Oña, 74
Infantazgo, 40, 43, 67, 95
Innocent II (pope), 21
Innocent III (pope), 77, 78, 80, 95, 105, 121, 122, 129
   correspondence with *Infante* Fernando, 9
Instancio, Pedro, Bp. of Ávila, 62

Jacopo di Palacio, father of Alderico, 52
Jerome de Perigord, companion of *El Cid*, 44, 85
Jiménez Monteserín, Miguel, 108, 109
John, K. of England, 8
Joscelmo, Bp. of Sigüenza, 25, 53, 110, 116, 126
Juan de Frantia, archpriest of Segovia, 90
Juan de Osma, 43, 87
Juan, Archd. of Palencia, 62
Jucar, River, 101
Julian-Jones, Melissa, 2

Ladero Quesada, Miguel, 106
Lanfranco di Palacio, brother of Alderico, 52, 59 ,62
Lara, Counts of, 5, 17, 20, 38
   Nuño, 89
   Pedro Manriquez, 20, 38
   Pedro Ansurez, 40
Las Navas de Tolosa, 1212 Crusade, 43, 89, 113, 116, 123, 127, 131, 132
   leadership, 91
   losses, 9

Lateran, Councils of
   first,
   second, 21
   third, 21, 47, 52, 56, 57, 59, 61, 66, 74, 90, 91, 96, 121
   fourth, 21, 79, 80, 123, 124
Leonor Plantagenet, Q. of Castile, 4, 6, 7, 9, 24, 125
   Dower lands in Gascony, 8,
Liber extra, 32, 80
Linehan, Peter, 12, 13, 29, 35, 38, 44, 98, 110, 129
Lisbon, 137
de Leucat, Pedro, 18
Logroño, 43, 45
Lomax, Derek, 35, 46, 55
Lombardo, Master Giraldo di, 57, 59, 62
Lope, Bp. of Sigüenza, 125
López de Pisuerga, Martín, Abp. Of Toledo, 16, 76, 85, 93, 94, 96, 99, 102, 115, 118, 119, 120, 122, 133, 140, 141
   cavalry raid in 1194, 7, 86, 87, 88, 89, 98, 116
   confirmation/expansion of *Fuero* of Belinchón, 25
   cultivation of patronage, 92, 96, 98
   investigation of the age of Gutierre Rodríguez Girón of Segovia, 89, 90, 91, 92, 98, 131
   papal judicial delegations, 94, 95
   purchases of property, 96, 97, 98
   reform of the chapter of Toledo, 94
   role in the reform of Cuenca, 93, 94, 98
Loperráez Corvalán, Juan, 82
Loud, Graham, 14, 110
Lucius III (pope), 55, 60, 78, 79, 134
Lugo, diocese of, 9

Madrid, 26
Maffei, Domenico, 59
Maladones, 40
Manes, uncle of Dominic of Osma, 60
Marc of Toledo, 135, 136
March Pact of 1204, 3
ibn Mardanish, Muhammad ibn Sa'd, K. of Murcia, 101
Martínez Díez, Gonzalo, 59
Martínez, Anton, 108
Martín, Bp. of Zamora, 62
Martir Riço, Juan Pablo, 109

Mathé, Juan, bp. of Burgos, 9, 123, 132
Mathé, Marino, bp. of Burgos, 54, 61, 74
Mathé, Mateo, bp. of Burgos, 81
Mauricio, bp. of Burgos, 104, 135, 138
Medinaceli, 53, 105,
   conflict with bishops of Sigüenza, 54, 116, 117, 118, 119, 120, 122, 123
Melendo, Bp. of Osma, 135, 138
Mende, Adalbert of, 97
Mérida, 3
Miguel of San Pedro de Arlanza, Bp. of Osma, 29, 71, 137
Miguel the Priest, *merino* of San Esteban de Gormaz, 72
Minguella y Arnedo, Toribio, 119, 125
Miller, Maureen, 14, 63, 106
Molina, Counts of, 7
Mondoñedo, diocese of, 9
Muñoz, Miguel, 115
Murcia, 4, 9
   Taifa kingdom of, 4

Nakashian, Craig, 49
Nalle, Sara, 107, 108
Nickson, Tom, 104
Nicolás "the Priest," Canon of Toledo, 31

Olstein, Diego, 31, 102, 103
Orvieto, 14, 137
Osma, 135
   archives, 11
   cathedral chapter, 71, 78, 79, 93, 133, 138
   chapel of Santo Christo, 82
   chapel of Santo Domingo de Guzmán, 82
   conflict with Sigüenza, 10, 20, 21, 54, 73, 134
   diocese of, 3, 9, 71, 75
Ourense, diocese of, 9
Oviedo, diocese of, 9, 54

di Palacio, Alderico, Bp. of Sigüenza and Palencia, 15, 51, 56, 62, 96, 126, 134, 140
   early life and family, 52, 53, 66
   Bishop of Sigüenza, 53, 54, 55, 56, 60, 66
   Bishop of Palencia, 54, 55, 66
   cultivation of patronage, 53, 58
   papal judicial delegations, 53, 54, 55, 60, 61, 62, 74
   reform of the chapter of Palencia, 55
   relationship with the *studium* at Palencia, 56, 57, 62
   relics, 51, 62, 63, 64, 65, 68, 108
Palencia, 54, 85, 97, 108, 135
   archives, 11
   attempts at archiepiscopal elevation, 55
   Capilla de las Reliquias, 64
   cathedral chapter of San Antolín, 42, 55
   cathedral structure, 45
   chapel of Sana Cruz/Immaculate Conception, 63, 65
   Concejo, 41, 42
   diocese of, 3, 9, 37
   dispute with Segovia, 54, 134
   dispute with Valladolid, 62
   Fuero, 40, 41, 42
   lordship by bishops, 37, 40, 41
   Museo Diocesano, 64, 65
   Studium at, 16, 56, 57, 58, 59, 60, 61, 109,
Parens, Master, 58
Pascasio Dominguez, 125
Peantes, 105
Peces Rata, Felipe-Gíl, 22
Pedraza, 39, 40
Pedro (St.) of Osma, 28
Pedro, Treasurer of Toledo, 60
Pedro, Prior of Sigüenza, 114
Pedro Pérez, Bp. of Burgos, 43, 54, 66
Peñafiel, Master Guillermo de, 57, 58
Peñas, 105
Pérez, Gonzalo, Abp. of Toledo, 55, 60, 71, 98, 110
Peter II of Aragon,
   alliance with Castile, 75, 76
Petrus, Papal Subdeacon, 23
Plasencia, 16, 125, 129, 132, 134, 135
   archives, 11, 16, 82
   diocese of, 3, 9
   founding of new diocese, 7, 10, 72, 86
Poema de Almería, 48
Polo, Alonso, 109
Ponce de Minerva, 36
Ponç, Master, 59, 60, 61
Powers, James, 6, 26, 106
de Pozancos, Arnaldo, 115

Quesada, 89

Raimond of Toledo, Abp. (1126–1152), 19
Ramón Berenguer III, C. of Barcelona, 36

Ramón Berenguer IV, C. of Barcelona, 36
Ramón II de Minerva, bp. Of Palencia, 15, 21, 35, 39, 48, 54, 66, 68, 89, 134, 140
  cultivation of patronage, 39, 40, 55
  early life and family, 36, 37, 49
  Fuero of Palencia, 40, 41, 42
  negotiations at Henry II of England, 45, 46, 47
  papal concerns about conduct, 28, 42, 43, 44, 49, 50
  personal conduct, 44, 45
  recruitment of *magistri* for *studium*, 57
  reform of the cathedral chapter, 55
  Tutor regis, 5, 36, 38
Reilly, Bernard, 1, 12, 19, 115
Ripoll, Monastery, 76, 77
de los Ríos, Pedro, 108
Rivera Recio, Juan Francisco, 44
Rodrigo, bp. of Oviedo, 54, 61
Rodrigues, Martin, Bp. of Porto, 78
Rodríguez Girón, Gutierre, Bp. of Segovia, 89, 90, 91, 110, 131
Rucquoi, Adeline, 14, 58, 59
Ruiz, Teofilo, 39

S., priest of Segovia, 90
Sahagún, 1157 Treaty of, 37
Salamanca, diocese of, 9
Salvatierra, 9
Sancha Raimúndez, sister of Alfonso VII, 36
Sánchez Portocarrero, Diego, 113, 123
Sancho III, K. of Castile, 4, 5, 17, 19, 20, 36, 37, 38, 55
Sancho I, K. of Portugal, 78, 86
Sanç VI of Navarra, 46, 47
Sanç VII of Navarra, 75
San Cristóbal de Ibeas, 76
San Esteban de Gormaz, 72, 82
San Isidoro de León, 39
San Juan de Burgos, 61, 76
San Millán de la Cogolla, 57, 69, 70
San Pedro de Arlanza, 81
San Pelayo de Labedo, 81
San Salvador de Campo Muga, 65
San Salvador de Oña, 61, 74, 81
San Salvador de Pinilla de Jadraque, 124
San Sebastián Parish, 72
Santa Cruz de Coimbra, 138
Santa Cruz de Juarros, 76
Santa María de Huerta, 124, 126

Santa María de Nájera, 39
Santa María la Real de Las Huelgas
  foundation of monastery, 7
Santiago de Compostela, 18, 58, 134
  archdiocese of, 3, 9
  Archbishop as metropolitan, 10, 11, 72, 77, 78
Santiago, Military Order of, 54
San Zoilo de Carrión
  monastery of, 6, 35, 37, 38, 42
  control of Castilian territory, 5, 17, 23, 43, 45, 70
Sares, Master, 59
Sasso, Ugolino da, 59, 135
Saxony, Jordan of, 56, 57
Sayers, Jane, 14
Scot, Michael, 136
Segovia, 54, 89, 98, 126, 135
  archives, 11
  cathedral chapter, 90, 91
  dispute with Ávila, 54
  dispute with Palencia, 54, 134
  diocese of, 3, 6, 9, 129
  1166 Synod of, 5, 22, 23, 34, 44, 47, 131
Serrano, Luciano, 43
Seville, 9, 88
Sicily, 14
Sigüenza, 55, 106, 122, 123, 126, 135, 138
  Capilla del Doncel, 126
  conflict with Osma, 10, 20, 21, 54, 73, 134
  damage to Cathedral during Civil War, 11
  diocese of, 3, 9, 75
Soifer Irish, Maya, 26, 40
Soria, 71

Tagacete, 105
Tairbroch, Pedro de, 10
Tarazona, 76, 123
Tarragona, 76, 77
ben Tauro, Julián, 16, 101, 102, 103, 104, 105, 107, 119, 133, 141
  cultivation of patronage, 103, 105, 106
  reform of the cathedral chapter, 83, 93, 94, 105
  relics and cult, 63, 108, 109, 110, 111
Téllez, Juan, Bp. of Osma, 21, 28
Téllez de Meneses, Tello, Bp. of Palencia, 56, 63, 122
Temple, Military Order of, 96, 97
Tierra de Campos, 43, 66, 67, 95, 96

Toledo, 19, 122, 123, 135
  archdiocese of, 3, 6, 9
  archives, 11, 90
  cathedral chapter, 56, 60, 89, 138
  financing conquest of Cuenca, 6, 101
  hospitality toward Andalusi bishops fleeing the Almohads, 48
  jurisdictional disputes, 54
  Mozarabic community, 16, 31, 32, 48, 92, 94, 97, 102, 111, 141
  primacy and Metropolitanate, 14, 23, 25, 93
  province, 71, 72, 77
  revolt of the clerics, 92, 93
  royal burials at, 19
  translators and "School of", 59, 60, 135, 136
Tordehumos, Treaty of, 7, 72, 86, 87, 95
Tortosa, 77
Tours, 1163 Council of, 20, 21, 32, 47
ibn Tumart, 136
Túy, Diocese of, 9
Túy, Lucas of, 56, 57
Tyre, William of, 138

Úcles, 64
Urraca, Q. of Portugal, 7
Urraca, Q. of León and Castile, 49, 57

Valderón, 75, 83
Valenzuela y Velazquez, Juan Bautista, bp. of Salamanca, 109
Valladolid, 43, 85, 126
  1155 Legatine Council of, 21
  dispute with Palencia, 62
  Santa María de, 40
Verona, 14, 137
Vic(h), 14, 135
Villamuriel, 40, 41
Villaniel, 40

Worms, Burchard of, 138

Ximénez de Rada, Rodrigo, Bp. of Osma and Abp. of Toledo, 56, 70, 89, 98, 99, 113, 122, 123, 126, 131, 135, 138
  Archiepiscopate, 31
  De rebus Hispaniae, 38, 43, 56, 57, 87

Yagüe, Bp. of Ávila, 132
Yáñez, Juan, Bp. of Cuenca, 60, 102, 103, 104, 106

Zamora
  diocese of, 9
  ecclesiastical jurisdication case, 77, 78, 129